W9-ACS-318

"Rx for ailing screenwriters: Read this tonight and call me in the morning."
—Tony Bill, Actor-Director-Producer, Producer of *The Sting*

"Linda Seger has written quite simply the most brilliant and useful book on screenwriting that I have ever seen." —William Kelley, Academy Award-winning Co-Writer, *Witness*

"Linda Seger's updated *Making a Good Script Great* is an invaluable tool for beginning writers, as well as a go-to manual for seasoned professionals. I plan to keep it very close at hand." —Fern Field, Producer, *Monk*

"The first edition of *Making a Good Script Great* is sufficiently timeless, but perfectionist Dr. Linda Seger makes "great" "greater" and even sensational in this edition." —Dr. Lew Hunter, Writer-Producer and Screenwriting Faculty Chair Emeritus, UCLA

"*Making a Good Script Great* clarified for me what a great screenplay should be. After I read it…I was ready to go. Like a great script, it is clear, concise, has great dialog, and is a compelling read. In a crowded market, this one is essential." —David Gleeson, Writer-Director, *Cowboys & Angels* and *The Front Line*

"A must-read for every writer, beginning or professional." —Barbara Corday, Co-Creator, *Cagney & Lacey*

"If they handed out Olympic medals for books on screenwriting, Linda Seger would take gold every time. As if her classic, pioneering text *Making a Good Script Great* wasn't already good enough, she's written a new edition and in so doing has, predictably, brought us another winner. As perceptive, lucid, reader-friendly and eminently practical as all her writing, the third edition of this old friend arrives refreshed, invigorated and bang up-to-date with a wealth of examples from contemporary films and a range of new material… If you've read previous editions you'll find the new spin Seger achieves thought-provoking and inspiring… If you've never read *Making a Good Script Great*, you have a great experience ahead. You'll find a resource you'll return to across your entire career. When in doubt, see what Seger has to say. Compulsory reading for novice and veteran alike." —Linda Aronson, Author, *Screenwriting Updated* and *The Twenty-First Century Screenplay*

"There have been many books on writing, but none that have the depth and accessibility of Linda Seger's. It's a marvelous book for producers and executives as well as writers." —Renee Valente, Producer, *Blind Ambition* and *Love Thy Neighbor*

"An invaluable tool for the working writer." — Richard Walter, Screenwriting Faculty Chair, UCLA

"*Making a Good Script Great* is the quintessential go-to book on rewriting your screenplay. Though not limited to just the rewrite process, it also teaches how to organize yourself prior to putting pen to paper and offers practical hands-on tools to identify problem areas once your screenplay is written. We recommend it to all our students and feel it is the right game plan for writers, executives, and producers to tackle the ever elusive writing process." —Rona Edwards and Monika Skerbelis, Authors, *I Liked It, Didn't Love It: Screenplay Development from the Inside Out*

"A classic that guides you through the specifics of writing, revising, and polishing your draft into a commercially viable project. Sensible, thorough, and empowering!" —Dave Trottier, Author, *The Screenwriter's Bible*

"*Making a Good Script Great* is the gold standard of screenwriting books, a must-have ... Linda Seger has surpassed her own standard with this latest edition that includes not only the basics, which she covers so well, but also new information and examples. Use it and you can raise the standards of your script and go for the gold." —Pamela Jaye Smith *Power of the Dark Side, Inner Drives*

"Whether you're on your first script or your tenth one, screenwriting can be such a bumpy and solitary road. But the journey certainly can be made much smoother with the latest edition of Making a Good Script Great." —Kathie Fong Yoneda, Author, *The Script-Selling Game*

"*MGSG* is one of those books that does what it says—it enables any writer to improve. Linda makes the difficult seem achievable." —Julian Friedmann, Literary Agent and Editor of TwelvePoint.com (formerly *ScriptWriter* magazine)

MAKING A GOOD SCRIPT GREAT

Other books by Linda Seger:

Creating Unforgettable Characters

The Art of Adaptation: Turning Fact and Fiction into Film

From Script to Screen: The Collaborative Art of Filmmaking
(coauthored with Edward Jay Whetmore)

*When Women Call the Shots: The Developing Power and Influence of
Women in Television and Film*

Making a Good Writer Great: A Creativity Workbook for Screenwriters

*Advanced Screenwriting: Raising Your Script to the
Academy Award Level*

And the Best Screenplay Goes to ... Learning from the Winners:
Sideways, Shakespeare in Love, Crash

MAKING A GOOD SCRIPT GREAT

3rd Edition

LINDA SEGER

SILMAN-JAMES PRESS Los Angeles

Copyright © 2010 by Linda Seger

All rights reserved. No part of this book may be used or reproduced in any manner whatsoever without permission from the publisher.

Acknowledgment is made to the following for permission to reproduce the material indicated: MCA Publishing Rights for excerpts from *Back to the Future*, copyright © Universal Pictures, a division of Universal City Studios, Inc., courtesy of MCA Publishing Rights, a division of MCA, Inc.; MCA Publishing Rights and Peter Benchley for excerpts from *Jaws*, copyright © Universal Pictures, a division of Universal City Studios, Inc., courtesy of MCA Publishing Rights, a division of MCA, Inc.; Paramount Pictures excerpts from *Witness* copyright © Paramount Pictures; Columbia Pictures, Don McGuire, Larry Gelbart, and Murray Schisgal for excerpts from *Tootsie*.

Library of Congress Cataloging-in-Publication Data

Seger, Linda.
Making a good script great / Linda Seger. -- 3rd ed.
p. cm.
"1st Silman-James ed."--T.p. verso.
Includes index.
ISBN 978-1-935247-01-2 (alk. paper)
1. Motion picture authorship. I. Title.
PN1996.S384 2010
808.2'3--dc22
2009051981

Cover design by Arthead, adapted from first edition cover design by Hal Siegel.

Printed and bound in the United States of America

Silman-James Press
www.silmanjamespress.com

R0450141185

Dedication

To three of my drama teachers,
who taught me that loving drama was a good thing to do:

To my mentor, Dr. Wayne Rood, who taught
me to be bold and to be kind;

To Harold Zahorik, who taught me balance
and generously filled in the gaps;

To Irma Forsberg, who taught me to keep
going even if the roof falls in.

Contents

Acknowledgments

With many thanks to my publishers—Gwen Feldman and Jim Fox—for agreeing to do a new edition, and for all they've done to make the first two editions successful. And many thanks to Jim for his excellent editing.

Thank you to Alvin Shim, my college intern, for his invaluable help on researching, brainstorming with me, discussing films with me, and doing a month of hard work to help me finish this project on time.

Thank you to my wonderful readers who gave me feedback: Elizabeth Copley, Devorah Cutler-Rubenstein, Elona Malterre, Lori Marrett, Kim Peterson, Ellen Sandler, Dr. James Schaap, Pamela Jaye Smith, and Elizabeth Stevens.

Thank you to the students at Dordt College in Iowa who provided me with examples: Jesse Brauning, Bree Brouwer, Kelly Cooke, David De Wit, Laura Heckmann, Andrew Hornor, Daniel Kauten, Luke Kreykes, Jon Nederhoff, Jeffrey Niesen, Daniel Palmer, Emily Sajdak, Dale Vande Griend, Ryan Van Surksum, Matt Turner, Joel Veldkamp, Hani Yang.

Thank you to my friends and colleagues Heather Hale, Carolyn Miller, Treva Silverman, and Kathie Fong Yoneda for discussing concepts, answering questions, and providing me with examples and definitions.

Thank you to writer David S. Ward for permission to quote extensively from his script *The Sting*.

Thank you to Universal and Amblin Entertainment, along with Bob Gale and Robert Zemeckis, for permission to quote from *Back to the Future*.

To my assistant, Sarah Callbeck, who keeps me organized, for her efficient and effective help and for coming through for me when all else fails.

And always, to my husband, Peter Hazen Le Var, for his constant kindness and support of my many endeavors.

Preface
to the Third Edition

When the first edition of *Making a Good Script Great* came out at the end of 1987, few screenwriting books had been published. I expected fairly new writers to be the book's main readers, but soon learned that wasn't true. All sorts of writers were using the book: Those who had never written a script used it to learn the basics; experienced writers read the book and then used the questions at the end of every chapter to recheck their work; producers and directors used it to help understand why scripts they planned to film worked, or didn't. To this day, executives at studios and production companies often have the book on their shelf, to refer to when a script is stuck.

Ron Howard was given the book by his father, and he told me he used it on every one of his films beginning with *Apollo 13*. Other experienced writers, including a number of award winners, mentioned they had read the book and found it very useful for their work.

I noticed how often people told me they *used* the book. Clearly they weren't just reading it, but trying to apply its concepts to help them make better scripts. As several people told me, "It can make a bad script passable and a good script great!"

As I started to write the third edition, I wanted above all for the book to be practical for writers, whether new or experienced, whether in college and university classes or using it in screenwriting groups.

As I rethought the book, I decided to take out the mythology chapter that was in the first two editions. When I first wrote that chapter, there were no books on the market in the area of myth and screenwriting (although there were seminars on the topic). Now there are several excellent books on mythology by people who have carved their niche in this area and studied it far more than I have. Chris Vogler's book *The Writer's Journey* came out shortly after mine. Pamela Jaye Smith now has three books on the subject—*Inner Drives, The Power of the Dark Side,* and *Beyond the Hero's Journey.* Sarah Beach wrote *The Scribbler's Guide to the Land of Myth: Mythic Motifs for Storytellers,* and James Bonnet wrote *Stealing Fire from the Gods.* The mythology chapter from *Making a Good Script Great* has been reprinted in the textbook *Signs of Life in the USA,* edited by Sonin Maask and Jack Solomon.

For the present edition of *Making a Good Script Great,* I updated my examples to newer films, except for several classics such as *Some Like It Hot* and *The Sting.* As I picked new examples, I usually tried to choose films that both did well at the box office and achieved some sort of critical acclaim. I've also occasionally cited films that are not particularly great films but provide good examples of some aspect of screenwriting. Don't presume that because I mention a film in the book I think it's perfect. There are few perfect films; even Academy Award winners often have flaws. Although most of my examples come from films that I think are very good, if not necessarily terrific, I also believe we can learn from many different types of films, and even a mediocre one sometimes does something well.

This edition also contains three new chapters: discussions of point of view and of creating cinematic images and dialogue, and a new case study of screenwriter Paul Haggis. Throughout the book, I extended my coverage of some concepts, but if I felt my coverage of a topic in the previous edition was thorough and said what needed to be said, I often updated the examples but left the discussion as it was. In all my decisions, I took the position that "If it ain't broke, don't fix it!"

I chose to add a case study of a writer, Paul Haggis, to this edition. Paul is one of the most successful writers in Hollywood. He has been nominated for three Academy Awards for Best Screenplay (*Million Dollar Baby, Letters from Iwo Jima,* and *Crash*) and won for *Crash.* He has won two Emmys for his television writing for *thirtysomething* and *Due South.* And he's been nominated for a number of awards in many genres—including for the films *Casino Royale* and *In the Valley of Elah.*

I hope this book continues to be enjoyable and useful and makes many good scripts great, and helps create many great films.

Introduction

Screenwriting, like any other art form, is both an art and a craft. Writers express themselves through the stories that drive them, the characters they want to bring to life, the ideas they want to convey, and the styles they choose to express their personalities, values, and individual takes on life. Learning to write includes learning to speak in a personal voice. You become an artist by putting yourself into your work. Your work becomes compelling and deep because of the personal and artistic odyssey you take in the writing process.

But it isn't enough to simply express oneself. Screenwriting is also a craft. A screenplay's form is vastly different from a novel's or a short story's. One has to know how to convey the elements of drama in a way that serves the particular mediums of dramatic writing—film, television, theater, and Web. It isn't enough to write well. One has to write well for a visual medium. To become not just a great artist, but great at the *craft* of screenwriting, a whole new set of skills needs to be learned. These skills include knowing how to tell a story, with a beginning, middle, and end, that is clear upon the first viewing and can be told within a specified time limit. This might mean telling a story in a few minutes for a short film, in twenty-two to thirty minutes for a sitcom, in forty-two to sixty minutes for a television series, or in ninety minutes to two hours for most films.

Screenwriters need to learn how to integrate their themes and ideas into stories without getting preachy or giving a lecture about the meaning of life.

Screenwriters need to learn how to use the cinema—how to tell a story through action, conflict, and images.

The screenwriter has to learn to reveal characters succinctly through a story's twists and turns, through the telling gesture, through the small character details that show us what makes a character tick.

These are part of the craft. They can be learned, and when integrated with the art of screenwriting, they can lead to the making of a great film.

Making a great script is not just a matter of having a good idea. In screenwriting it's the art and the craft, the writing and the rewriting, that make a good script great.

Art without craft is simply self-expression. Craft without art is predictable and by-the-book. But the two together? That's where great films come from.

* * * * *

If you're writing your first script, this book will help develop your skills at telling a compelling and dramatic story. If you're a veteran screenwriter, this book will articulate the skills you know intuitively and, hopefully, give you some additional skills you hadn't thought about. And if you are currently stuck on a rewrite, this book will help you analyze and solve your script's problems and get it back on track.

This book will take you through the complete screenwriting process, from the first spark of an idea through a full script's rewriting. You will learn how to organize your ideas, how to create a compelling story, and how to make your characters dimensional and worthy of our company for two hours. You'll also learn how to rewrite your script when you're finished. Because if you write, you will rewrite—that's the nature of the business. Unless you're a writer who writes purely for himself and stashes his scripts in a box in the garage, you will find yourself rewriting your scripts—again and again. First, you will do it to get your first draft "just right." Then your friends will have a few suggestions, and you'll rewrite "just to make it a little better." Your agent will have some suggestions about how to make it more marketable, and you'll incorporate those. The producer and development executive will want you to do another rewrite so that they can put their own stamp on it. And, once your script is in production, the actors will have ideas about "what works for them" and want you to give them "just a little bit more."

At every stage of the process of rewriting, input from others will influence your choices. As it should. Screenwriting is ultimately a collaborative process, combining solitary hours of self-expression with working in tandem with other artists to realize a vision through a visual medium.

This is all well and good, provided you know what to rewrite and provided that every rewrite improves the script. Unfortunately, this rarely happens. Many people feel like the man who decided to become a writer because he saw so much bad writing on television and in film. He declared, "Certainly I can do better than that!" After submitting his script to a producer who turned him down, he protested, "But it's much better than anything else I've seen!" "Of course," said the producer. "Anyone can write better than that. The trick is to write so brilliantly that after everyone ruins it in rewrites, it's still watchable."

And it's true. Many scripts get worse and worse in the rewrite process. The further a script gets from its inspirational source, the more muddled it becomes. It begins to lose its magic. By the fifth rewrite, certain elements no longer make sense. By the twelfth rewrite, the story is completely different, and no one wants to do the film anymore.

The solution might seem to be "Don't rewrite!" Unfortunately, that is not an alternative. Most first-draft scripts, regardless of all the creativity and magic that their writers put into them, don't work. Many are overwritten—they're simply too long to make a good, salable film. In the heat of the creative moment, many writers lose sight of essentials—paying off a clue, completing a character's transformational arc, finishing off a subplot. A writer may have a germ of an idea running through the script that needs to be strengthened. Rewrites will clarify all these elements and repair those that are ailing.

Is there a particular trick to rewriting? Yes! Only rewrite what doesn't work, and leave the rest alone. This often means working against the temptation to do more and more. It means not getting carried away by new and different ideas that are exciting but don't fix your script's problems. It means following suggestions that are designed to get the script on track, not off. It means holding back on a new creative stamp because the writer's original creative stamp is "just fine, thank you." If it ain't broke, don't fix it! And if it is broke, do something!

So how is this done? This book is designed to discuss just that. It's designed to discuss what "on track" means, and to look at concepts that can be applied from the beginning of the writing process through the rewrites to help make a good script better. It's designed to teach you how to write and rewrite effectively, without losing the magic needed in the important last draft—the shooting script.

My career as a script consultant has focused almost exclusively on how to get the script on track so that problems are solved and the original creativity is preserved. I've worked on several thousand scripts for feature films, as well as television scripts and plays. I've worked on miniseries, television movies, dramatic series, and sitcoms, and on horror films, action-adventures, sci-fi, mystery, comedies, dramas, and fantasies. Whether I work with writers, producers, directors, or executives, the challenge is always the same: How can we make the next draft work? Together, our job is to define the script's concepts, analyze its problems, and find the solutions to those problems that will create a workable draft. I've worked with many of the most creative and successful people in the business and realized that everyone, no matter how experienced, suffers from problems in writing and rewriting.

Rewriting difficulties usually occur because the script's problems aren't well defined or analyzed before starting the rewrite. The producer might say, vaguely, "It's the second act," so a rewrite is done to fix the second act. Then the director says, "Now I see we have a problem with the main character," so another rewrite focuses on the main character. Next, another rewrite is undertaken to fix the subplot. But the subplot rewrite throws the main plot off track, so another rewrite tries to fix that.

Since the script works as a whole, changes in one part of it may require changes in another. My job as a script consultant is to identify and analyze the script's problems *before* the rewrite and to work with the creators to make sure that all the problems get solved, without introducing even more problems. I've discovered that the process of rewriting a script is not just an amorphous, magical, "maybe-it-works, maybe-it-doesn't" kind of process. There are specific elements that make a good script great, elements that can be consciously analyzed and improved.

Naturally, since every script is unique, every script's problems are different. It's not possible to write a book that you can follow point by point to create the perfect script. The creative process is not a paint-by-the-numbers process, and this book is not designed to give you some simple rules and formulas to apply by rote.

This book is about concepts and principles, not about rules and formulas. It's about what works and why it works. It's about appreciation of the art of film and the techniques used to express this art. It's also about problem solving. It is about combining intuition and creativity and one's instincts with certain concepts and principles to make sure a script is not just fresh and original, but that it *works*.

In my many years of experience, I've seen the same kinds of script problems occur again and again. Problems in exposition. Problems with structure, with shaping the story. Problems with momentum. Problems with an insufficiently developed idea. These are all problems that can make the difference between a sale and another rejection letter, between commercial success and box-office failure.

To understand how these problems have been solved in great scripts, I'll discuss some of the most satisfying films throughout a long period of film history. I've chosen films that are good teaching films. They're well structured with strong dimensional characters and a well worked-out idea. But they are not formula films. They're creative, artistic, and well crafted. If you haven't seen these films, you can rent them and study them, again and again. Many of the scripts are now found on the Internet. And, of course, while discovering why they work and how they work, you will also be entertained.

It is my belief that it takes both a good write and a good rewrite to create a film that entertains, has something to say, and is of high quality. With some creativity and a strong idea you can create a good script. This book is about making that good script great!

CHAPTER ONE

Gathering Ideas

You're a writer. You've got a great idea for a film. You think it's as good as *E.T.*, as original as *Babel*, as intimate as *Juno*, as action-packed as *Die Hard*, and as genre-stretching as *Letters from Iwo Jima*. You know it's not just the idea but the execution of the idea that counts. You want to do it right. Where do you begin?

Or you're an executive. You saw an article that gave you some ideas for a story. You want to assess the story for its cinematic possibilities. How do you do it?

You're a producer in the last stages of the rewrites for your next picture. You sense that something in the script is not yet working. How do you identify the problems and solve them?

You're a director. You've never written a script before, but you have a storyline that's been pushing at you for a year or two. You want to get the story down in treatment or script form, then maybe you'll find a writer to collaborate with you. How do you start?

* * * * *

Rarely do script ideas appear full blown. Most scripts begin with a spark, a snippet of images. Perhaps yours begins with a situation you want to explore. Maybe it starts with a character you've known or imagined. It could begin with parts of a story that pull at you, demanding to be told.

Your spark might be as small as a one-line idea—"Something about a circus." It might be epic: "My grandfather told me many stories about fighting in the Russian Revolution." But somewhere between your initial idea and 120 pages of script, your story will need to take form. It will need to be shaped, fleshed out with characters, and built with images and emotions. How well you accomplish this will determine whether your screenplay is muddled, merely competent, or brilliant.

As with any other art form, writing a script begins with a certain degree of chaos. Ideas are half-baked. Storylines can bog down at any point. Characters might seem inconsistent, one-dimensional, too predictable, or too much like a character you've seen a hundred times before. You don't know yet where you're going and how you're going to get there.

The process of writing is a process of moving from chaos to order. How quickly you move will depend on how fast you write, how much you know about the process and the craft of writing, how disciplined you are, the difficulty of your idea, the amount of research you need to do, and how much you value your own creative process. Some of you may be fast-thinking, organized, with ideas spilling out as quickly as you can write them down. Others may need time to mull, season, consider, ruminate over ideas. There is no right way to be creative. There is no one process that will work for everyone.

GETTING THE IDEA

Where do ideas come from? The world is brimming with fascinating stories, dramatic characters, and intriguing ideas and issues. Part of your training as a writer consists of finding the clues, hints, small threads that can form the basis for a great script. Many writers find ideas in newspaper articles, which are filled with conflict, drama, dynamic characters, and important issues. Your own immediate family—good or bad—contains myriad situations that can be explored. Friendships, marriages, problems at work—whether from your own life or situations you've heard about—can be used. The adventures, and misadventures, of you or your friends can be a catalyst for story explorations. And your dreams, fantasies, hopes, and goals (as well as your failures, disappointments, and betrayals) are all grist for the creative mill.

Many situations, when coupled with a good dose of imagination, can lead to new ideas. You might ask, "What if I had followed him to Africa?" or "What would have happened if I had taken the job in Lebanon right before the bombs started falling?" or "Suppose I had gone to that boarding school for the wealthy and my parents became bankrupt?"

Many writers keep file folders filled with possible stories. Some have hundreds of one-liners in a file on their computer. Others have notes scattered about. Eventually, one story from among many story ideas begins to call out and heat up one's imagination. It *demands* to be told.

ORDERING YOUR IDEAS

There are many ways to start, and many ways to order your thoughts. Some writers will think about an idea for a while, play around with it before writing it down. But it's important to get your idea on paper in order to look at what you have, and to begin deciding where to go with it. Getting it down on paper also means transferring certain ideas out of your mind so that there's room for more to emerge. Ideas connect with ideas, and—Eureka!—a story begins to take form.

A script can be divided into five major components: the storylines, the characters, the underlying theme or idea, the images, and the dialogue.

Each of these elements takes form at different times in the process. Some writers are particularly good at imagining and building characters and may start their work there. They let the story emerge from getting to know their characters' decisions and actions.

Other writers are driven by storylines. They're intrigued with sequences of events. They like action, people doing exciting things.

Other writers might begin with a concept they want to explore. Perhaps they're fascinated with questions of justice, identity, and integrity and the lure of greed and corruption.

No matter where you start, at some point all of your script's major components need to come together. And, since they're all related, you can't work on characters without story ideas emerging, and you can't work on story ideas without some images beginning to blossom. So you want to bring together your ideas while still letting them be fluid, with plenty of opportunity to grow, change, and take new shapes.

To do this, some writers write their ideas down on index cards.

THE INDEX CARD APPROACH

Since a storyline will rarely come to a writer full blown, it's necessary to find some flexible method to get down and organize (and reorganize) all the idea snippets that will add up to the script. Many writers use index cards, or write their ideas in a loose-leaf binder, to help them get started. Index cards are colorful, chaotic, and fluid—all of which can be conducive to the creative process.

Many writers buy index cards in many different colors. As they order their thoughts, each color represents different elements in the script. Perhaps you're writing a mystery, and the white cards are used for all the scenes about the investigation. You use the pink cards for all the scenes about the love relationship between the detective and the witness. Yellow cards might contain notes on characters—including biography, relationships, physical descriptions, and unusual habits. Blue cards might be notes on images—New York City's gritty streets *(Taxi Driver)*, water images *(The English Patient)*, desert images *(Babel, Syriana)*, or all the different ways to make traveling in a car interesting *(Pulp Fiction, Little Miss Sunshine)*. The notes on any one card may be short ("Upset, she calls the police"), or they may be more extensive, describing the mood of the scene and some of the action. You might have separate cards that give research information: What happens at a crime scene? Where might a detective find fingerprints? What is gunshot residue, and where do you find it?

Since the creative process wants to move from chaos to order, your mind will naturally begin to see relationships among your cards. You might find that your note about working relationships goes with your note about your character's desperate passion, which seems to fit well with your cards that describe images of victory and defeat in the oil fields (*There Will Be Blood*). So you reorder your cards to integrate your story, images, and emotions.

You might play around with the best place to put your love scene so it has the most dramatic impact (*Enchanted, Brokeback Mountain, When Harry Met Sally, Slumdog Millionaire*).

Using index cards allows your ideas to emerge and find natural connections with other ideas. With the index card method, you don't need to force the creative process by trying to write your script before you're ready. You don't force yourself to make up a part of the story that isn't yet clear to you. Index cards allow you to shuffle around ideas from act to act or scene to scene in myriad different ways—until one way eventually "feels right."

Many writers display their index cards on a bulletin board, moving them around from act to act and studying them daily for new possibilities—new connections, new orderings. Some put their index card information on their computers.

The danger of the index card method, of course, is having nothing but a lot of different idea fragments with no overriding order. That might happen at first, but your mind eventually will find natural connections between your cards. And your story will emerge organically, as a natural, creative, exciting discovery.

You don't know how many index cards you'll need before your story, characters, theme, and images take shape. You may require fifty or a few hundred. But, at some point, the story will start begging you to write it down. Then you may want to write an *outline*.

THE OUTLINE

An *outline* is simply a few lines about each of the scenes (in chronological order) that make up a story. You may write it down on a few pieces of paper, on your computer, or in a loose-leaf binder (allowing a paragraph or a page for each scene). A complete outline might consist of fifty to one hundred sentences, although you may not find it necessary to write out all your key scenes before beginning to write your script.

If you were to outline the beginning of *Little Miss Sunshine*, it might look like this:

```
Olive watches, over and over, the Miss
America pageant on television. She copies Miss
America's gestures.

Sheryl goes to the hospital to pick up Frank.
Establish Frank's slit wrists, and everyone's
concern about whether he'll do it again.

Frank comes back with Sheryl, meets Dwayne.
Establish their room. Keep tension alive.

Dinnertime—begin Richard's small subplot about
getting his book sold with phone call.

Olive comes to dinner—establish that she and
Grandpa are practicing her routine off-screen.

Establish phone call—telling them that the
first-place winner just forfeited her position—
and Olive is next in line.

Establish discussion about when they're going
to the contest, who's going, etc.
```

With just this much information, it's possible to begin writing a script, although some writers might choose to first expand on each scene with more character and story information. Some writers will continually revise their outlines as new ideas take shape. Other writers will write scenes as they organically emerge and use the outline as just a general guide.

THE TREATMENT

Instead of index cards or an outline, some writers begin with a treatment. Treatments take two different forms in Hollywood.

(1) There's the treatment that is a selling document meant to quickly show a possible buyer the potential of the story. This type of treatment is a selling tool, not a writing tool. It usually consists of a one-sentence *logline*, a one- to three-page synopsis of the story, and possibly even a *marketing hook*.

A *logline* is a one- or two-sentence distillation of a story. It usually tells us who the protagonist is, what challenge or conflict or situation the protagonist will confront, and when the story takes place if it isn't set in the present. Used by writers to keep themselves on track or as a marketing tool to pique the interest of a producer or an audience, a logline is not meant to tell the whole story or to reveal a surprise ending.

A logline for *Jaws* could be, "A shark threatens a seaside town on the Fourth of July weekend." A logline for *Little Miss Sunshine* might be, "In spite of innumerable obstacles, Olive and her family are determined to get to the Little Miss Sunshine pageant on time."

As a marketing tool, a logline hooks a producer into reading your script by being memorable and easily digestible. Producers get it immediately. Later, a logline is used in advertising, and on movie posters, to hook an audience into coming to your film.

A *marketing hook*, as opposed to a logline, is anything that entices an audience into a theater. In *Transformers*, *Toy Story*, and *G.I. Joe*, the marketing hooks were the toys themselves. In *Spider-Man* and *Iron Man*, the marketing hooks were the familiarity many moviegoers would have with the comic books. The marketing hook for *West Side Story* could be "A modern day Romeo and Juliet set among the gangs of New York." Sometimes a marketing hook puts together two successful elements, so if you did a film about a predatory lion in Africa that kills people, you might say it's "*Jaws* meets *Out of Africa*."

(2) In the early stages of writing a script, some writers work out a story in *treatment* form—a fairly brief (eight to fifteen pages) synopsis.

It's basically a short story, and it tells the beginning, middle, and end of the tale. A treatment is a creative tool you can use in many ways. If, for example, your story has come to you fairly full blown, writing a treatment is an opportunity to set it down in logical order. Then, by stepping back and looking at your treatment—your story's narrative line—you'll be able to see if your story makes sense and has movement and direction. If one event doesn't seem to relate to another event, you may have gone off on some tangent that has nothing to do with the story. If your story bogs down, your treatment will help you feel exactly where action is missing. If the climax isn't clear, you'll be able to see that your story doesn't build or has lost direction toward the end.

Some writers use the treatment as a form of stream-of-consciousness writing—letting all their ideas gush out. They might write for five pages about the feeling of an apartment or about why two people are attracted to each other, and then sum up the next eight scenes with a line or two. In this way, a treatment can get a script's initial spark down on paper. It can be an opportunity to let ideas simply pop out or to start getting into the flow of dialogue or to begin feeling out the style of the story.

Treatments can help you formulate your story by seeing its problems. It's important to keep your treatment a fluid document that can change and grow as it is rewritten. For some writers, once something is written down, it's *the truth*. There's something pretty about a neat and cleanly written page of beautiful words, even if the story is not yet worked out. If this is the case for you, write on the back of scratch paper. Then if you need to crumple the paper and toss it out later, you'll only be throwing out used-up paper anyway. This can free you up to continue to make changes in your treatment and storyline until you feel it's "right"—clear, interesting, and well structured.

KEEPING A JOURNAL

While treatments can be good for getting a clear sense of your story, they are sometimes less helpful for character and thematic development. That's why some writers work with journals before writing their scripts. Journals give writers the opportunity to explore characters and themes in the same way they might explore their own lives and issues.

Just as you might keep a journal about your own inner thoughts, you may find that the journal approach to your script takes you deeply inside your characters and helps you find their bodies and voices—find what they think, how they feel, what bothers them, what they care about, and how they react.

Your journal might be written in first person, as though you're the character writing your thoughts and experiences, or written as a third-person account, as though the characters are your friends or people you're observing. It might contain character descriptions and actions as well as associations. It might answer questions: How much money does the character earn? What's his family like? What kind of school did she go to?

You might create a character by writing about people you know and how your character is like them. Think of character traits that interest you. Why does a character do what she does? Maybe you'll write down your feelings about the woman who left you five years ago and base a story on that experience. Or maybe you'll remember a summer romance and write down details that give that story a new twist. And as you work through your ideas, something sparks inside of you. You get more excited, ideas come. Maybe you use them. Maybe they take you somewhere else. Scripts contain ideas, and ideas need to be worked through as much as your story and characters. If your theme is about the spreading negative influence and connections of violence *(Babel)*, you might make journal entries about the various ways and the various levels that violence affects your different characters. You might explore the seemingly universal attraction to violence. You might discuss bonding through violence—wartime bonding or bonding through gangs.

You might find that, as you develop your story, questions emerge. Perhaps you have a cop character, and realize that you don't know enough about police investigation. Perhaps part of your story takes place in New York, and you haven't been to New York for twelve years. You need to do more research.

RESEARCHING THE STORY

Writing a script is a back-and-forth movement between imagination and logic. Every story, even a sci-fi story, has an inner logic that has to make sense. Often stories demand that part of the writer's preparation will include research. It may be that the writer has a scene that takes place in an operating room, and she realizes that the only operating rooms she's seen have been on television and in films. She wonders if that's what they really look like. She might need to spend some time at a hospital, find a surgeon who will show her around, and perhaps even be allowed to watch an operation to get the scene just right.

Maybe a writer has set his story in a small town, even though he grew up in New York and has lived in Los Angeles his whole adult life. He realizes he knows little about small towns, so he decides to spend a few weeks wandering around one, talking to the locals, and getting the feel of such a place.

Perhaps a writer is writing about the early gangs of New York (*Gangs of New York*), or Berlin in the 1950s (*The Reader*), or space flight (*Apollo 13*). The facts uncovered during research will affect a story's direction. In many cases, if its facts aren't accurate, the story won't work.

Research can include library research—looking at books, articles, diaries, and newspapers, and consulting librarians for other resources.

It can include talking to someone who knows the arena, whether it means making friends with a psychologist to write about mental illness (*Rain Man, A Beautiful Mind*) or talking to people who have lived through a particular historical event and can help you get the facts and emotions correct (*Munich, Hotel Rwanda*).

Sometimes it's important to live an experience in order to understand it. People live in drastically different worlds. The vocabulary, the relationships, the pressures, and the issues for doctors are different from those for cowboys or teachers or artists or scientists. What particular people do in their spare time, what they drink after work, whether they shower at night or in the morning, are all part of the details necessary to make a character ring true.

Research determines your character's vocabulary. Does the character go to a restaurant, supper club, a hamburger joint, a diner, or a private club for dinner? Does the character play the violin or the fiddle? If characters want a drink, do they go to a bar, a pub, a tavern, or a lounge? The art is in the details, and the writer needs to know how those details change, depending on a character's occupation, historical period, culture, and geographic location.

Research may take a few hours, a few days, or years. Some writers say they research for months and can write the script quickly as a result. Some writers are never able to finish the script, because either they're not willing to research or their imaginations fight against the facts. There's more than one script that has failed because the research was off.

In most cases, your story will be based on something you know about. Writers write what they know about, because the script then rings true, and the writer brings his or her own personal voice and personal knowledge to the project. But most scripts will require some research to make sure that a particular character detail or piece of vocabulary is accurate.

RECORDING YOURSELF

You may have tried several of the preliminary scriptwriting approaches mentioned above and now find that your characters have begun to talk to you. If so, you might want to get out a tape recorder or some sort of digital audio recorder and try another technique.

Every day of your life, you talk. You're used to it. Talking to an audio recorder can be very freeing, letting your ideas flow in an uninhibited way. Perhaps you're beginning to think of chunks of dialogue for your characters. Their voices are coming at you. They're talking so fast you can barely get them down on paper. Perhaps you're driving in your car or stuck in traffic or you wake up in the middle of the night with a piece of dialogue. If something is working well in your mind, no matter what your situation, you want to get it down while it's hot. An audio recorder gives you the opportunity to capture words and ideas whenever they come. It also allows you, when playing back your recordings, to hear them spoken (as they will be onscreen), rather than just see them written.

You might play around with dialogue to express attitudes or to think through ways to express the issues in your script or to explore character relationships. The dialogue may come full blown, or your imagination may hear a few key words or a turn of phrase while reworking other things.

Of course, there is a disadvantage to recording yourself. You need to transcribe what you said. But you don't need to transcribe everything. If you like something you've recorded, transcribe it. If not, you don't need to transcribe it now, but don't delete it. Later, you may want to go back to your recordings to revisit your dialogue inspiration or the relationship of one idea to another. It may be important to remember why your words originally came out in a particular order.

GETTING IT DOWN

You may decide that instead of trying various preliminary methods to organize script ideas, you just want to get to work writing. And there are good writers who take that approach.

Some ideas come to writers in one great rush. They see almost a whole movie in their head. If that's the case with you, start *writing* your script immediately. At some point you may get stuck and need to pick up one of the aforementioned techniques, but, if not, simply sit down and write your script.

Perhaps you're a first-time scriptwriter. You're ready to write your first script, but writing over 100 pages of script seems overwhelming. In that case, if you have a storyline, you may want to start by simply getting your story down in script form, without preparation, and then rework it.

Until you find your own creative process, you naturally will have fears. Can I actually write a whole script? Is this going to be worth my time? How long will it take? Turning out 120 pages or so, no matter how good or bad they are, gets rid of the "I wonder if I can do it!" problem. Rarely will an initial draft be workable, because there is little craft in its creation. But it may have some artistic, magical scenes or dialogue. You may need to start all over again from the beginning, preparing and crafting the story. But the knowledge that you've done it once makes the next time easier.

Most experienced writers, however, work out their stories and characters very carefully before starting to write a script. The more time spent planning a script, the faster it gets written. You might decide to apply the getting-it-down technique after employing all of the previous preparation methods. In that case, once you begin writing, keep writing. Some writers, once they start writing, don't go back to edit and rewrite their work until they've finished their script. They recognize that once the script starts flowing, it's not productive to interrupt the process to change grammar, fix typos, or play around with several approaches to a scene. They want to just get everything down.

COMPUTER PROGRAMS

We live in the Information Age. Most writers write on a computer. It's only natural that a variety of screenplay computer-software programs are now on the market to help writers write and rewrite their scripts. I'm not talking about programs for formatting your script (such as Movie Magic Screenwriter, MovieMaster, and Final Draft), but programs designed to help you organize and prepare to write your script (such as John Truby's Blockbuster and Dramatica). For some writers, these programs are controversial. They feel that the programs apply a paint-by-number approach to scriptwriting, telling writers where to place every event and assuring them that if they follow everything in the system, they'll have a "perfect" script. Other writers see these programs as a catalyst for creativity, a guide to keep them on track, and a help in determining what to do next.

What does a screenplay program do? When can it work for you? What do you need to beware of?

At the very least, a screenplay program can help you organize your thoughts and put all your information together in one place. Instead of index cards or scratch pads with copious notes, all the information you amass on story and character and premise and theme are in one place, to be worked and reworked as new ideas emerge.

A screenplay program can help you maintain awareness of the issues that you need to address as you write your script. There are hundreds, if not thousands, of elements that make a script work. Experienced writers know many of these elements subconsciously, but the new writer probably doesn't. A good screenplay program asks the writer: Have you clearly worked out your characters' biographies? What are the traits of your main characters and supporting characters? Do you understand your characters' wants and what actions they're going to take to get them? What problems do your characters need to solve? Do your characters' choices make sense? What's the dramatic conflict? Who's the audience?

A good screenplay program works as a partner that keeps moving you forward in your thinking. Most of them will contain definitions, analyses of great scripts, and information about how a script's elements interact. So, they serve as teaching tools as well as writing tools.

Some of them have room for playing around with ideas. Many of them organize material so that you can see the relationship of elements within the script. Most are designed to ask you questions at various points in your story creation.

Some of the questions posed by a good screenwriting program are similar to the questions you'll find at the end of each of the chapters of this book. Like these questions, they are designed to keep the writer cognizant of the issues that need to be resolved to make a script work.

Remember that every system is based on the dramatic theory of the designer. To use such a system effectively, you'll have to learn its designer's vocabulary. There may be a number of concepts to learn before you can even begin to write.

Implicit in a screenplay program is a certain logic. A computer program needs to be constructed rationally, even though your approach to writing may not be overtly rational. Maybe you want to begin constructing your character from a piece of dialogue or a sense of a character's energy and rhythm or the color of a character's dress. But when you pull up the character questions, you see the same questions each time, which may make you think that there's only one way to go through the process of creating the script. A screenplay program can't take into account the hundreds of different (and unusual) starting places, or the thousands of different processes that can get you to a good script.

Ultimately, the test of any method is whether it's an effective tool for you. Any system is only as good as the artistry of the writer using it. If a writer simply fills in the blanks, the result may be a so-called workable script, but it will probably be *predictable* and *derivative*. If the method doesn't help you shape and structure your story, or create exciting and imaginative characters, then it's not the system for you. A good system should be flexible and have room for your own creative process. It should work as a creative collaborator, helping you understand the issues as well as shape your script.

THERE'S NO ONE RIGHT WAY

Many writers will utilize different methods for different scripts. The art of writing includes having many different techniques to get you into your story. If one doesn't work, hopefully another will. But remember, the object of these techniques is to serve the actual writing of a script. Some writers have hundreds of ideas, thousands of index cards, but no script. At some point, these aids need to lead to a script.

The creation of the script will require not only your knowledge and craft, but also your art—your particular voice, your vision, your perspective, your experience, and your unique attitudes. All methods that help you craft your story should also be catalysts to help you become a better artist.

STAYING TRUE TO THE PROCESS

Many writers, particularly new writers, say "I don't like to write, but I like being done with writing." The process from conceiving the story to writing the script to selling the script takes so long that if you don't find joy in the work itself, you'll have trouble getting through the many periods of impatience and confusion, not to mention the many rewrites necessary before a script is ready to be shopped to potential buyers.

Writing is a process, and if a writer stays true to the process, the script will proceed. This means the writer needs a writing discipline that is steady and consistent. Professional writers write every day, sometimes two hours a day and sometimes eight hours a day. Most non-professional writers don't have the time, or the money, for daily writing, but the good ones still have some kind of a writing discipline. Some get up very early, perhaps at 5 or 6 a.m., and write a few hours before work. Some write at night, often late into the night. Some write on weekends, perhaps a few hours in the morning. The amount of time is not as important as the fact that you're writing.

Most times, writing a screenplay takes far longer than a writer expects. It might take years to get a story to work. If you expect it to happen next week, or next month, you'll be destined for years of frustration.

The amount of time needed to write a script varies from writer to writer. For some, writing a script from the idea through the first draft takes six months to a year, although many writers may take a year or three or five on their first script, and maybe a year or more on other scripts. I know of some writers who have written a script in a few months, but most writers take much longer. Rewrites might take an additional two months—or two years. There is no time limit that you must follow to create your script.

There is no one creative process.

APPLICATION

Questions to Ask Yourself about Your Script

There is a reason why you're writing a script. Certain questions can help you remain in touch with your passion, your creativity, and the methods that can best help you prepare your thoughts before writing a script.

Before beginning to write your script, ask yourself:

What's the one thing that makes me want to write this story?

What research is necessary for me to tell this story?

Have I thought through all the elements of my script— story, theme, characters, images, and dialogue?

Do I hear the voices of my characters? Are they beginning to talk to me so that when I start to write the dialogue, I'll have *real* characters talking? Have I incorporated specific syntax and word choice as part of those voices?

Have I taken enough time to explore the story and characters without rushing ahead to write the script?

Have I superimposed rules onto my story and characters, or have I tried to allow them to grow organically?

Am I focusing on my passion, my art, on what I really want to say? Or am I being overly concerned about marketing the script, how commercial it is, how much money I'm going to make, and how famous I'll become? Am I planning my Oscar-acceptance speech before the script is written, or am I willing to wait for the nomination?

Have I remembered to keep my eye on the process rather than trying to find fast results?

EXERCISES AND THINGS TO THINK ABOUT

(1) Watch a favorite movie, and outline it. Then transfer your outline to index cards. Then write a synopsis/treatment of the film. Then do the same with your own story ideas. Which of these methods do you find the most creative and the most helpful?

(2) Practice with an audio recorder, speaking your thoughts and storyline and bits of dialogue. Does this help, or hinder, your creative process?

(3) Watch several movies. Are there scenes that must have needed research for accuracy? If you were writing one of those scenes, how would you have researched it?

CHAPTER TWO

The Three-Act Structure:
Why You Need It and What to Do with It

You're a screenwriter. You've got your story worked out and you've just finished writing 115 pages of script. It's good. You know it's good, You've shown it to several friends who tell you it's really great—and might even win an Academy Award. But you have a gnawing feeling that something isn't quite right. Someplace, maybe in the second act, it seems like some of the elements don't fit. Something doesn't add up. You begin to doubt your work.

You're a producer who wants desperately to option a specific script. It's unique, it's funny, and it would make a great vehicle for one of the hottest stars in town. But the script seems inconsistent, the ending is much better than the beginning, and there seem to be too many characters. You don't want to let the deal go, but you can't commit to an unworkable story.

You're a development executive, three weeks away from shooting. The script still is a hefty 138 pages, the second act is lagging, and the star doesn't like the way her character develops in Act Two.

All of these are normal situations that must be confronted in order to make a good script great. They're all basically structural problems. It's not that the story isn't good. The problem lies with the construction of the story. The script doesn't yet work—but where to start?

THE THREE-ACT STRUCTURE

Writing and rewriting is a process that demands both a clear overview and great attention to detail. Like a script itself, the writing process has a beginning, a middle, and, thankfully, an end.

Part of writing and rewriting a good script includes finding a strong structure that will support your story. This means constructing your story in a way that will give it direction, momentum, and clarity. This means finding ways to help your audience "get with" your story and involve themselves with it all along the way. This means crafting your story into dramatic form.

Dramatic composition, almost from the beginning of recorded drama, has tended toward the three-act structure. Whether it's a Greek tragedy, a five-act Shakespeare play, a four-act dramatic TV series, or a seven-act Movie-of-the-Week, we still see the basic three-act structure: beginning, middle, and end—or the setup of the story in Act One, the development of the story in Act Two, and the build to a climax and a resolution in Act Three.

For movies, this is true whether a film is from Europe, Australia, Africa, Asia, or South America. The pacing might be different (often slower in non-American films). There might be less conflict in non-American films. Non-American films might be more character-driven than plot-driven. But a good film from anywhere in the world will still have a *sense* of the *three-act structure* to help it maintain clarity and momentum. (See "What Is Script Momentum?" in Chapter 4.)

Television artificially stops a show for commercials, creating two-acts (for sitcoms), seven acts (for a two-hour television movie), or four acts (for a dramatic series). But in a good television show, the three-act structure is still contained within these more artificial act endings. There is still a clear *setup*, *development*, and *resolution*.

Although there are no actual stopping places in feature films, an act structure is there—helping to move and focus the story. As a result of these similarities in all dramatic forms, all the comments I make about feature film structure are equally relevant to television and theater and even interactive storytelling.

These acts for a feature film usually include ten to fifteen pages of story setup and about twenty pages of development in Act One, an Act Two that might run forty-five to sixty pages, and a fairly fast-paced Act Three of twenty to thirty-five pages. Each act has a different focus. The movement out of one act and into the next is usually accomplished by an action or an event called a *turning point.* If we were to graph the three-act structure, it would look something like this:

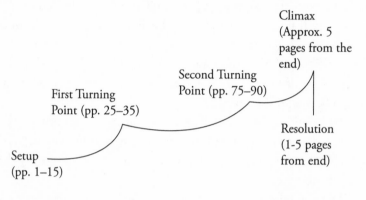

Climax
(Approx. 5
pages from the
end)

Second Turning
Point (pp. 75–90)

First Turning
Point (pp. 25–35)

Resolution
(1-5 pages
from end)

Setup
(pp. 1–15)

Act One   **Act Two**   **Act Three**

Written out, this structure is:

Act One
> Setup (page 1 to about page 15)
> Act One Development (from about page 15 to some where between pages 25 and 35)
> First Turning Point (somewhere in the neighborhood of pages 25 to 35)

Act Two (from about page 35 to page 75 or 85 or 90)
> Second Turning Point (somewhere in the neighborhood of pages 75 to 90)

Act Three (from around page 90 to page 115 or 120)
> Climax (approximately 5 pages from the end)
> Resolution (usually 3 to 5 pages from the end)

This structure provides balance among the parts of the script and can be applied to any dramatic writing. Regardless of how long the script is (a film short, a television series, a miniseries), approximately half of the total script is Act Two. About one-quarter of the script (or slightly more) is Act One and a bit less than one-quarter of the script is Act Three.

For an average-length feature film, Act Three needs to be at least eighteen to twenty pages in order to build up the drama and intensity of the act. If it's more than thirty or thirty-five pages long, the drama will usually dissipate and lose its structure and focus. The third act of *The Godfather: Part III* is about thirty-five minutes long—but then, there's a lot of killing to do, and the act preserves the urgency and drama because of its intercutting.

The length of the acts will depend upon the length of the overall film. In *Amadeus*, the first turning point (the burning of the crucifix and Salieri turning his focus to defeating Mozart) occurs at forty-three minutes into the film.

The page numbers I specify for the various parts of a script are approximate, since some scripts play faster than others. Although one script page usually equals around one minute of film, a comedy with rapid dialogue exchanges might go faster, and a script with long descriptions that must be acted out (such as "the army moves the elephants across the Alps") will obviously take much longer than a minute per page.

* * * * *

Each part of the three-act structure has a different purpose. The setup accomplishes different goals from the second turning point. The development of Act One is different from the development of Act Two. Act Three has to accomplish different objectives than Act One and Act Two. Reworking the script is more manageable after identifying the setup, the turning points, and the resolution.

THE SETUP

Creating the Context

The first few minutes of a story are often its most important. Many scripts have problems with the setup. It's unclear, unfocused. It sets up everything but the story.

The purpose of the setup is to tell us the vital information we need to get the story started. Who's the protagonist? Who are the main characters? What's the context? Where is it located? When does it take place? What's the genre? Is it comedy, drama, sci-fi, horror, action-adventure, thriller, or a combination genre?

Usually the first few minutes of a film show the context of the story. They establish the world of the film, and help the audience know where they are. Is it a war story? If so, which war? World War II looks different from Vietnam or a story that takes place in Iraq or in a South American country. One big American city, such as Atlanta, will look quite different from another, such as San Francisco. A small town in South Dakota looks different from one in Alabama.

The writer tells us, or implies, what year it is. For contemporary stories that clearly look contemporary, nothing needs to be said—just show us our recognizable world. But for films that take place a long time ago, such as 1776 or 10,000 BC or in Biblical times, the writer may need to let the audience know with "30 AD" emblazoned on the screen. For movies in the future, we may not need to know specifically whether the year is 2050 or 3008, but the look of the spaceships, electronics, and uniforms should tell us we are well into the future.

When establishing a context, the writer needs to set out the details that make the script's world believable and accurate.

If a film takes place in a context that is immediately recognizable, there may not need to be many details and not much needs to happen before the script moves from context to starting to tell the story. But in most films, the audience needs to see a few minutes of context before anything happens. It's the opportunity for the audience to settle in and get oriented, so they can enjoy the show without asking such questions as "What's going on?," "Where are we?," "What are those characters doing?," "Why are they doing it?"

Beginning with an Image

In most good films, context is shown through images. As a film begins, we see visual cues that give us a strong sense of its place, mood, and texture, and sometimes its theme. This first image could be a space battle (the famous first scene in *Star Wars*), street gangs in New York (the famous first scene in *West Side Story)*, Wall Street (*Wall Street*), Amish farmers walking down a road (*Witness*) or the famous floating feather in *Forrest Gump.*

Films that begin with dialogue, rather than well-chosen visual images, tend to be more difficult to understand—and slower to draw in the audience's attention. This is because the eye is quicker at grasping details than the ear. If important information is given verbally, before the audience has adjusted to the film's style, place, and sounds, the audience may not know how to incorporate them into the story.

In some films, we need a few minutes (or even longer) to adjust to the characters' accents before we can begin to understand the story. It might be a film with accents from northern England (*Billy Elliot*) or with lower-class Irish accents (*In Bruges*) or with Appalachian backcountry accents (*Nell, Matewan*) or with a Boston accent (*The Departed*) or a Baltimore accent (the HBO series *The Wire.*) If the audience isn't used to the dialect or accent, it's helpful to keep dialogue to a minimum early in the film and give the filmgoers a few moments to determine where they are, before they slowly begin to hear the language of the story.

So begin with an image that will quickly and powerfully convey a sense of where we are and a sense of the film's pacing style. Tell us as much as you can with this image. Get us into the mood of the piece. If possible, create a visual metaphor for the film, telling us something about its theme.

Creating the Style from Page One

Most great writers will create the style and the feel of their stories with more than just images and dialogue. They will also use a script's descriptive passages. Although the audience never sees these descriptions, the readers (including producers, directors, actors, cinematographers, and production designers) do. If it's a comedy, the beginning images and descriptions and first pieces of dialogue should have some sense of comedy, or at least a comic tone, to them.

The beginning of the script of the classic comedy *Some Like It Hot* (written by Billy Wilder and I. A. L. Diamond) gives a sense of tone and period:

```
FADE IN:

CITY AT NIGHT

A hearse of late-twenties vintage is proceeding
at a dignified pace along a half-deserted
wintry street.

Inside the hearse, there are four somber men
in black—and a coffin, of course, with a
wreath of chrysanthemums on top.
```

In this first scene, as the hearse proceeds, a police car starts chasing it. There's a hail of bullets, a chase, and a shooting—of the coffin. Liquid spurts through the coffin's bullet holes, and as its lid is removed, we see the inside is packed with booze. On the screen is superimposed: "Chicago, 1929."

The first line of dialogue comes at the bottom of page 2, after the hearse arrives at Mozarella's Funeral Parlor. We see a "mourner" as the coffin is taken inside. Mulligan, a federal agent, talks to Toothpick Charlie (who is so named, according to the script's description, "because his name is Charlie, and because he has never been seen without a toothpick in his mouth"). Charlie tells Mulligan the password for getting inside: "I come to Grandma's funeral."

Although the description is not all-out comedy, there are touches in the script that establish a humorous tone: the hearse moves at a "dignified pace," there's a "wreath of chrysanthemums"—"of course." The tone is still not absolutely clear, but there's an exciting car chase and plenty of bullets, yet no one gets hurt. The booze in the coffin is a punch line. By this time, the audience knows this is not meant to be a serious crime drama. The style has been set. The period is set up by the era of the car, followed by the onscreen date. Most of the beginning is images, not dialogue.

The film *The Lord of the Rings* had to set up a place that's not inhabited by humans. The script did this by beginning with a chant in the Elvish language: "I amar prestart sen." Images then show us three rings being forged at the Noldorin Forge and given to the High Elves, who have unusual names such as "Galadriel."

Just from the words used (Elvish, Noldorin Forge, Galadriel), we know immediately this is another world. The chanting, the sense of something magical happening with the rings, begins the story.

Juno starts simply, but its script's descriptions contain very precise words to set its character and tone. The first line of dialogue implies this isn't a heavy drama, although as the story proceeds, we can see it's dealing with an important subject

The images begin by showing us sixteen-year-old Juno on a street, looking at a leather recliner, abandoned on the curb. Juno says, "It started with a chair."

Nothing need be said about the year or about the city. It's contemporary. Within another page, the story has begun—Juno is pregnant.

Finding the Catalyst

After the initial images that begin a film, we need to move from context to story. And some event needs to set the story in motion. I call this event the *catalyst*.

The catalyst begins a story's action. Something happens—a crime occurs, a letter arrives, Aunt Mary appears on the doorstep—and from that moment on the story is defined.

Until the catalyst kicks off the story, the only information the audience has is where and when the film takes place. But once an event happens, the story suddenly has focus and direction.

Sometimes this catalyst presents a problem that must be addressed (there's pollution or someone is ill) or a need (the need for a cure, the need to find the killer, the need to find someone who will commit to a true love). Sometimes the catalyst is a disturbance, something jarring that starts an extraordinary journey.

The strongest catalysts are specific *actions*. In many crime stories, detective stories, and mysteries, a very strong action somewhere in the setup will explosively begin the story. In television shows, such as *CSI* or *Law & Order*, *The Mentalist*, *Without a Trace*, and *Ghost Whisper*, the catalyst (usually a crime) takes places in the first few minutes of the show. In such films as *The Dark Knight*, *The Fugitive*, and *State of Play*, a crime is one of the first images on the screen. In *Jaws*, the first shark attack begins as the credits end. In *Crash*, the first scene introduces the accident that will set the flashback story in motion. In *Capote*, the first scene introduces the crime that will be the catalyst for both the crime story and Capote's book *In Cold Blood*. In *Pulp Fiction*, the first scene is the beginning of a robbery, although the scene is interrupted and isn't completed until near the end of the film.

In many other crime stories, the crime happens after a few scenes have set up the movie's world—a big city (*The Naked City*), a small town (*In the Heat of the Night*), a foreign country (*The Man Who Knew Too Much*), or a family or community (*Changeling*, *Witness*) that will be forever changed by some event. In such films, the crime can happen anytime until the end of the setup, which might be at four minutes, twelve minutes, or fifteen minutes. If the crime takes place after the setup, the audience will simply be watching context, without the story getting underway, and there won't be adequate time to develop the crime's investigation.

Sometimes the catalyst can be a piece of *information* that a character receives. Such a catalyst orients the audience to the subject of the story through dialogue (including via a phone call or a letter that's read aloud) rather than action. Perhaps a character is told that she is eligible for the beauty pageant (*Little Miss Sunshine*) or that her daughter-in-law has died (*The Queen*) or that she must leave the convent to teach seven children (*The Sound of Music*) or that he's given a chance to fight the champion (*Rocky*). Although this type of catalyst isn't as forceful as an event, in relationship-based stories it might be very appropriate.

Sometimes a catalyst is *situational*, made up of a series of incidents that add up over a period of time. This sort of catalyst is rare, because hinting at action is usually not a strong way to start a story. Three films that have situational catalysts are *Tootsie*, *Back to the Future*, and *Some Like It Hot*. *Tootsie*, for instance, introduces the New York theater world, showing how difficult it is to get a job. Then it shows Sandy preparing for and going on an audition for a soap opera. Then it shows that Michael is difficult, so nobody wants to hire him. These small catalysts culminate at the moment when Michael decides to try out for the woman's role in the soap opera. At twenty minutes into the film, Michael takes on the persona of Dorothy, and the story is now focused.

In *Back to the Future*, Marty goes into the future at about twenty minutes into the film. But several small catalysts prepare us for this. We first find out that the crazy inventor is working on some visionary creation. He then asks Marty to meet him at the mall. After which they try out the time-travel car. And, at twenty minutes in the film, Marty time travels back to the past.

Some Like It Hot begins with a series of small catalytic incidents. It introduces the cops chasing the gangsters and raiding a speakeasy, putting two musicians out of work. Then it shows that these two impoverished musicians have trouble landing other jobs. Then one big event draws together and focuses all these little incidents: The musicians witness a mob hit, which forces them to flee town immediately.

When very skillfully handled, this sort of a situational catalyst can shade in a movie's style and context and imply that something dramatic is ready to happen. But be careful of this type of setup. It demands that the audience find the film's context exciting enough to stay engaged with a story that's taking a long time to begin. In most scripts where you find overly long setups, the writer is not trying to create a situational catalyst, but simply overwriting.

Raising the Central Question

The introduction of the catalyst does not complete the setup. The opening images have oriented the audience, and the catalyst has begun the story, but there's one more ingredient necessary before the story is fully underway—*the central question.*

Every story, in a sense, is a mystery. It asks a question in the setup that will be answered at the climax. Usually, a problem is introduced or a situation that needs to be resolved is presented. This situation or problem raises a question in our minds, such as "Will the detective find the murderer?," "Will these two beautiful young people fall in love and get married?," "Will the mountain climber reach the summit of Everest?," "Will the woman get promoted?," "Will the man get cured of his terrible disease?"

Once it is raised, everything that happens in the story relates to that question, which keeps coming up throughout the story. With each turning point and each setback and each step forward, the question is repeated subconsciously. At the story's climax, there's an answer, which is almost always "yes." Will the detective solve the crime? Yes. Will the lovers get together? Yes. Will the mountain climber reach the top? Yes. But since we don't learn the answers until the end, we remain interested in what will happen along the way and how the objective built into the central question will be accomplished.

Once the central question has been asked, the setup is complete, and the story is now ready to unfold.

ACT ONE DEVELOPMENT

By the end of the setup, we are usually about ten to fifteen minutes into a full-length film. It's important to keep the setup tight because the audience will become impatient if they don't have some sense of the story after fifteen minutes. The longer a story waits to get started, the more danger there is that it might not have a strong narrative line, sometimes called the *spine* of a story, or that the audience won't find it.

There are, of course, a number of foreign films and some American films that make the audience wait much longer than fifteen minutes for a sense of the story spine. And although some of these films may be artistic successes, rarely are they box-office successes. Since I believe that you can have scripts that are both artistic and well crafted without compromise, I recommend a tight, clean, clear beginning.

After the setup, more information is necessary to orient us to the story. We need to learn more about the characters. We need to see the characters in action before we see them develop in Act Two. We might need to know more about a character's *backstory* (i.e., what took place in a character's life before the point at which the movie picked up his or her story) or physical situation. Where is the character coming from? What's motivating the character? What's the central conflict? Who's the antagonist? This is *Act One development*.

Once there's a catalyst to define the story, Act One proceeds with Act One development. This section of the script gives us all the additional information we need before the story *opens up* into Act Two. Act One development might, for example, give us more information about a crime, perhaps even taking us down a wrong road as investigators try to solve it. It might introduce the protagonist's family and friends, or tell us more about the protagonist's challenge(s) ahead. In a film about some terrible disease, it might include losing all hope for the patient before exploring an alternative cure during Act Two. Whatever information we *need* to know that isn't in the setup, generally becomes part of Act One's development, since Act Two must develop the *story* and usually doesn't have time for a great deal of *expositional* information.

Beats

To analyze Act One, we need to understand the important *beats* that prepare us for the story's unfolding. The word "beat" in drama tends to be somewhat vague. Actors sometimes use the term to designate a pause, as in "I want to take a beat after I pick up the knife but before going after my victim." Writers may use the term to define a *series of events*, big (a murder) or small (taking a tomato out of the refrigerator). For example, a writer might decide to create six beats to show a meeting between the two soon-to-be lovers: Beat #1: A cute guy comes into a café. Beat #2: A gorgeous waitress asks him if he wants a cinnamon cappuccino or a mint latte. Beat #3: She brings him his coffee. Beat #4: She knocks it over. Beat #5: They both jump to clean up the mess. Beat #6: They bang heads; their eyes meet under the table, and it's clear this is love at first sight.

For writers, a beat works in a script much as a beat works in a piece of music. In a song, single beats are grouped to make up a measure. By adding more beats (thus more measures) you create a phrase, and eventually an entire melody. In the same way, single dramatic beats or moments, placed together, create a scene. And the beats in a scene, together, create the beats of an act, and the beats of an act, together, create an entire film.

CREATING THE TURNING POINTS

A good story always is interesting from beginning to end. It retains interest because of unpredictable and intriguing twists and turns in the action along the way to its climax.

Although twists and turns can happen throughout a story, in the three-act structure there are two turning points that must happen to keep the action moving—one at the beginning of Act Two and one at the beginning of Act Three. These help a story move forward by introducing changes from the expected, the norm: New events unfold. New decisions are made. As a result of these two turning points, the story achieves momentum.

Generally, the first turning point happens about a half-hour into the film, with the second one coming about twenty to thirty minutes before the end of the film. Each accomplishes a variety of functions:

It turns the action in a new direction.

It raises the central question again and makes us wonder about the answer.

It often requires a decision or commitment on the part of the main character.

It raises the stakes.

It *pushes* the story into the next act.

It takes the audience into a new arena, where a character's actions may be seen with a new focus.

A particularly strong turning point will accomplish all of these functions, although many successful turning points accomplish only some of them.

DEVELOPING ACT TWO

Act Two plays out the central action of the story. Act Two advances the story, develops the conflict, explores the theme, and builds the relationships before Act Three shows the consequences of Act Two's actions.

If you're writing a detective story or crime story, Act Two is usually about the investigation of a crime or the planning of further crimes or the exploration of criminal motivation or corruption. The action can be done with the twists and turns of *L.A. Confidential*, with the chase-action combined with crime investigation of *The Fugitive*, with the threats and danger of *The Departed*, or with the intertwining of crime story and interrogations of *The Usual Suspects*. In crime stories and mysteries, it's the writer's job to make sure that the investigation is not played out in a derivative, predictable way.

If you're writing a love story, the second act develops the love relationship, unless it's a film such as *Sleepless in Seattle*, where the second act develops the *desire* for a love relationship. If it's a sport story, Act Two usually shows preparation and practice for a big contest that will take place in Act Three.

By the beginning of Act Two, if not in Act One, it's important to give the audience some sense of what the plan will be for Act Two. This plan is sometimes called the "mission" or the "objective" or the "intention." Clarifying the protagonist's mission, and therefore the story's objective, helps the audience stay up to speed and invested in the story. If the protagonist telegraphs even a loose agenda, the audience then knows what that character will try to accomplish and what kinds of obstacles and risks may loom ahead. In *The Proposal* (2009), for example, the main character makes it clear that she's going to stay in the United States, no matter what it takes. In *Julie & Julia*, Julie announces her plan to cook her way through Julia Child's cookbook and write a blog. Julia is also clear about her problem in Act One (that she wants to do something) and about its solution (she'll go to cooking school). In *The Lord of the Rings*, the mission—to throw the ring into Mount Doom—is clearly announced in the trilogy's first part, and accomplished at the end of the third part. In *Quiz Show,* the mission is clearly suggested to Charles Van Doren: Go on the show; you'll surely beat the doofus. In *(500) Days of Summer*, as well as many other love stories, the protagonist's mission—find true love—is clear. In many cop films, the mission (get the bad guy or make sure justice is done or get revenge) is announced fairly early in the picture.

When a script is too vague about the journey ahead, the audience can only watch passively, without worry, anticipation, and anxiety about the final outcome.

The Second Turning Point

After about an hour of developing the story in Act Two, a second turning point changes the action around once again, forcefully moving the story into Act Three. It accomplishes the same things as the first turning point:

> It turns the action in a new direction.
>
> It raises the central question again and makes us wonder about the answer.

It often requires a decision or commitment on the part of the main character.

It raises the stakes.

It *pushes* the story into the next act.

It takes the audience into a new arena, where a character's actions may be seen with a new focus.

But the second turning point does one thing more: It gives a sense of urgency, or momentum, to the story, speeding up the action to make the third act more intense than the first two. It *pushes* the story toward its conclusion.

Sometimes, a second turning point is a "ticking clock." In most James Bond films, an explosion or crime that will cause great havoc is put into play here, and Bond has just a few hours, or minutes, to diffuse the bomb or stop the madman. *The Dark Knight* has two ticking clock devices in the third act: (1) Batman has to decide who will he save in the little time left, and (2) The Joker is preparing to explode the hospital, which needs to be evacuated in minutes. Tick, tick, tick…

Sometimes the second turning point is in two beats. These beats are often (1) a *dark moment,* followed by (2) a *new stimulus.*

In a mystery, a dark moment might be when the detective has almost given up—despairing that the case is unsolvable. The new stimulus is the moment that suddenly occurs a bit later—after perhaps a few false steps—when the detective sees the solution. Then the third act proceeds as he finds the villain. In a horror film, the dark moment might be when the scientist realizes that he'll never be able to destroy the monster. But, a few moments and a stroke of genius later, a new plan—the new stimulus—is hatched.

If you use a two-part turning point, whether for your first or second turning point, make sure its two events—the dark moment and the new stimulus—occur close together. I have not yet seen a two-part turning point that worked when its two parts were separated by more than five minutes. If they're too far apart, the audience will be lost between acts, stuck in limbo, and the film will lose its direction.

Although a two-part turning point is rare, if done well it can be very effective and can add an extra structural punch. *Witness* uses a two-part first turning point. The first part occurs when John Book realizes that Schaeffer is in on the crime. This moves us out of Act One, since it now begins to focus the crime and the antagonist. John escapes. But we're not yet in Act Two, since it seems that John's intends to simply drop off Rachel and Samuel at their Amish farm and go hide out somewhere. That would then define Act Two as, perhaps, "hiding out in a cheap motel." The second part of the turning point occurs when John is forced to stay at the Amish Farm because he's hurt and passes out in his car. Now the focus of Act Two is set—it will take place at the Amish farm—and a new direction is defined.

There's a two-part second turning point in the movie *L.A. Confidential.* Police Captain Dudley Smith shoots Jack Vincennes (dark moment), bringing an end to Act Two as we realize the Captain is one of the bad guys. But we don't know yet the direction of Act Three. Not until Ed Exley adds up the clues (new stimulus), is the direction for Act Three set, allowing the story to start rolling again to its climax and resolution.

FOCUSING ACT THREE

Act Three is the consequence of Act Two's development. You can't get to Act Three without going through Act Two, although writers occasionally try to do so. If the story is a crime/detective story with an investigation in Act Two, the second turning point often is the moment when the detective figures out the identity of the guilty party and sets out to capture the criminal. But the criminal is not so easily nabbed. So, there occurs another hunt or another elaborate plan to trap the bad guy.

If you have a social issue story, sometimes Act Three is the trial of the corrupters or polluters or bad corporate guys. If your story is about a terrible disease, Act Three might be the tryout of a new cure.

Act Three generally has more urgency and more tension than the previous acts. The story is moving toward its big finish. If it's a thriller, the audience should be on the edge of their seats, with sweaty palms and wide-open eyes. If it's a tearjerker, now the audience gets out their three hankies to weep throughout the act.

In competition movies, the third act is the big contest—climb the mountain, ice skate to fame, play at the big piano competition, step into the ring at the boxing or wrestling championship, or vie for the big dance trophy.

The Big Finish

The *climax*, which usually happens one to five pages from the script's end, is the end of the story: It's *the big finish.* It's the moment when the problem is resolved, the central question is answered, the tension is released, and we learn that everything will be all right. The detective captures the criminal. The boy and the girl get together. The working girl gets the long-wanted promotion. The man is cured. The villain is done away with.

Once the climax is reached, the party is over. It's time to go home. But the third act still has one last part—the *resolution*, which is usually two to five pages long. Its purpose is to tie up all the story's loose ends, answer all the story's questions, and even finish up subplots. It's like a runner's brief cool-down. Yes, the show is over, but the audience needs a moment to regroup before leaving the theater.

It's important to keep a resolution short. By the time the climax occurs, there should be little else to say (and it's a good idea not to say it). There's no more time to develop the story or to overwhelm the audience with information about what happened next. Occasionally, there are extra pieces of information offered during the ending credits (as in *Unforgiven*), but in most cases, after a short resolution, it's time to write "The End."

In addition to crafting a story into three acts, there are other ways to add structure to a script. Among these script-shaping tools are the midpoint scene and the opening credit sequence.

THE MIDPOINT SCENE

The *midpoint scene* occurs just where you'd expect it—about halfway through the script. Syd Field, in *The Screenwriter's Workbook,* says that it divides the story in half, introducing an event or line of dialogue that helps structure Act Two.

In my work consulting on more than 2,000 scripts and teaching many of the best films, I don't find a midpoint scene in every film. But when I do find one, it functions as an excellent tool to help structure a difficult second act.

Besides dividing the entire script in half, the midpoint scene divides the second act in half, creating a change of direction for the second half of Act Two while keeping that act's overall focus, which was determined by the first turning point.

When a midpoint scene is used, one half of the act usually shows everything going smoothly, and the other half shows obstacles and danger and all sorts of problems. In most cases, the first half will be smooth, and the second half will show increasing trouble. In *Apollo 13*, the really big problems occur around the midpoint, with increasing trouble in the second half of Act Two. In most thrillers and cop movies, the danger escalates after the midpoint. In the film *Beauty and the Beast*, this is reversed. The first half of Act Two shows Belle having all sorts of problems and frustrations about and resistance to the Beast, and in the second half, everything goes smoothly (except for the problem with the wilting rose). He saves her life at the midpoint, and she falls in love in the second half.

Some of the best midpoint scenes can be found in mysteries, thrillers, and gangster films. In *The Fugitive*, the midpoint shows both Kimble and Gerard starting to investigate the murder, which leads to another level of action in the second half of the act, dimensionalizing the chase action with investigative action.

Finding the midpoint scene can be confusing for many writers. In my consulting work, I've discovered that many writers mistake the midpoint for the first turning point, thereby throwing the structure off and creating scripts where the second act doesn't begin until halfway through the script. However, if the writer begins by first creating a clear three-act structure, often a midpoint scene will naturally emerge. Then, in the rewriting process, the writer can strengthen and focus this scene.

THE OPENING CREDIT SEQUENCE

Although it's not necessary for a script to even mention the opening credits, sometimes they can lend added structure to a story's beginning, or give the audience information that prepares them for a story.

A movie's opening credits can begin in four ways.

(1) A movie might begin with several minutes of purely graphic (and typographic) credits, and then the story starts. These credits can be as simple as white print on a black screen (most of Woody Allen's films) or more involved, such as intriguingly or beautifully designed (and sometimes animated) credits. Many old films start with a short list of credits, and then the movie begins. This is still occasionally done, although credits have become increasingly creative. *A Room with a View, The Age of Innocence,* and *The Sting* had very classy titles that helped set the style of the film. Alfred Hitchcock often used his opening credits to give a sense of the suspense that would follow. *Vertigo* opens with an extreme closeup of a woman's lips, from which the camera pans up to one of here eyes as spiraling graphics are introduced to the frame. *Family Plot* shows mist and credits swirling in a crystal ball. *Psycho* shows jagged looking credits as a violin screeches on the soundtrack. However, if the credits are graphics and begin before the movie begins, there is no reason for a screenwriter to even mention them. (Note: Saul Bass was a master designer of opening credit sequences, including three of the ones mentioned above—*Vertigo, Psycho,* and *The Age of Innocence.* It might be worth your while to seek out some of his other classic credit sequences, including *Walk on the Wild Side, West Side Story, Anatomy of a Murder,* and *North by Northwest.*)

(2) Often, the opening credits appear over important images (and actions), usually without dialogue. In the classic Western *Shane,* for example, we see Shane ride toward the ranch. *Witness* begins with images of Amish life. Hitchcock's *Frenzy* has images of the Thames under the credits, and, once the credits end, a floating dead body is discovered. Hitchcock's *Rear Window* shows the all-important courtyard underneath the credits. *Frost/Nixon, Milk,* and *The Wrestler* give context by displaying footage and text taken from news archives—real or fabricated—to set up the ambitions and past glories of the protagonists.

Sometimes opening credits appear over photographs, as in *Norma Rae,* or a voice-over with photographs, as in *Field of Dreams.* By putting credits over images, a filmmaker can set up a great deal of context or other important information before a story has even begun. But, if not done carefully, this practice can be problematic, since the audience's focus is pulled in two different directions—reading the credits and watching the images. Credits work best over images when the audience is not asked to absorb complicated information beneath the credits.

Occasionally, a story's catalyst may happen under the credits, and then the story evolves immediately afterwards (*The Fugitive*).

(3) Since perhaps the 1980s, another approach to opening a film has gained some popularity—the *pre-credit sequence.* In most cases, this amounts to two or three minutes of montage or scenes that show a story catalyst such as a crime (*Crash, Spider-Man*), or set up characters (*Broadcast News*), or set up a context or situation. These initial scenes and/or images are followed by opening credits that are either written (*Pulp Fiction*) or appear over action (*Eternal Sunshine of the Spotless Mind*). Then, after the credits, the main characters and main focus of the story are introduced. Occasionally, pre-credit sequences can run rather long: *Born on the Fourth of July* and *WarGames* have pre-credit sequences of about seven minutes. In both cases, the pre-credit sequence sets up the film's context, but the story doesn't really begin until after the credits. In some films that exploit a pre-credit sequence, the catalyst—a crime or problem or disturbance—happens before the credits (*A Shot in the Dark, The Dark Knight*).

The movie *The Fugitive* uses a hybrid of opening credits styles: Some credits appear under the murder that begins the film, then, after the story proceeds, the credits return at eleven minutes into the film. This return of credits serves to separate the action of the setup (murder, arrest, trial) from the core of the story, which begins with the train crash and escape.

(4) Some films just begin, and all credits appear at the end. Some films have only minimal opening credits, such as just the title of the film (*Angels & Demons, Garden State*). This was fairly rare in the early 1990s, when Barbra Streisand did it with *The Prince of Tides*, but in the last few years this has become more and more popular.

Although many executives, producers, and directors tell writers that the credits really are not their business (and in most cases, there is no reason for a writer to write anything about the credits), there are times when the credits are part of the shape of the film. It then becomes necessary for the writer to communicate this structure to the reader and the producers.

SO WHAT DOES THE STRUCTURE LOOK LIKE?

If a film's script is well structured, you can leave the theater with some sense of its structure because you understand the story's focus, as well as its setup and big finish. You're fairly clear about how the story evolves. You're able to recount the story accurately to someone else.

Here are the basic three-act structures of a few successful films— some classics, some recent hits.

SHANE

SETUP: A stranger, Shane, rides up to the Starrett ranch house.

CATALYST: A neighboring rancher, Ryker, wants Starrett's land.

Shane decides to stay to help Starrett. (5 minutes)

ACT ONE DEVELOPMENT: Many of the other ranchers want to leave because of Ryker's harassment.

FIRST TURNING POINT: The good-guy ranchers meet and decide not to be driven off by Ryker. They form a group. (25 minutes)

ACT TWO: Confrontations develop.

MIDPOINT: Jack Wilson, a gunslinger, arrives. (About 50 minutes, just before the halfway point of the film. This works as a midpoint since it raises the stakes further without turning the direction of the focus of Act Two).

Ryker decides to bait Starrett. His men kill Starrett's friend and neighbor Stonewall. (75 minutes)

SECOND TURNING POINT: Starrett gets ready to go to town to have it out with Ryker. (90 minutes)

ACT THREE: The shootout between Shane and Wilson and Ryker.

CLIMAX: The bad guys are done away with. (110 minutes)

RESOLUTION: Shane rides away. Starrett's son, Joey, cries after him, "Shane, come back!" (115 minutes)

APOLLO 13

SETUP: Introduction of the astronauts and their families and Jim Lovell's desire to go to the moon.

CATALYST: Lovell gets the assignment. (10 minutes)

ACT ONE DEVELOPMENT: The astronauts prepare for their journey. Ken Mattingly is exposed to the measles and is taken off the list. Fred Haise will go in his place. (20 minutes)

FIRST TURNING POINT: Blastoff. (35 minutes)

ACT TWO—FIRST HALF: All goes smoothly until "Houston, we have a problem!" (50 minutes) Then, "We just lost the moon." (57 minutes)

MIDPOINT: The astronauts' oxygen levels are low. They haven't lost just the moon; they may lose their lives. NASA tries to figure out what to do. Ken Matttingly is asked to help. (77 minutes)

ACT TWO—SECOND HALF: The astronauts and the men at NASA try to figure out what to do to save them.

SECOND TURNING POINT: New ideas are tried. One works. They think it will save the lives of the astronauts. (99 minutes)

ACT THREE: The men are on their way home. Will they make it?

CLIMAX: The men are safe! The space capsule lands safely in the ocean. (130 minutes)

RESOLUTION: Voice-over epilogue. (132–134 minutes)

CHICAGO

SETUP: A crime is committed, Roxie is charged. (10 minutes)

ACT ONE DEVELOPMENT: Roxie is taken to jail. She meets Mama and Velma.

FIRST TURNING POINT: Roxie hires attorney Billy Flynn to defend her. (35 minutes)

ACT TWO: Roxie tries to make sure the case and the trial will make her a star.

SECOND TURNING POINT: The trial is ready to begin. (78 minutes)

ACT THREE: The trial.

CLIMAX: Roxie gets off. (95 minutes)

RESOLUTION: Roxie gets a job singing with Velma. (105 minutes)

STATE OF PLAY

SETUP: There are three crimes, including Sonia Baker's murder. (1 to 8 minutes)

ACT ONE DEVELOPMENT: Reporters Cal and Della are assigned to follow the case. Congressman Stephen Collins and the PointCorp Corporation are introduced.

FIRST TURNING POINT: Cal connects Sonia with the corporation. (30 minutes)

ACT TWO: Cal realizes the case is bigger than he thought.

SECOND TURNING POINT: Bigham is getting ready to go shoot someone (Cal, we presume). Cal begins to suspect that Collins is part of this. (All these beats are around 90 minutes.)

CLIMAX: Collins is arrested. (120 minutes)

RESOLUTION: The story is printed in the paper (under the closing credits). (127 minutes)

Notice that the catalyst comes in fairly quickly in each of these stories. The first turning point is about thirty minutes into each story, and the second turning point is about twenty to twenty-five minutes before their climaxes. The resolutions are fairly short, except in *Chicago*, in which Roxie's desire to be a star needs to be resolved, and since it's a musical, there needs to be one more musical number.

Many writers will lay out their stories in an outline form, similar to my structural analyses above, mapping out the simplest structures and then filling in information for each act.

BUT WHAT ABOUT...?

Although it may seem that the three-act structure is a form that would create predictable and boring films, it needn't be. Just as composers continue to create works of immense variety from simple classical structures (the sonata, the rondo, etc.) and artists continue to create paintings on simple squares and rectangles of canvas, writers learn to tell three-act stories that aren't just a meaningless series of episodes, but a compelling narrative that pulls in and engages the audience.

At first look, some films don't seem to fit the three-act model at all. But they usually turn out to be variations on the simple structure. And these more difficult films usually are not written by first-time writers but by those who have learned the basics of conventional form and can experiment with it without having their stories fall apart.

Sometimes a film such as *Psycho* kills off the person who seems to be the main character. But notice where she's killed in *Psycho*—at the first turning point. The story then opens up by focusing on the murder and the detective who will solve the murder. Notice that this film builds suspense from the beginning, setting up its horror/thriller genre with a murder.

A similar technique was used in *Fargo*. Marge, the main character, doesn't enter the story until the murders of the men in the car. Notice, again, where this occurs—at the first turning point. When Marge begins her investigation, she isn't investigating the kidnapping that was set up in Act One, she's investigating the murders. The kidnapping story and the murder story separate at the first turning point, creating two plotlines that intertwine at times and then come together at the end.

No Country for Old Men begins with a monologue from Sheriff Bell, but it might seem that Llewelyn Moss is the primary protagonist. These two characters are closely related in motive, but they never share the screen. Llewelyn's character might be more accurately described as the catalyst (a humanizing catalyst) because he's a victim, running from the villain, with the hero (the Sheriff) bringing up the rear. It is Llewelyn who sets the chase in motion when he stumbles across the battle in the desert. When he is taken out of the film about two-thirds of the way through, the audience still has Sheriff Bell to follow, since he was so clearly established at the beginning.

Some films seem to belie the three-act structure because they work with four events: *Four Weddings and a Funeral, Frost/Nixon* (which has four interviews), and *Four Christmases* all have a similar structures. In these films, the fourth repetition (the last wedding and the funeral, the fourth interview, the fourth Christmas) takes place in the third act. The first event either takes place in the first act with the next two in Act Two, or, as in the case of *Frost/Nixon*, three interviews take place in Act Two. In these films, the fourth event raises the stakes and usually has a sense of urgency to it, as it works its way toward a resolution.

I often hear, "But this film doesn't follow the three-act structure!" Well, sometimes the places where a film doesn't follow that structure are its weakest. However, in remembering a film, we often recall only its particularly good and creative and engaging parts. Our memory of these often leads us to consider such a film great.

In the film world, one of the best-loved films is *Cinema Paradiso*. The first half of this Italian film is beautifully structured. Toto loves films. Alfredo allows him to sit by him in the projection room, but he doesn't allow him to do what he really wants to do: work the projector. At the first turning point (about thirty-three minutes into the film), Alfredo is taking an exam and doesn't know an answer. Toto agrees to give him the answer if he allows him to work the projector. Alfredo says yes. In the first half of Act Two, Toto works the projector and continues to work with Alfredo, watching wonderful films while censoring the kissing scenes. At the midpoint, Alfredo is blinded in a fire. During the second half of Act Two, the story wanders and begins to lose the first half's tight structure. Toto goes into the Army and then comes out. Toto falls in love with Elena and stands by her window for many days. These are detours that have little to do with Toto's love of movies and slow up the movement of the film. Although there's no problem with adding a love subplot, little happens in this subplot and Elena is not a very interesting character. At the second turning point the story comes back into focus, as the adult Toto decides to go back home to attend Alfredo's funeral. Although the third act is long and drags a bit, it refocuses on Toto's love of movies and contains the memorable scene of Toto watching the kissing scenes that were originally censored.

The director's cut of the film adds scenes to Act Three, showing Toto meeting Elena again and, well, on and on. It won its Academy Award for Best Foreign Film based on the 123-minute version of the film. You may want to think about which scenes you loved the best, and then check to see if these scenes are in the well-structured part of the script, or in the more episodic second half of Act Two.

I'm often asked, "What is your favorite film?" Most of those who ask the question probably expect me to mention a great film, such as *Casablanca* or *Citizen Kane* or *Amadeus,* or *Gone With the Wind.* But one of my favorite films is the classic musical *Seven Brides for Seven Brothers,* which I first saw when I was young. Regardless of my love of this film, I'd be the first to mention that the setup and Act One and first half of Act Two are strong, and the second half of Act Two lags. The Third Act needs a bit more development to extend the tension that starts at the second turning point (the fathers are coming to get their daughters!).

We love films for many reasons, and they all aren't structural. But structure, which can keep an audience focused and engaged, is one aspect of a film that you, the writer, can control.

WHAT GOES WRONG WITH STRUCTURE?

Rarely will you see a film in which each act is equally well structured. Not everyone in Hollywood knows how to structure a script, nor is every brilliant writer necessarily a brilliant structurer. As a result, most films will have flaws in one or more of their acts.

Sometimes, you'll see a very slow setup (*Tender Mercies*).

Some films wait too long for their first turning point, which leads to a lag in the action in Act One and condenses the development of Act Two, which can easily lose audience interest (*Awakenings*) or not lead audiences to a satisfying ending.

Some films place the second turning point too early, causing Act Three to lag, or place it too late, so that there isn't sufficient time to develop tension and suspense leading to the big finish. (Notice in *Awakenings* that Act Two gets squashed between the first and second turning points, not giving the old folks long enough to be happy in order to balance out their more catatonic time.)

Some films, even some great ones, have overly long resolutions that continue, on and on, after the climax has been reached (*The Color Purple* and *A Passage to India*). Watch the final installment of *The Lord of the Rings* trilogy, where the resolution had a great many ends to tie up. Did you feel it was too long? Did you notice any places to make cuts that could tighten it? How might you reapproach the last few minutes of the film to get a great deal of information into a small amount of time?

Rewriting often is a time of cutting and condensing and shaping. Images are made clearer and context is sharpened. Turning points are tightened if an act is overwritten and seems to drag. The climax is built up. The resolution is condensed. Many times, great economy of writing is called for to get an act shortened, or a writer needs to think of further details to develop an act so it's played out to its fullest.

Sometimes the structure in a film is very strong and clear, but too predictable. You know exactly what will happen before it happens. There are no surprises. Other times, films are artistic and original, but difficult to follow or too unfocused. They might be beautiful pieces of art, but they're not well crafted. A great writer brings together art and craft into one seamless whole.

Studying well-structured films helps writers write well-structured scripts. Some well-structured films worthy of study include *Witness, The Fugitive, Fatal Attraction, Romancing the Stone, The African Queen, Tootsie*, and *Back to the Future*. Some more recent films with a tight structures include *Erin Brockovich, Little Miss Sunshine, Shrek, Slumdog Millionaire*, and *Shakespeare in Love*. You can also see a very strong structure in the nontraditional film *Crash*, which I analyzed in my book *And the Best Screenplay Goes To…* The turning points in *Crash* are not readily apparent during a first viewing. However, the test for films like it, and for any film or script, is the same: If you feel focused throughout, without any lags in your interest or in the movement of the story, you can be fairly certain that the script is well-structured.

APPLICATION

Questions to Ask Yourself about Your Script

Much of the work of a rewrite is restructuring the story. The three acts of a first-draft script are rarely clear. Usually, one act is stronger than the others. Sometimes a turning point is misplaced. Or a turning point might be weak, hindering the movement of the script from act to act.

As you look through the structure of your script, ask yourself the following questions:

Did I begin with an image?

Does that image give a sense of the story's style and feeling?

Do I have a clear catalyst to begin the story? Is it strong and dramatic, preferably expressed through action?

Is the central question clear? Does the central question set up the climax of my story? Does each turning point bring up the central question again?

Do I have a clear first turning point? Does it lead into the action of Act Two?

Is my second turning point clear? Does it set up the climax?

Is my climax a big finish? Is my resolution quick?

EXERCISES AND THINGS TO THINK ABOUT

(1) Watch the beginnings of five to ten films. Identify the context and the catalyst and the central question in each one. When does the catalyst occur? Were there any parts of the context or the catalyst that you believe demanded research from the writer in order to get it right?

(2) Consider the catalyst and two turning points in a film or television show you like and in one you don't like. Do they imply the action that will follow? Do they imply so much that the story becomes predictable, or not enough, so it seems that the story took detours?

Compare and contrast the use of these elements in a film, such as a detective/mystery, and a television series that has similar subjective matter, such as *CSI* and *Law & Order.*

(3) Identify the turning points in a mystery, a comedy, a drama, and perhaps several films in other genres. Time the films to see where these occur. Do they all work? Are they all action points, or are some dialogue points?

You've reworked your major plotline. It's consistent. It's dramatic. It moves. But rarely will you have only one plotline. Integrating subplots is the next important step.

CHAPTER THREE

What Do Subplots Do?

A workable subplot adds dimensionality to a script. Subplots give the protagonist an opportunity to smell the flowers, to fall in love, to enjoy a hobby, to learn something new. Subplots are usually relationship stories, whereas the plot is usually an action story.

A good subplot *pushes* the plotline, often changing the plot's direction. In *Chicago,* Roxie's desire to be a star (subplot) keeps pushing her relationship with Velma, and pushing her decisions about how to handle her murder case, which is the plotline. In *A Beautiful Mind,* the love-story subplot raises the stakes and pushes both John Nash and his wife Alicia to resolve his mental illness (plot) in order to save his reputation and his family. In *Shane,* the very small subplot about Shane and Marian Starrett helps us care more about Shane; it gives him dimension by showing his yearning for a kind of family life he will probably never have.

The plot and subplot then interweave. A good subplot not only pushes the plotline, it also intersects it. Subplots aren't free floating, and they aren't detours—they're connected to the plot. They may be connected because the love interest on the subplot line pays off on the plotline. Perhaps the love interest (a subplot) in a detective story is a fellow detective who is working on the case (the plot) or is a witness or some other person who holds an important clue to solving the case. Perhaps the protagonist has a hobby or avocation (a subplot), such as jogging, mountain climbing, or kayaking, that pays off in the main story (the plot) by becoming the means by which the protagonist escapes danger.

A good subplot carries a story's theme. The plot is what the film is about, but a subplot shows what the film is *really* about. Many times writers write scripts because of their interests in the significance of their subplots.

Subplots can be about almost anything. Often they're the love story that tells us something about the nature of love. Sometimes they carry important individual themes of identity, integrity, greed, or "finding oneself."

Sometimes a subplot reveals a character's vulnerability. We often see this in detective films in which the macho detective has to be strong and prepared for anything on the plotline. But when he's with his girlfriend or mother, we see his vulnerable side. Sometimes we see a character's goals, dreams, and desires through subplots. It's as if the character is too busy "doing" the plot to tell us much about himself or herself. Subplots give characters a chance to relax, to dream, to wish, and to think about larger visions.

A subplot can show us the transformation of characters. It can show us the beat-by-beat development of a character's identity, self-esteem, or self-confidence. It can help us see why and how a character changes.

I have occasionally worked with writers who don't want to discuss the plot, because they're not interested in it. They have it because they need it. But their concerns are about making their subplots work.

Many times, subplots are the most interesting part of a film because they add dimension to the story. Sometimes a subplot is what we remember most about the film, what moves us, what interests us. However, without a well-structured plotline, subplots won't work, so both need to be attended to carefully.

How Many Subplots Do You Need?

Most films will have at least one or two subplots. Some films may have as many as five or six. If a film has no subplots, it's in danger of being too linear, without dimension. If it has too many, they can muddle the script as well as take time away from the development of the "A" story, which is the main plot, and the "B" story, which is the main subplot.

Subplots can work well to complicate a storyline that may be too predictable. Movies such as *Tootsie, As Good as It Gets,* and *Ruthless People* are unusual, since they have five or six or seven subplots. They get many of their complications from the interest of the subplots. Each subplot turns the direction of the story, creating humor and unpredictability.

If you want a great many twists and turns in your script, look to subplots to help you. If you want a good deal of development of the main plot, you'll want fewer subplots, since the more subplots you have, the more time is spent away from the main story.

How Much Time Does a Subplot Take?

The plot usually is given the most screen time because it's the main story, the story that gives direction and momentum to your script. This is certainly true in almost all mystery, detective, thriller, action-adventure, and sci-fi movies, where it takes considerable time to develop the plot, build the excitement, and set up and pay off information or clues.

Occasionally, a subplot or a combination of subplots may take more screen time than the plot. In *Stand by Me,* the story that gives the movie direction is about the search for a dead body. But the movie puts most of its screen time into the friendships between the boys. Yet, without the direction-giving story (the plot), the movie would just be a series of episodes from the lives of four friends.

October Sky is similar. It has an important main story (plot) about Homer Hickam's love of rockets and desire to follow his passion. It also has several relationship stories that carry the film's style and emotions and theme.

In *Slumdog Millionaire,* the main story could be defined as the quiz show. It gives direction to the story and raises the central question: "Will Jamal win the million rupees?" The quiz show, however, is presented in fewer beats than the subplots about the police interrogations, the love between Jamal and Latika, the relationship of the two brothers, and Jamal's epic background story about his struggle with poverty and oppression. Although we root for Jamal to answer the questions correctly, without all the background provided by the subplots, we wouldn't care as much about the hope that the money offers to him.

In love stories that have a strong love relationship, the subplot might seem to be the whole movie, and it may be difficult to define a main plot. This is rare, however, since even love stories usually have a main plot about some goal other falling in love that has to be accomplished. In *Sleepless in Seattle*, it may seem that there isn't a main plot, but Annie Reed's journey—trying to find the man she had heard about—is the plot that gives direction to the story. But there are exceptions. *When Harry Met Sally* is a love story without any real outside goals. In that case, the love story is the main plot that gives direction to the story, with subplots about the characters' relationships with friends and each other. Movies like *Crash* and *The Big Chill* and *Traffic* seem to be only subplots, yet *Crash* has an investigation that gives forward direction, and *Traffic* has the drug trade that gives direction, and *The Big Chill* has the goal of getting pregnant. Although such a goal-oriented story may be small, it can still advance the action.

Pride & Prejudice seems to be mainly relationship stories, but there's a clear goal that is set up from the beginning—the mother needs to get her daughters married off. Although the film focuses on relationships, these are all part of the mother's bigger plan. Although a film like *Enchanted* seems to focus on relationships, there are still the questions about whether Giselle will return to her fairytale world, and whether her wicked stepmother will succeed in foiling Giselle's happiness.

THE STRUCTURE OF SUBPLOTS

Just as the plot has a beginning, a middle, and an end, so too does a subplot. A good subplot also has a clear setup, turning points, developments, and a payoff at the end. Sometimes the turning points of a subplot reinforce the plotline by occurring right before or right after the plot's turning points. This is often used in non-American films, especially those that don't have a strong plotline but rely on their subplots for interest. The subplots' turning points might be clustered around the plot's turning points, reinforcing what might have been weak turning points in the plot.

A subplot's turning point might occur in the middle of Act Two or Act Three. This gives a film extra twists and turns, since the plot's first turning point twists and propels it into the second act, while its subplots' turning points can offer extra story twists partway through an act.

Sometimes a subplot doesn't even begin until the plot's first turning point. In such films as *Romancing the Stone, Tootsie, Unforgiven, Back to the Future, Shrek, King Kong,* and *Ratatouille,* a subplot begins at the plot's first turning point.

The intersection of a subplot and the plot would look something like this (we will call the plot the "A" Story and the relationship subplot the "B" Story):

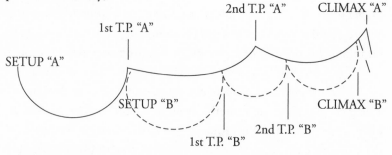

Here, characters meet at the first turning point (as in *Romancing the Stone* and *Tootsie*), beginning a relationship subplot, which has its first turning point in the middle of the script and its second turning point near the "A" Story's second turning point. After that, the climaxes of the "A" and "B" Stories come together.

OR, the intersection of a plot and a subplot might look like this, where the subplot begins in Act One and follows much of the structure of the "A" Story:

"B" Story

"A" Story

BREAKING DOWN *AS GOOD AS IT GETS*

Few traditionally structured films contain many subplots. One that does is *Tootsie*. Another is *As Good as It Gets*, which I discussed in my book *Advanced Screenwriting*. Some nontraditional structures can be found in films based almost totally on subplots, such as *Crash*, which I analyzed in my book *And the Best Screenplay Goes To...*

One of my favorite films, and a film that seems to get richer with each viewing, is *As Good as It Gets*. Every subplot in it (and there are many) has a clear three-act structure and helps Melvin's transformation. At first glance, this film seems to lack a clear "A" Story. It seems as if the movie is made up of nothing but relationship stories. I believe, however, that the "A" Story that gives the film direction is the story of the worst guy in New York, afflicted with an obsessive-compulsive disorder and an inability to relate to others, who gets better. This getting-better plot works on two levels—Melvin has to be willing to take some pills and to relate better to others (to like, perhaps even love, others). This transformational getting-better plotline is very simple, and all other subplots relate to it in one way or another.

"A" STORY: MELVIN GETTING BETTER

ACT ONE/SETUP: Melvin doesn't love anyone. He has an obsessive-compulsive disorder, as evidenced by the many times he locks his doors and washes his hands. (4 to 5 minutes)

FIRST TURNING POINT: Melvin starts to change when he changes his seat in the restaurant, therefore showing that he likes the dog, and he seems to also like Carol. (35 minutes)

ACT TWO: Melvin begins to make small changes. He goes to see the therapist, and gets pills that help him. (42 minutes)

Melvin tells Carol he wants to be a better man. (100 minutes)

SECOND TURNING POINT: Carol leaves him. She doesn't think that he's good for her. (115 minutes)

ACT THREE: Melvin tells Simon he's not sure if he wants to change. Simon says, "Then get in your jammies and I'll read you a story." Melvin decides to go to see Carol.

CLIMAX: He pays Carol a compliment, kisses Carol, and, for a moment, steps on a crack. (131–132 minutes)

We can look at all the subplots in terms of how they help Melvin get better:

"B" STORY: MELVIN AND CAROL

Melvin wants to get better because he likes Carol. So Carol's character, as a good, forgiving, kind person, helps push Melvin to make some new decisions.

ACT ONE/SETUP: Film establishes that Melvin has a favorite restaurant where he eats breakfast every day. Carol is the only waitress that isn't afraid of him and can tolerate him. Carol establishes her boundaries: He is not to talk about her son! (15 minutes)

FIRST TURNING POINT: Melvin asks Carol about her son. It's the first time he has shown an interest in someone else. He and Carol talk. (23 minutes)

ACT TWO: He and Carol begin to talk more often at the restaurant.

Carol and Melvin go out on a dinner date at a beautiful restaurant. (92 minutes)

SECOND TURNING POINT: Carol leaves him. She doesn't want to be around him. (115 minutes)

CLIMAX: He and Carol kiss. They go to the bakery together. (131 minutes)

"C" STORY: MELVIN AND SIMON

ACT ONE/SETUP: Establish Simon, an artistic gay neighbor with a dog that Melvin doesn't like. But then, Melvin doesn't like anyone, as Simon states. (2 to 6 minutes) Frank confronts Melvin, and lets him know that Frank will think of some way for Melvin to make it up to Simon for his meanness.

FIRST TURNING POINT: Simon is robbed and beaten. Melvin will take care of his dog. (24 minutes)

ACT TWO: Melvin takes care of the dog while Simon recovers.

Simon returns. He must give the dog back. Melvin cries. (38 minutes)

EARLY MIDPOINT: Melvin is asked whether he can walk the dog. (55 minutes)

SECOND HALF OF ACT TWO: Melvin comes to walk the dog and sees Simon in his depressed state. Melvin softens and tells Simon why the dog comes to him—it's the bacon.

Melvin agrees to drive Simon to his parents to ask for money and help.

SECOND TURNING POINT: Melvin arranges for Simon to come and live with him, since Simon has to give up his apartment. (115 minutes)

ACT THREE: Melvin and Simon are roommates.

CLIMAX: Simon encourages Melvin to go after Carol. Clearly they are getting along.

"D" STORY: MELVIN AND THE DOG

ACT ONE/SETUP: Melvin doesn't like the dog. (1 to 2 minutes)

FIRST TURNING POINT: Melvin is asked to take care of the dog. (28 minutes)

ACT TWO: Melvin has to give back the dog. (38 minutes)

MIDPOINT: But then he's asked if he'll walk the dog. Yes, he will. (55 minutes)

SECOND TURNING POINT: Melvin is worried about the dog. But the dog is in a kennel, so Melvin is able to help Simon by driving him to see his parents. (This turning point is discussed, but we don't see the dog.) (72 minutes)

ACT THREE: The dog is not discussed. The focus moves to Melvin and Simon.

CLIMAX: Melvin and Simon come home to Melvin's apartment. The dog is there. "Mummy and Daddy are home!" (116 minutes)

"E" STORY: MELVIN AND SPENCE

As a result of his fondness for Carol, Melvin becomes interested in her son, Spence.

ACT ONE/SETUP: Melvin mentions Spence, and Carol tells him to never mention her son again. (13 minutes)

FIRST TURNING POINT: Melvin meets Spence and finds out more about his life. (45 minutes)

ACT TWO: Melvin takes Carol and Spence to the hospital. (48 minutes)

AN EARLY MIDPOINT: Melvin arranges for Spence to get help from Dr. Betz. (52 to 54 minutes) This changes Carol's as well as Spence's life. She is grateful to Melvin.

She wants to thank him. If she wants to thank him, he insists she chaperone Simon when he drives Simon to go to see his parents. She likes the idea of a convertible and a ride in the country.

This pushes the relationship of Carol and Melvin.

CLIMAX: Carol calls Spence. He's playing soccer. (90 minutes)

Notice that there isn't a second turning point in this smaller subplot, nor is there an Act Three that leads to a resolution. Once the doctor has helped Spence, the Melvin-Carol story gets a push, and the Melvin-Spence subplot just needs to be completed by letting us know that all is well.

The Melvin-Carol subplot is also pushed by the Melvin-Simon subplot.

Simon has his own subplot—about his relationship to his art. It's Simon's desire to be an artist that sets up a number of different events that push the story.

"F" STORY: SIMON AND HIS ART

ACT ONE/SETUP: Simon is an artist. He has an art party in the first scene. Introduce Frank, who shows Simon's work. (6 minutes)

FIRST TURNING POINT: Simon is beaten up. He is losing everything he wanted. (25 minutes)

ACT TWO: Simon is in the hospital.

EARLY MIDPOINT: Simon is broke; his art show didn't go well. (50 minutes) Simon's feeling for art has died.

SECOND TURNING POINT: Simon sees Carol in the hotel bathroom and starts painting her. He regains his love of art. (108 minutes)

ACT THREE: Simon's art isn't mentioned again until the climax.

CLIMAX: Simon's art work has been moved into Melvin's apartment. Simon thanks him. (116 minutes)

As Good as It Gets has one plot with five subplots, all of them working hard to help Melvin transform, to change into a better person. Notice: The smaller subplots tend to drop out a turning point or the action of an act, but they still have development, movement, and a sense of a beginning-middle-end.

Creating the Smaller, Shorter Subplots

Major subplots will usually have strong turning points. As you start constructing "D" and "E" stories, however, turning points might drop out, although they will still have a beginning-middle-end.

For a subplot to feel integrated into the story, it usually has to thread its way through at least two acts of the film. If it's crushed into one act, it will usually feel truncated and undeveloped. Yet, there have been a few times when a subplot has been effectively worked into only one act. *Hannah and Her Sisters* puts one of the love stories into the third act. Although the character was introduced earlier, the actual subplot love story was all played out in the third act.

When I was the consultant on the movie *Luther*, we ran into a subplot problem because Martin Luther didn't meet Katharina von Bora until shortly before the climax of the story. Originally the writer had threaded Katharina throughout the script, recognizing that playing the whole subplot in Act Three could be problematical. As a result, the drama of Luther's story before he met Katharina was interrupted to show Katharina in the convent, although she had little interaction with Luther at that time (other than, perhaps, hearing about him). Historically, she never came into the story during much of the turmoil of Luther's story. I felt we could make it work if we constructed it in a very tight three-act structure with strong turning points that fit within Act Three. During one rewrite, a turning point dropped out and the love story subplot fell apart. By putting the turning point back, we created a third-act love story with a beginning-middle-end.

Doing a whole subplot in one act is not the preferred model, but if you need to do it, it works best by creating a very well-structured subplot.

If the subplot lines are carefully worked out, a good film can work with a great deal of complexity and handle anywhere from three to seven subplots. However, if the story has multiple subplots that are not well integrated, it becomes muddy, unfocused, and weighted down with too much going on.

Subplots versus Throughlines

Sometimes a subplot is mistaken for a *throughline*. A throughline is a recurring character or relationship that doesn't develop and doesn't turn a story's direction. A throughline might be about Mom, who has come to visit and cooks in the kitchen and occasionally drives to the grocery story. There are no fights, no confrontations, no events that happen that change the direction of the relationship she has with anyone. She is simply there in the story. She might still have a function and a pay-off (e.g., Mom is going to hit the burglar over the head with a frying pan—a weapon she knows well!), or she might serve as a contrast with her daughter who is trying hard to find her own identity (since Mom already has an identity—she's a great cook) or she might be there to take care of the kids (and cook for them) when the couple has to leave for some big adventure. She's a recurring character, but not a subplot.

Or a throughline might be the morning bicycle rides that the protagonist takes with his next-door neighbor. The bicycle gives the character dimension and keeps him in good shape for the physical activity he'll need to do in the third act, but it's not a subplot. There are no accidents. Nothing new happens between the protagonist and the neighbor as a result. The bicycle doesn't change the direction of the plot. It's a recurring scene, but not a subplot.

SUBPLOT PROBLEMS

Subplots are responsible for many script problems. These problems seem to fall into several categories. First of all, many subplots lack structure. They ramble, they're unfocused. They disorient the audience, which doesn't know what the story is really about or what's going on. They are episodic rather than part of a strong narrative line.

Sometimes a film has problems because the subplot doesn't integrate with or intersect the plot, so it doesn't seem to have any bearing on the story. Although the subplot might be interesting, it seems to float, unconnected to anything else happening in the story. Sometimes there's no resolution and no payoff. In *Star Trek* (2009) there is a subplot between Kirk and Uhura that revolves partly around her first name. But her first name never pays off, and she's suddenly with Spock, although this hasn't been set up. In *Places in the Heart*, the Wayne-Vi subplot has little relationship with Edna's story, even though Edna is the protagonist and subplots generally need to intersect.

Some films have problems because of a misplaced subplot. Instead of carrying it throughout the story, interwoven with the plot, sometimes the subplot is played first. As a result, the plotline begins long after we've become convinced that the subplot is our main story. In *Out of Africa* there's a strong Karen-Bror subplot that then drops out. As a result, the major subplot between Karen and Denys doesn't begin until late in the story (around seventy minutes into the film.)

APPLICATION

As you work with your subplot, separate it from your main storyline so that you can clearly see how it works. If you're not sure which is your "A" story and which is your "B" story, ask yourself, "Where is the movement of the story coming from? Where is the most action? Which storyline gives a goal to the protagonist, or a problem that must be solved?" Chances are this is your plotline. Then ask yourself, "What are the relationship stories that help me add dimensionality to the characters?" Chances are these are your subplot lines.

By separating your subplot and plotlines, you can see how you've structured each one of them. Look for the setup of the subplot. Clarify what happens in Act One, Act Two, and Act Three. Usually, it's more difficult to see clearly the structure of a subplot line. You may need to ask yourself, "What is the development of this subplot?" Once you know that, trace the development back to where it begins. That is probably your first turning point. Then see where the development takes another turn. Is there a place where the subplot becomes more urgent or more intense? If so, this might be the second turning point. Make sure that once the plot's climax has occurred, the climaxes of the subplot(s) happen quickly.

Questions to Ask Yourself about Your Script

Making your subplot work is one of the most important writing tasks. Ask yourself the following questions as you tighten and clarify your rewrite:

> Do I need this subplot? Does it add to my story? Does it intersect the story? Does it dimensionalize the story?

> How many subplots do I have? If I have more than three or four, are there any that I can cut in order to give more focus to the plotline and the "B" and "C" stories?

> Do I have a clear structure for each subplot, with a clear setup, clear turning points, and a clear climax, particularly for the "B" and "C" stories?

Does my subplot resolution occur close to the climax of the plot?

Are some of my subplots small but without turning points? If so, do they still go through at least two acts? Do they have a sense of a beginning-middle-end?

EXERCISES AND THINGS TO THINK ABOUT

(1) Look at a number of love stories to see if you can find the plotlines that give the stories direction while the focus is often on their subplots. These might include *Some Like It Hot, Knocked Up, Enchanted, Fever, Roman Holiday,* and *50 First Dates.* Look at *Working Girl* and *Big* to see how their business plots balance their relationship subplots.

(2) Read a book that has been made into a film (such as one of the Harry Potter books) and determine which subplots have been left out and why. Are there any that could have added more depth to the film?

Look at strong action films that don't seem to have a subplot, such as *The Fugitive* and *The Day of the Jackal.* Is there time for a subplot in these films? Imagine adding a subplot to *The Fugitive.* Imagine creating a subplot for *The Day of the Jackal.*

(3) Watch *Ruthless People, Tootsie, As Good as It Gets, Crash, The Big Chill, Syriana,* and *Traffic.* Can you identify each film's "A" Story? Is there one in each film? Can you map out the structures of all the subplots? How does each subplot intersect and push its "A" Story?

If your subplot is tightly structured, if it dimensionalizes the story, and if it intersects the plot, you probably have a workable and dramatic subplot that can go a long way toward helping you say what you want to say. Now the challenge is keeping the script moving, particularly in the difficult second act.

CHAPTER FOUR

Act Two –
How to Keep It Moving

A ct Two can seem interminable. For writers, it means keeping the story moving for forty-five to sixty pages. For moviegoers, an unworkable second act is a time to snooze, to buy popcorn, and to vow never to see a film by that filmmaker again.

Most Act Two problems come from insufficient momentum and lack of focus. The movie doesn't move! We're unsure what's happening and why.

A second act might not work for many reasons. Sometimes the script has moved off track. It has taken a detour, circled around, and then decided to come back to the main storyline. Perhaps unrelated scenes are muddying and slowing the story. Perhaps the characters are talking, not acting. Perhaps the story is developing too quickly—or too slowly—and is missing or skipping critical beats.

A clear setup and Act One development will help the clarity of Act Two. A strong first turning point will do much to give a needed spur for Act Two's movement. But other elements are necessary if the second act is going to keep audiences interested for an hour or more.

What Does the Second Act Do?

The second act has a job to do: develop the story and create strong action that has a direction and will resolve itself in Act Three. It's important that Act Two have a lot of action, not just a lot of talk. If the movie is a mystery or detective story, this is probably investigative action (*The Fugitive, State of Play, The Da Vinci Code, Angels & Demons*). If the movie is about explorations of new territories or visiting unfamiliar lands, then the main action is about the journey (*K2, Into the Wild, The Man Who Would Be King, Seven Years in Tibet*). If it's a love story, then the main action of Act Two will be about falling in love, and probably getting together in Act Three (*When Harry Met Sally, The Wedding Date, The Wedding Planner, Must Love Dogs*). If it's a sports story, Act Two action will probably be the preparation leading up to a big competition in Act Three (*Rocky* films, *The Karate Kid* films, *Cool Runnings, Remember the Titans, Invincible, Hoosiers, The Wrestler, Tin Cup, National Velvet*).

Some other main Act Two actions might be trying to get a new job or a big promotion (*Working Girl, Big*), or trying to get cured or find a cure for some hideous disease (*Lorenzo's Oil, I Am Legend*), or preparing for court or having a trial (*A Few Good Men, The Reader, Adam's Rib*), or about trying to get to Paris (*Revolutionary Road*) or going to Paris (*An American in Paris, Forget Paris*) or lovers in Paris (*Paris, je t'aime.*) If the film's a war story, the second act actions may be preparations for the big battle that will take place in Act Three (*Gallipoli, Platoon, Zulu*).

In Act Two, characters *do* things, they just don't talk about them. They take actions to reach objectives. The second act keeps them busy trying to attain their goals. In Act Two, characters don't *kind of* or *sort of* want something, they prove that they desperately need something. Either they'll fail at the end of the story or they won't, but they can't get to their goals without all the work they'll do in Act Two.

They have to care enough about their objective to stay busy throughout the act. If they don't put out great effort to achieve their goals, the audience won't put out any effort to cheer them on.

What Is Script Momentum?

To make Act Two work, the writer needs to keep it moving. It needs *momentum*. Momentum in a script is the sense that one scene propels us into the next scene, which propels us into the next. Each scene implies the development in the scene that follows it. Each scene contains seeds that will grow in the following scene. When connected in such a cause-and-effect relationship, every scene advances the action and brings us ever closer to the climax.

This is a very simple way of describing something that's very complex. Some scenes have only small story points and might focus on subplot or character revelation. Certainly, if every scene were taking us forward in a straight path, always advancing toward the climax, the story would lack subtlety and dimension. But, for now, think of momentum as the product of action-reaction scenes. (As I discuss idea and character later, I'll integrate Act Two's complexities.)

Any good film can demonstrate this action-reaction or cause-effect relationship. In *Little Miss Sunshine* there's a clear goal: get to the beauty pageant by 3 p.m. Sunday. As a result of Olive's desire to be a beauty queen, she's entered a contest and now can compete in the Little Miss Sunshine pageant. *As a result* of this opportunity, the family has to decide how to get to California. *As a result* of this need, they decide to all go together, in spite of all the family problems. *As a result* of having to take the old van, they meet obstacles—such as the clutch going out. *As a result* of Grandpa being old and addicted to heroin, he dies. *As a result* of him dying, they have to figure out a way to keep his death from impeding their California journey. *As a result* of resolving this problem by sticking him in the trunk of the car, they are in danger of being discovered by the authorities.

Olive's original desire to become a beauty queen set in motion many actions. There are no arbitrary detours. Everything moves in one direction, in spite of the obstacles met along the way.

Action Points

An *action point* is a dramatic event (an action, not dialogue) that causes a reaction and, thus, drives a story forward. The reaction, in turn, usually causes another action.

One might further define an action point as an event that is strong enough to *demand* a response: Someone shoots someone else and the police come in as a response. They can't let it go. They have to pursue it. Or a guy meets the girl of his dreams. He can't let his dream go. It demands that he do something. Or someone has an opportunity to compete in a championship sports event. They can't just dismiss it and pretend it doesn't matter. They have to respond.

A good storyline has many possible action points (dramatic events) that can be played onscreen. If, for example, a writer is doing a sports movie, the protagonist will need to do a great deal of practice to prepare for the big competition. The writer might make a list of all the different exercises the protagonist does, and how often each practice is done. Obviously, all of them can't be put on screen. We aren't going to watch the protagonist's every exercise session. So the writer must decide which action points should be shown.

Onscreen action points imply off-screen action points. Sometimes a writer chooses not to show a particular action, but to show the response to it. Instead of showing every crime in a detective story, a writer might decide to imply a crime by showing the detective talking to the police captain. Instead of showing a person dying, the writer might choose to show the response to that death. Instead of showing a date, the writer might choose to show a character's response to a terrible date.

In every case, the action or the response works best when it's visual, dramatic, and strong enough that the protagonist can't ignore it.

These action points are part of a chain of events in which one action flows out of another. Different actions and/or reactions would start a totally different chain of events. What's important here is that there is a connection between scenes. They should not be episodic. Each scene should come out of the previous scene, creating a tight story that moves forward to the story's climax.

Using the Implied Scene

As noted above, action not only comes from what we see onscreen, but also from implied scenes, which occur offscreen yet push the story forward. An implied scene can be described as a scene that is set up or suggested, but isn't played on the screen. It clearly exists in the string of beats that make up the storyline, but we don't see it. We simply know it happened (or perhaps it's ready to happen). The writer chooses which scenes to play, and whether to play out only the action points or also play out the response to them.

If a seedy-looking guy sitting in a bar turns to a cute tart next to him and says, "Let's get out of here," and the writer immediately cuts to the guy and the tart driving down the road in a car, we know that there were scenes in this chain of events that the writer didn't show. It's implied that these two people walked out of the bar, got into the car, and started driving. The cut to them driving down the road uses the language of film to hop from one scene to another that takes place several minutes (or hours or days or years) later. Some writers say, "I use the cut to take me over the boring scenes in order to get to something more interesting."

If two people in a script come home late at night, wearing beautiful party clothes, and enter a beautiful mansion, it's implied they've been to a party. The writer decided the party wasn't as important as what happens after the party, and that's where the writer takes us.

If a group of people walk down the street carrying protest signs that say, STOP THE VIOLENCE NOW! it's implied that someone has been doing violent activity and that the protest is a reaction to an implied scene. The writer decides whether we need to see the violence. Sometimes it's the violence that erupts at the demonstration that's more important than the violence that has gone before.

We see a clearly strangled body wash up on shore, so we can be pretty sure that a murder took place (Hitchcock's *Frenzy*). The writer chose not to put the murder scene onscreen, but it's implied. Now we see the police show up. So we know that, offscreen, somebody informed the police about this event. The writer chose not to show us all this; the dead body and the arrival of the police are enough.

Some scenes imply actions that will follow. In the case of most detective stories, it is implied that after the police discover a crime they will return to their precinct house and start working on solving it. It's also implied that a detective will be assigned to the case, and that the detective will start questioning others. The writer must decide which, if any, of these implied scenes will be played out onscreen.

In some cases, a strong piece of dialogue will imply the action that will follow, and helps the audience anticipate the second act. In *The Fugitive*, at the first turning point, Sam Gerard says, "Our fugitive's name is Dr. Richard Kimble. Go get 'im!" Now the second act's action is implied—this will be a cat-and-mouse chase. The dialogue revs us up and makes us look forward to how Sam will end up getting Richard.

Although action points can be used in any act, they are particularly important in Act Two, where a script needs the most momentum for the longest amount of time. Several types of action points can be used. We've already discussed turning points that are action points at the ends of Act One and Act Two and the midpoint scene that occurs in the middle of the script. Other action points include the *obstacle*, the *complication*, the *reversal*, and the *twist*.

The Obstacle

In many movies, a character tries something—perhaps follows a clue or performs an action—that doesn't work because it doesn't lead anywhere. The character has hit a barrier. An *obstacle* is an action point because it *forces* a character to make a decision, to take an action, or to move in a new direction.

Notice how obstacles work. They stop the action for a moment, and then the character goes around the obstacle and continues. The story doesn't develop out of the obstacle itself, it develops out of the decision to try another action. For example, if I were a saleswoman, I might knock on Door 1 to try and sell my product. The customer says no. That's an obstacle to getting my objective. Then I knock on Door 2 to try to sell my product again. The next customer says no. That's another obstacle. Finally, I knock on Door 3, and somebody buys. As a result of this sale, I might take off early and celebrate with my boss. In the course of the celebration, my boss gives me a promotion. As a result of my promotion, I get an office and I am no longer selling door-to-door.

We can see that these obstacles led to further actions, but the real development and momentum came as a result of the last action—*overcoming* the obstacle.

In *Gone with the Wind,* Scarlett tries to get money from Rhett to pay taxes on her home, Tara. When he says no (an obstacle), she marries Frank Kennedy to accomplish her goal.

Little Miss Sunshine is built on obstacles designed to keep the family from getting to California on time. They have the problem with Sheryl's suicidal brother, who can't be left alone. They have to get around this obstacle. They have the problem with the son who refuses to go to California. They have to deal with that. They have the problem with the clutch that won't work. They have the problem with the grandfather who has overdosed on heroin. When they arrive at the hotel, they have problems with parking and one-way streets and barricades. They then have the problem of arriving a minute late. If it's not one thing, it's another. Each obstacle threatens to keep them from reaching their goal, and each obstacle leads to new action.

Obstacles are basic to drama. If used sparingly, they can do much to push a story forward. Several in a film can be workable—but if too many are used, a story will feel repetitive. Instead of giving a story momentum, an overabundance of obstacles will slow it down.

How Many Obstacles Are Too Many?

The writer needs to decide if obstacles are getting in the way of the development of the story. If in doubt, invoke the *Rule of Three.*

The Rule of Three is based partly on joke construction. A joke is (1) set up, (2) developed, and (3) finally paid off. Think of jokes such as those about the priest, the rabbi, and the preacher. Each of these three people, in turn, reacts to the same situation, but the humorous payoff is always the third character's reaction.

If you want to make the point that a beautiful young woman has really tried dating but only ended up with weird guys, you don't need twenty guys. Showing three bad dates will do it.

In *The Fugitive*, when Kimble sneaks into the hospital's computer room to research one-armed men who might have killed his wife, his search first brings up 121 names, then 21 names, and finally only 5 names that best fit the profile. He then pays off his search by printing out the last list, which ends the scene. In the next scenes, he begins following up on the five names.

In sports movies, sometimes we see two practice competitions, and then the big game. We don't need to see dozens in order to get the point.

Not all films need to use the idea of threes, but if in doubt, this will usually be the most workable.

The Complication

A *complication* is an action point that doesn't pay off immediately. Something happens (an action), but the reaction to it doesn't come until later. We have to wait and anticipate the inevitable response.

In *Shrek,* Donkey discovers that Fiona is actually an ogre. This is a complication. We realize that Shrek, too, will eventually discover that Fiona is not the beautiful princess. When Shrek finds out, this will complicate the journey. When the Prince finds out, this will complicate the wedding.

Tootsie presents another example of a complication. Michael has dressed up as a woman and become Dorothy Michaels in order to get a job. That was his only intention—to work. But during the first day on the set, he sees Julie. Nothing happens immediately, but we know that it will. Julie's presence has complicated Michael's intention. We guess that he will fall in love with her, which will jeopardize his work. But his first meeting with Julie and his anticipated response are thirty-two pages apart.

In *Tootsie,* we see another complication when John Van Horn (the soap's Dr. Brewster) meets Dorothy and decides that he wants her. Again, the payoff of this action point isn't immediate. It happens far into Act Three, when he comes to serenade Dorothy and forces his affections on her.

Further complications develop when Julie's father, Les, falls in love with Dorothy. He meets her early in Act Two, but little happens until

Dorothy visits his farm at the end of the act. They sing together, dance together, and that leads to the proposal.

A complication is not your ordinary garden-variety action point. It's actually quite rare. You don't see it in many scripts. Sometimes, when it's there, it's quite subtle. In looking for a complication, check for three elements:

A complication doesn't pay off immediately, so it adds anticipation to the story.

A complication is the beginning of a new throughline or subplot. It doesn't turn the story around; instead, it keeps the story moving forward, but with a new twist.

A complication gets in the way of a character's intention.

Because of Julie, Van Horn, and Les, Michael can't continue to be Dorothy Michaels, even though his career is blossoming. His original intention—to be successful—continues. These people haven't interfered with his overall intention. But they have interfered with (complicated) his willingness to continue as Dorothy.

The Reversal

The strongest kind of action point is the *reversal*, which changes a story's direction by 180 degrees. It causes a story to make a U-turn, to move from a positive to a negative direction or from a negative to a positive direction. It's stronger than most turning points, which turn the action but do not reverse it.

Reversals can work physically or emotionally. They can reverse action or a character's emotions. In many horror films, a reversal occurs because characters think they've killed the monsters, or defeated the aliens, but just as everything seems calm and resolved, the monstrous aliens appear at the window or down the street. In *Jaws*, the townspeople think that they've caught the shark, so they start celebrating. But their celebration is reversed when Matt informs them that the captured shark isn't the killer.

In *Chicago,* Roxie fires Billy Flynn but reverses herself almost immediately, when she discovers that women who don't hire Billy Flynn lose their cases and are hanged.

In *Little Miss Sunshine,* the family is told they've arrived too late and Olive can't enter the pageant, but one of the officials reverses that position and allows Olive to compete.

In *Changeling,* Christine is told they've found her son, but the situation is reversed when she sees the boy and realizes he's not hers.

Playing a reversal at the first or second turning point can be a particularly good way to build momentum into the second and third acts. But reversals can work anywhere. In a detective film, we see a reversal when the discouraged detective suddenly puts two and two together and realizes how to solve the case.

In a romance, we see reversals at work when a lost soldier unexpectedly returns to his sweetheart, or when a beloved one, on her deathbed, suddenly recovers, or when the two lovers break up over a misunderstanding and then get back together again as if nothing had happened.

Whereas an obstacle pushes a story forward by forcing a decision, and a complication pushes the story forward by leading to an anticipated payoff some time later, a reversal *catapults* a story in the opposite direction, causing new developments. Because a reversal creates such momentum, you rarely need more than a couple of them in a script. One or two have the power to push the story through that difficult second act.

The Twist

A *twist,* one of the most difficult action points to pull off, is an event that pushes a story in a new direction because it reverses *expectations.* We *think* we're moving in one direction, and then discover nothing is quite what it seems. This ploy isn't the reversal I discussed above, because it might not lead to a 180-degree turnaround. But it might catapult us to another place, or set us on a whole new track. It's not unusual when a film hits a twist to hear an audience gasp, or even hear an "oh" or "ah" in the audience.

There are very few workable twists in films. The first turning point of *Witness* has a twist when we discover that the police chief is in on the crime. The second turning point of *L.A. Confidential* has a good twist when we discover (yes, the same thing) that the police chief is in on the crime. The very end of *The Usual Suspects* has a twist when we discover that the seemingly dumb guy is really the clever one and that we have actually been seeing the whole story from his point of view, and the story was not at all what it seemed. *The Illusionist* has almost the same kind of twist as in *The Usual Suspects*: The chief inspector finally has an *aha!* experience as he realizes that Edward is fine, and now with the love of his life.

There are twists in *The Prestige*, when we discover that Alfred Borden is not really dead, even though we thought we saw him hang, and that Robert Angier is not really dead, even though we thought we saw him drown.

To make a twist work, the audience's *expectations have to be set up*, but it's important that they're *not contradicted*. This isn't a matter of manipulating the audience by telling them one thing and then letting the audience know the writer didn't really mean it. A writer can't *tell* the audience that someone is alive when they've really been dead the whole time (*The Sixth Sense*, of course). But the writer can *imply* that a person is alive, when that character is really dead. We, the audience, then add it up and realize we formed a conclusion and we were wrong. Provided it is *not a contradiction* of something that has been clearly established, the twist can work.

Usually a twist works when the audience takes a particular path hinted at by the writer, only to realize later that nothing had actually forced them down that path. They simply followed it, and ended up learning that things weren't what they seemed. Or, occasionally, as in films about magic, it is allowing the audience to buy the illusion, and then reversing it. We buy it, because the film is about illusions.

One of the best films for twists is *The Sting*, which contains at least four of them. The first twist occurs just a few minutes into the film. We see a mugger running away from the robbing and stabbing of a man who we later learn is Luther Coleman. Two people witness this event: a bookie joint bagman carrying an envelope containing thousands of dollars in cash and a likeable, helpful young man, Johnny Hooker, who thwarts the crime and recovers Luther's wallet. Luther, clutching his wounded leg, asks the two passersby to help him make a $5,000 payment that's due to a loan shark in just minutes. The bagman agrees to do it, so Johnny shows him how to hide Luther's packet of money—*together with* the bookie joint's envelope—under his belt.

We next see the bagman get in a cab and drive off with no intention of delivering Luther's packet, which he soon discovers contains nothing but shredded paper, as does his own envelope from the bookie joint. It's at this point that we realize this was all a con, and that Johnny and Luther and the mugger were in on it together. Luther's wound wasn't real. Johnny pocketed the bookie joint's money when he showed the bagman how to hide the two envelopes in his pants. We thought it was just what it looked like—a violent robbery stopped by good Samaritans, but it wasn't.

The second twist occurs twenty minutes into the film when Johnny is confronted by Lieutenant Snyder, who wants a cut of Johnny's money in exchange for not arresting him. Johnny unwillingly (so it seems) finally agrees to pay Snyder $2,000. But when he takes out his roll of money to count it out, Snyder grabs all of it. Just when we're thinking *that lowdown cop!*, Johnny tells his friend it's counterfeit. Things, again, were not what they seemed.

Another twist occurs when we discover that Loretta, the waitress, is a plant, and is really Salino, a hit man who was mentioned earlier. We never expected the hit man was a woman, and that the hit man was the woman that Johnny slept with the night before. We also thought the hit man was the person following Johnny, but this was really the man assigned to watch over him.

And a fourth twist occurs at the very end, when we discover that FBI Agent Polk is actually part of this con. Doyle never discovers that, but the audience does.

Notice that these films with good twists—*The Sting, The Sixth Sense, L.A. Confidential,* and *The Usual Suspects*—never make the audience feel stupid for not figuring out the twist sooner. In fact, when the twists are revealed, the audience often has a moment of appreciation for the clever surprise. We are never snookered by the writer; we're led carefully, so the twist is unexpected without contradicting the facts we've been given.

Structuring and Shaping the Scene

Just as an entire story, as well as each of its subplots, can be constructed as a three-act structure, some scenes are structured in three acts too. This structure that gives momentum and direction to the whole film can also do so for individual scenes. A three-act structure is not found in every scene, nor should it be. If every scene were a three-act structure, the movie would drag, rather than gain momentum. But certain important scenes can be given extra shape and focus if given a clear beginning, middle, and end with turning points.

In *Little Miss Sunshine*, Olive's performance in the third act has a three-act structure:

ACT ONE/SETUP OF SEQUENCE: Olive is announced as the next contestant and enters the stage.

ACT ONE DEVELOPMENT: Olive begins her performance. She shakes and shimmies and moves like a stripper. She throws off her hat, strips off her pants, takes off her blouse. The audience and judges are shocked. Some girls walk out.

FIRST TURNING POINT: Richard sees the problem and begins to clap. He changes the direction of the scene.

ACT TWO develops further as Frank joins in. The family begins to clap as Olive continues to dance and twirl and run and shimmy. The emcee chases Olive to try to stop her, but she just keeps going. The judge tells him to get his daughter off the stage. Act Two is about the *action* of Olive's family cheering her on.

SECOND TURNING POINT: Richard goes up on stage and begins to dance as a backup to Olive. He changes the direction of the scene, adding another dimension. Olive keeps going.

ACT THREE: Frank joins them, as do Dwayne and Sheryl. The family dances with Olive, who is relentless in her moves. Act Three is about the *action* of the family dancing onstage.

CLIMAX: The music stops.

RESOLUTION: One person in the audience stands up and claps.

The performance scene is about five minutes long. Following it is the scene that shows the *film's* climax—the family in the office in a police station, where they are told they can leave if they promise never to enter their daughter in a pageant in the State of California again. They agree and then leave for home.

Together, the two scenes—the performance scene followed by the film's climax scene—total seven minutes. They make the themes of love and family clear, and although Olive didn't win the pageant, they end the movie on a high note. Few in the audience really care whether she won, because Olive won our hearts, and something more important was going on here.

Creating a Scene Sequence

Occasionally, action-reaction scenes are grouped together in a *scene sequence*—a series of scenes about the same subject—that has a beginning, a middle, and an end. This type of multiscene structure provides momentum.

A scene sequence might be a series of exciting chase scenes filmed all around town, ending when the villain's car finally crashes or the villain is caught. It might be a sequence of scenes that builds to a final explosion (*The Guns of Navarone*) or the developing scenes that lead to lovers reuniting (*When Harry Met Sally*) or scenes that work against time (Mozart finally finishes his opera in *Amadeus*).

Momentum is gained through a scene sequence because it's a sort of mini-story—with structure, momentum, and direction. Its chain of action-reaction scenes advance the mini-story to a climax.

Most scene sequences are relatively short, ranging from about three to seven minutes. Occasionally, two scenes sequences are placed together, to create a great sweep of momentum. In *The Fugitive*, for example, the bus and train sequences are placed one after the other. Each of these sequences is about three to four minutes long, and each has a beginning, middle, and end and turning points. The last act of *Witness* consists of two scene sequences placed one after the other: The first is about six minutes long, and the second is about eight minutes long. This pair of sequences is preceded by several scenes that begin Act Three and followed by a resolution scene at the film's end.

Many of the most memorable parts of films are scene sequences. The burning of Atlanta in *Gone With the Wind* is a seven-minute scene sequence. The last battle in *Star Wars* is a scene sequence,

In *Gone With the Wind,* two separate scene sequences in a row are probably the most memorable parts of the entire film. The first is "Melanie has her baby," and the second is "Atlanta burns." Each one is about seven minutes long. By studying them, we can see how a scene sequence works to give a story momentum.

"Melanie has her baby" begins deep into the siege of Atlanta. Knowing that the city will be taken by the Yankees, Confederate soldiers and local townspeople begin to flee. At this time, Melanie announces her labor pains.

SETUP: Melanie announces that she has labor pains.

FIRST TURNING POINT: Scarlett sends Prissy for the doctor.

DEVELOPMENT: Prissy returns, saying the doctor can't come.

SECOND TURNING POINT: Scarlett is told she must deliver the baby.

CLIMAX: Melanie's baby is delivered.

The "Atlanta burns" sequence works in the same way and follows the "Melanie has her baby" sequence.

SETUP: Prissy goes to get Rhett, asking him to help them escape Atlanta's chaos.

FIRST TURNING POINT: Rhett comes to help them flee the city.

DEVELOPMENT: Men try to stop their carriage and steal their horse. Rhett announces that they must get past the ammunition depot before it explodes.

SECOND TURNING POINT: They come to the ammunition depot, already afire, putting their escape in jeopardy.

DEVELOPMENT: They make their way through the flames.

CLIMAX: They escape just as the depot explodes.

RESOLUTION: They reach safety. Rhett leaves.

Scene sequences can come at any place in a story. Many times a scene sequence occurs shortly after the middle of Act Two, when the act is in danger of lagging. Occasionally, a scene sequence is found in Act One, either as a very exciting beginning setup (you'll find such sequences at the beginning of many James Bond films), or to push us toward the first turning point.

Steven Spielberg, that modern master of momentum, often uses scene sequences. You'll find a short one in *Back to the Future,* when Biff chases Marty and drives into a truckload of manure. *Jaws* has several scene sequences, such as "Harpooning the shark," "Using the shark cage," and, finally, "Victory." *Schindler's List* has several scene sequences, including "The Killing in the Ghetto," "Amon the Good," and "Moving to Czechoslovakia."

There is a tightly structured scene sequence in *Little Miss Sunshine* that I call "Stealing Grandpa." In it we can see a three-act structure with turning points.

This sequence begins right after Grandpa dies. The sequence's first act shows the doctor telling the family that Grandpa is dead. Sheryl explains this to Olive. A bereavement liaison, Linda, then appears to give the family a brochure for a grief recovery support group and funeral home information.

At the sequence's first turning point, Linda explains that they can't just leave Grandpa's body there. This statement from Linda changes the direction of the action, adds an obstacle to getting to the pageant, and forces the family to rethink their goal.

The sequence's second act is about the problem of Grandpa's body and figuring out how to get to the pageant on time. The family asks Linda if they can come back for the body later. No, they can't.

At the sequence's midpoint, Richard asks if they can view Grandpa's remains. This midpoint provides a slight change of direction, giving more structure to the sequence.

They look at Grandpa under the sheet. Richard gets angry and hyperventilates. Sheryl promises Olive that she can do the pageant next year. Richard now changes the direction of the sequence. Determined that they will make the pageant, he comes up with a new idea—he decides they'll sneak Grandpa out of there—the second turning point.

The sequence's third act shows them slipping Grandpa through the window. At the climax of the sequence they successfully get away in their VW bus. In the sequence's resolution, Sheryl assures Olive that Grandpa's soul is in heaven.

This scene sequence is about seven minutes long (as is the "Killing Alex" sequence in *Fatal Attraction*). The longest workable scene sequence I've seen is the "Going to the opera" sequence in *Moonstruck*, which is twenty-one minutes long, although there is some interruption of this scene sequence by subplots.

Scene sequences are not only well-structured mini-stories, they also may clearly illustrate how turning points work. In the "Stealing Grandpa" scene sequence, each act has a different focus. The sequence's first act is about "Telling the family the news." It would have continued with the same action (talking about Grandpa's death) until a turning point (a stronger action event) occurred to change the sequence's direction. When Linda comes into the story, she changes the sequence's direction. The second act of the sequence, however, would have continued to be about filling out paperwork and following Linda's orders until something new—another turning point—came into the story, changing the action's focus. One might think that going to see Grandpa's body is a turning point, but it doesn't add a new action to the sequence's third act. Not until Richard gets a new idea—stealing Grandpa's body—does the action turn again.

MOMENTUM PROBLEMS

Lack of momentum is one of the most common problems in films. Momentum problems usually occur because there's not a clear three-act structure with clear turning points to keep the story moving. Sometimes they occur because certain scenes take the story off on a tangent.

Often, momentum problems are misdiagnosed. As a result, the proposed remedies fail to solve the problems.

Most filmmakers try to fix momentum problems by adding more action. It's not unusual for a television detective series to add a car chase, a fistfight, or a shootout every time the story seems to slow down. But, these actions rarely solve the problem. Often, they interrupt the story's structure, thereby slowing its momentum even more once the added action is finished.

Sometimes, filmmakers confuse momentum with pacing and think that if they up the pace they will mend a momentum problem. But momentum is the result of the relationship of one scene to the next, creating action and reaction. It doesn't matter whether scenes unfold or move slowly or quickly, as long as they seem connected and keep the story moving forward.

Sometimes audiences say they think that certain European films work well, even though they don't have momentum. They may be confusing momentum and pacing. Such films might have momentum yet just move at a slower pace. This is often true for American films as well. *Signs,* although about great threats and dangers and mysteries and tragedy, was not a fast-paced film. Much of *Witness* was slowly paced (true to its setting on an Amish farm) but still kept its momentum going.

Sometimes, to solve a momentum problem, writers pick up a story's pace, sometimes hurrying the plot to the extent that there's no letup for the audience. If a movie's pace is too fast, the audience can't catch up with its story. Therefore, instead of being "with" the story, the audience feels as if the story is always ahead of them, unattainable. This can happen with the relentless action in some action-adventures.

When audiences lose interest in a story, the problem may have little to do with story movement. If a story is too predictable, audiences will lose interest. If there are no subplots to dimensionalize the story, or if the characters are stereotypes who fail to involve us, audience interest will diminish. In these cases, focusing on the development of the plot, subplots, and theme should perk up audience interest, provided this development itself has strong momentum.

APPLICATION

None of the above-mentioned script elements (action points, implied scenes, obstacles, complications, reversals, twists, scene sequences, momentum, pacing) can be imposed on a script. They must be integral to the story. But carefully working these elements can strengthen a script that almost has a reversal or almost has a complication in it or is developing toward a scene sequence.

In order to exploit these script elements positively and adeptly, it's important to know them when you see them. You might start doing this by watching films specifically to identify these elements. Many films rely more on one script element than another. Some use all of them! Once you're clear how they are used in particular films, you will find it much easier to identify and develop them within your own scripts.

Scene sequences can be created with very little rewriting after a script's first draft. Many times, action-reaction scenes revolve around several ideas rather than one. To create a scene sequence, the writer can find the scenes related to one idea and string them together to create a clear setup, development, and climax for the sequence.

A reversal can often be created by punching up and strengthening an existing action point. Think about the suddenness when the Ghostbusters lose their jobs—just when they've finally seen a ghost in the library. If this had been written without the story reversal, we would have seen the crew drift back to their office and talk a bit, followed by someone drifting in to tell them that they might lose their jobs. We might have all drifted out of the theater while waiting for some punch. Instead, this moment was played quickly as a physical and emotional reversal, rocketing the story forward.

You can create strong emotional reversals by looking for emotional moments that can be expanded or extended. If your main character is "kind of sad" before becoming "sort of happy," see if you can create a clear moment when despair leads to ecstasy. Or reverse the situation, moving from celebration to horror or fear.

Questions to Ask Yourself about Your Script

Look at your script and ask yourself:

How are action points used? Is my story gaining momentum through action points, or does it use dialogue to push itself forward?

What kinds of action points are used within my script? Obstacles? Complications? Reversals? Twists? Where do they occur, and how often?

Are there any scene sequences—or potential scene sequences—in my script? Where do they occur? How do they work to give energy to my story? Can I rework them to create a scene sequence?

Does my script go off on tangents, or does it stay focused on its plot and subplot developments?

EXERCISES AND THINGS TO THINK ABOUT

(1) Choose one or two action-adventure films. See if you can find scene sequences in the films. Are these scene sequences three-act structures? Can you find the setup, the turning points, and the climax? Just for starters, notice the number of barriers that Sam Gerard encounters while trying to find Richard Kimble in *The Fugitive*. Notice the use of reversals in *Chicago* and *Fatal Attraction* (when the sexually exciting second night turns into a suicide attempt). Notice the use of strongly structured scenes with beginnings, middles, and ends, such as the first long scene in the restaurant in *Schindler's List* and some of the long fight sequences in *Shane*.

(2) Select ten of your favorite movies. Identify any obstacles, complications, reversals, and twists that appear in them. How did these elements work?

(3) View a film that you don't like and try to follow its story, keeping track of when your mind wanders or when you lose track of the plot. How could these moments have been fixed?

Above all, remember that as long as you have a succession of actions and responses that are related to your story, your script will continue to move. You do not need big actions to move your story. Not every physical action needs a dramatic physical response to move your story. You can move your story through physical actions or dialogue or emotional responses. As long as there are connections between one action and another and as long as you have a structure that supports your story, your script will move.

Keeping this concept in mind, you needn't be concerned if your script is about relationships and slower-paced than *Rambo* or your average James Bond film, or if your fast-paced action-adventure slows down for a love scene. As long as it contains action-reaction scenes, your script will have direction, focus, and momentum.

Once your script has a solid structure and strong sense of momentum, you'll want to think of ways to connect your audience with your protagonist.

CHAPTER FIVE

Establishing a Point of View

A writer must engage an audience with a film. To do this, the writer needs to decide how much we, the audience, need to know to identify and empathize with the main character. The writer has to determine the breadth of our focus on the film. What do we know? Do we know only what the main character knows, or do we know more because we have a broader point of view than the protagonist? Through whose eyes do we see the story? Who do we follow? How much should we care about the main character? How big (or small) is the story?

Such decisions will be made in Act One. If the writer has made unworkable decisions there, they will haunt the rest of the script.

Early in a script's writing, the writer establishes the point of view (POV) from which the story will be told. At its most basic, *point of view* is a literary term describing whether a story is told in a first person, second person, or third person voice or view.

First Person Point of View

Since film can only show external events, a *first person* POV, sometimes called a *subjective* POV, simply means that every scene is shown through the eyes or voice of a main character.

In a novel, having a subjective first person POV would mean that a single central character tells the whole story. The character would say, "I did..." and "I felt...," and we wouldn't know anything more than that character knows. First person novels are not unusual. Detective novels, such as the Spenser novels by Robert B. Parker and Sue Grafton's Kinsey Milhone novels, are good examples, as are many romance novels that seek to draw the reader deeply into a steamy affair. A number of literary works, such as *Huckleberry Finn* and *Catcher in the Rye*, use the first person POV. It connects us, the readers, strongly with the main character. We feel with the protagonist, follow his or her story, and see the world through that character's eyes.

When a film utilizes the first person POV, its audience knows only what the protagonist knows. The film *The Wizard of Oz* follows Dorothy's story from a subjective first person POV. Although the story might swerve to another character for part of a scene, such as showing someone else walking through a castle, or going to the side of the yellow brick road, these are acceptably small diversions that don't really leave Dorothy's story. It's Dorothy's tale—and she's in every scene.

Memento uses a first person POV, as do many classics such as *It's a Wonderful Life* and *Sunset Boulevard,* the latter of which is told via flashbacks from the POV of a now-dead man. Although the first person POV usually permits the maximum identification between protagonist and audience, it can also present a problem—the protagonist doesn't know *everything* about the story. Even when the detective from whose point of view the story has been told has added up all the clues and tossed the bad guy in jail, there might still be lingering questions and doubts. If these are important or disturbing enough to the audience, they can lead to the need for third-act exposition in which some other character (or a narrator) must explain everything, including information about motives or how the bad guy was caught or missing links between clues.

In the Perry Mason television series, Perry almost always has some final explaining to do about how he figured out who the culprit was. This is done through third-act exposition. Although such a late-in-the-game exposition might be acceptable in books, in film, a medium that relies on action and not long discussions, this can very often be deadly.

In the film *Presumed Innocent,* a need for third-act exposition led to a long monologue in which the wife had to explain everything that the protagonist and the audience couldn't have known. The movie's POV wasn't broad enough to reveal the information earlier, so it had to be told at the end.

Few films are totally subjective first person stories, but when they use this perspective, they keep us identifying with the protagonist. Some films use a subjective first person POV that's suddenly interrupted (perhaps unintentionally) once or twice, creating a jarring aspect to the film. The film *Resurrection* (1980) has a very strong subjective first person POV (Edna's), except for one jarring scene that switches over to her boyfriend's POV for a few seconds. We have not been in his POV before, so it feels as if we are jolted away from Edna's story.

Fight Club used a subjective first person POV, but has two scenes from the POV of Tyler Durden. You decide if they're jarring or not. I recommend that once a writer commits to a POV, he or she should stay with it.

Few films use only the first person POV. Most films broaden their POVs to two or more persons in order to allow the audience to know more about the story than just what the main character knows, feels, and experiences.

Some films use first person POV in unusual ways. The film *The Hours* was told from the POVs of three characters (Virginia Woolf, Clarissa Vaughan, and Laura Brown). This would seem to create an *omniscient* (all-knowing, all-aware) POV, but the movie felt *as if* it had only a single subjective first person POV because, within each story, we felt so very close to each character. We weren't standing back, as is usually the case with an omniscient POV, watching the action unfold from a highly objective viewpoint. As we repeatedly returned to each story, each character's subjective first person POV adroitly drew us in.

For one of the ultimate subjective first-person movie experiences, watch *Lady in the Lake* (1947). In this film noir classic, the camera acts as the protagonist's eyes. In fact, this subjective view is carried so far that we only see the protagonist when he catches a glimpse of himself in a mirror or a store window's reflection.

Second Person (and Two-Person) Point of View

In literature, there is a *second person* POV that features a character that is "you" (instead of the "I" of a first person POV). Rather than the narrator standing in the shoes of the protagonist, the narrator watches the main character—you. This is very rare, although both *Beach Red*, an epic prose poem (described as a "novel" on the book's cover) by Peter Bownam, and Jay McInerney's novel *Bright Lights, Big City* use this device. *Beach Red* tells the story, in verse, of an Army unit's beachhead during World War II. *You* are the main character. The narrator tells the reader what you do. At the end of the book, *you die.*

Instead of the literary second person POV, movies are apt to use a *two person* POV, where the story follows two characters, usually the protagonist and the antagonist but sometimes two people falling in love. The films *In the Line of Fire* and *The Day of the Jackal* move back and forth between the scenes told from the protagonist's POV and scenes told from the antagonist's POV, although both films broaden these POVs occasionally.

The Fugitive has almost exclusively a two-person POV: Nearly all its scenes are from either Kimble's or Gerard's POV. In the beginning, Gerard is Kimble's antagonist. But as the film proceeds, we discover the new, *real* antagonist. A few very short scenes, however, take us into the POV of another character—the One-Armed Man—and neither Sam nor Richard is in the scene. The One-Armed Man's POV was set up in the murder scene that began the story, so we were prepared for his POV when it returned later.

A two-person POV allows a writer to create tension by intercutting between the two POVs. The audience knows more than the protagonist knows—they can see imminent threats creeping up and near-misses ready to happen. And they can see how each person moves to an inevitable collision with the other.

The *Die Hard* films often use two-person POVs: There is John McClane's, as he tries to save the day, and the POVs of the villains as they close in on him. In cases like these, the antagonist's POV is not just the POV of *an* antagonist, but of the *antagonist group*.

Love stories that create two almost-equal protagonists will often use the two-person POV. Such movies as *Thelma & Louise, When Harry Met Sally, Last Chance Harvey,* and *Adam's Rib* work this way, although some of these occasionally swerve off to a third POV. In *Thelma & Louise*, several scenes are from the POV of the detectives, and in *When Harry Met Sally*, one or two scenes are from the viewpoint of their friends.

Third Person (and Omniscient) Point of View

Most films use an omniscient POV that is similar to the literature's *third person* POV, in which an all-knowing narrator stands back to give us the big picture from all viewpoints. The third person POV allows the writer to tell the larger story, and to show us how all the pieces fit together. We see the story from the POV of the protagonist, but also in terms of what's going on behind the scenes. We might see the worlds of the detective and the villain, and then see what's happening in the city at large and what's happening in the world (past and present), showing a raging war or a political campaign or the machinations of a corrupt boss (*In the Line of Fire, Shane, The Sting, The Constant Gardener, Milk*). With an omniscient POV, a story moves back and forth between the narrow POV of the protagonist and the broad omniscient POV that sets up the movie's context.

Casablanca moves among the POVs of Rick and Ilsa and the occasional omniscient ones that show us the police closing in and the world at war. The film's first scene sets up this broadest POV by showing us a map of the world at war and telling us of the refugees fleeing Europe, passing through Casablanca. And then it moves in to focus on a more personal story.

Shane focuses on Joey's POV from the very beginning. But it also opens up occasionally to an omniscient POV, so we can see various confrontations between the bad guys and the good guys, even though Joey isn't in these scenes. At times, we also see the interplay between Shane and Joe (Joey's father) and Shane and Marian (Joey's mother), when Joey is not around.

Warning: An omniscient POV can get so broad that we, the audience, can lose our identification with the protagonist. In trying to show us everything, it can put the focus on the story more than the characters, often costing us our empathy for the protagonist.

Choosing the POV

A film's POV may evolve during the writing of its script. A writer may decide to use a subjective first person POV, but then find it necessary to open up the story in order to impart more information in Act Two and not be forced to talk about it in Act Three. The writer can then go back to Act One to set up and expand the POVs.

Whatever POVs are chosen, they need to be set up in Act One. Otherwise, the audience will find it jarring to look exclusively through one person's eyes for a good while, and later on suddenly switch the way they see the story. In literature, this is called "head hopping": We hop from one person's mind to another, sometimes only briefly, rather than staying with one POV. To resolve this effect in a film script, the screenwriter chooses a single POV and sticks with it. Then, if changes need to be made, the writer can rewrite Act One in order to set up clearly the chosen POVs. In this case, the writer might start or end an Act One scene with a supporting character's POV rather than the protagonist's, thus preparing the audience for a switch that will occur later.

Analyzing *Changeling*

A movie worth studying for its use of POVs is *Changeling* (2008). It did reasonably well at the box office and was nominated for three Academy Awards. The writer, J. Michael Straczynski, and the director, Clint Eastwood, held to a very tight and emotional subjective POV for much of the film, focusing on the feelings and actions of the mother, Christine Collins, whose son disappeared in Los Angeles in

1928. We see the beginning scenes from her first person POV. We see her son in the early scenes, but the focus is kept on her. We watch *her* world. We see her as a mother and a phone company supervisor. We see her riding the streetcar and talking to her boss about a promotion.

Suddenly, around ten minutes into the film, her son is missing. At twelve minutes into the film, we begin to realize that the story is bigger than just her personal story. The film's POVs expand to include that of Reverend Briegleb, who believes part of his job is to "expose the violent, corrupt, incompetent police department." We learn that Christine's treatment at the hands of the police, and their unwillingness to act promptly, is not unusual. A larger corruption story is suggested by Rev. Briegleb's sermon. Since he will figure prominently in the story as it proceeds, it was important to open up the film's perspective to include the reverend's POV.

The movie's POVs expand again in the next scene, showing us Police Chief James Davis and Police Captain J. J. Jones. There's clearly a bigger story here than just Christine's emotional torment over the loss of the son.

After fifty minutes, the film introduces yet another POV. The scene shows Detective Lester Ybarra driving to Northcott Ranch to find a boy who is said to be staying there. Now it's suggested that this ranch figures into the story. Later, the POVs will expand again, to follow the murderer, Gordon Northcott, who is visiting his sister in Canada.

As the story broadens, so does the inclusion of POVs. As the plot thickens and the mystery deepens, these POVs show us more of the story's many complicated elements.

The Act Two shift to Ybarra's POV was jarring to me. I wondered why this shift was jarring, when the shifts to Briegleb and the police officers were not?

I think there were two reasons why this POV shift didn't work as well as the ones in Act One. First, the shifts that were set up in Act One all focused on Christine's story: The police were working on her case. The reverend was commenting on her case. But the shift at fifty minutes seemed to have nothing to do with Christine's story. Only later did its relationship to her story become clear.

Second, these other POVs had been set up in Act One. The story about the Canadian boy hiding out at the Northcott Ranch was not set up early enough. It was mentioned in the background dialogue of an earlier scene, but then it didn't seem to have anything to do with Christine's case.

The Detective Ybarra character had been very briefly set up at the police station a few scenes earlier, but not until the third viewing of the film did I realize that the detective at the police station is the same person who drives out to the ranch fifty minutes into the film. In the earlier police station scene, background dialogue told us that a boy from Canada had crossed state lines, and that Ybarra agreed to take the case. The audience had about two seconds to memorize Ybarra's face among a group of other detectives who all dressed the same, wore the same hats, and had similar body builds. In order for his POV to be set up clearly, this scene in the police station needed to be connected with the scene of him driving the car out to the ranch.

Introducing Ybarra's POV was further complicated because the scene of him driving a truck out to the ranch began, not by re-establishing his character, but by showing a character we had never met—Gordon Northcott—with a broken-down car.

As you watch this film, see what you think of this shift of POV. Do you find it jarring or smooth and natural? If you find it jarring, you may want to imagine a better way of setting up Ybarra's POV, perhaps with an extra line of dialogue by Ybarra as he takes the case. Perhaps you would add an extra line of dialogue from the police captain that would connect him with the captain, whom we already know. Perhaps you would add Ybarra to more of the earlier police station scenes in Act One. You might add some very small interaction at the police station between Christine and Ybarra. Perhaps you would start the scene of him driving to the ranch from his own POV, seeing Gordon's broken-down car, rather than starting the scene from Gordon's POV.

The changing POVs in *Changeling* allow it to shift repeatedly to the big story and back to an intense personal and emotional focus on Christine.

What Can Go Wrong with POVs

You might want to watch both *Duplicity* and *The International* to see how they used POVs, and consider whether they encountered point-of-view problems. Both demanded that the audience learn considerable information to understand their backstories.

Duplicity used limited POVs, focusing on the two main characters and their relationship, using flashbacks to tell us about their backstories. As a result, because I was seeing so much of the back-and-forth of the subplot, I found I didn't always know what was going on and why. A broader use of POVs would have helped.

The International had the opposite problem—too many POVs. The film focused on the many people who were related to the overall plot, but placed little emphasis on the main characters. Therefore, since the male and female main characters were shown with little relationship to each other, and since the male seemed to be a particularly isolated individual, I found it difficult to become engaged in the story. It left out the personal POVs that help us connect and identify with the protagonist.

USING VOICE-OVERS

A *voice-over* (V.O.) is any offscreen voice that talks to the audience, narrating an event or giving voice to a character's unspoken thoughts. A writer can show deep aspects of a character's subjective world through the use of first person voice-overs. Much like a novel, which can take us into a character's thoughts, the first person voice-over can take us inside a film's character.

In films, a voice-over can work in two ways: subjectively or objectively. It can be a true first person voice that tells us what and how a character thinks. Or it can be a third person voice—a narrator of some sort—who tells us a story or part of a story.

A number of films are known for subjective voice-overs that pull us into the mood and psyche of the protagonist. *Sunset Boulevard* begins with a V.O., which we soon learn is the voice of the now-dead protagonist, Joe Gillis.

> JOE GILLIS
>
> Yes, this is Sunset Boulevard, Los Angeles, California. It's about five o'clock in the morning. That's the Homicide Squad, complete with detectives and newspaper men. A murder has been reported… You'll get it over your radio, and see it on the television - because an old time star is involved. One of the biggest. But before you hear it all distorted and blown out of proportion, before those Hollywood columnists get their hands on it, maybe you'd like to hear the facts, the whole truth… Let's go back about six months and find the day when it all started.

And the story is then told as a flashback.

American Beauty has a voice-over in several places, including the end, where it gives us insight into the transformation of the character and the theme: It pulls us into Lester Burnham…

> LESTER
>
> …I guess I could be pretty pissed off about what happened to me, but it's hard to stay mad, when there's so much beauty in the world. … I can't feel anything but gratitude for every single moment of my stupid little life. You have no idea what I'm talking about, I'm sure. But don't worry. You will someday.

The Shawshank Redemption and *Forrest Gump* use voice-overs to pull us into their characters' attitudes and philosophies. *Annie Hall* helps us understand how Alvy is thinking and feeling through voice-overs.

Sometimes a voice-over is used in juxtaposition with action, belying it, letting us know that things aren't quite what they seem. In *Michael Clayton*, Arthur Edens begins his voice-over as we view the posh environment of a major law firm. It is in stark contrast to the visuals, because Arthur is raging with despair after years spent endlessly "fixing" a particular lawsuit. We see an office full of people doing their corporate thing, but we hear an intelligent, articulate man damning the very work that these people are doing.

What we hear at this point is actually lifted from later in the film. And when we hear it later, we realize that we've come full circle, to the point that we, too, view the "fixer" from Arthur's perspective. By the end of the film, we also have come back to a scene from near the beginning of the film. But now we have a context for the scene. The second time we see it, we know why Clayton's GPS is blinking, who is in the other cars on the road, why he stops to meet the horses, and why his car explodes.

A similar technique is used later in the story, when Karen Crowder prides herself on her eloquent impromptu speaking but actually spends inordinate amounts of time prepping herself for her performances. One scene shows her in a hotel room, revamping answers to anticipated questions.

In *Notes on a Scandal*, the voice-over is used to juxtapose Barbara Covett's public and private personas. We *see* her public one and *hear* her private one—Barbara's detailed diaries, through which we are able to peer deeply into her.

In *Stand by Me*, the V.O. comes from an adult Gordie, looking back to the moment when he was twelve and first saw a dead body—a turning point in his life, which the adult Gordie puts in perspective. This V.O. adds a reflective tone to the story, with ideas about fathers and sons and Gordie's dead brother. It begins the movie and comes back at the end to tell us about what he's writing. It also comes in several times during the film as a connecting link, to remind us that the adult Gordie is still telling the story, and to maintain the story's reflective quality.

Probably the most famous first person voice-over in television comes from *The Wonder Years*, where the older character's V.O. brings a reflective thematic quality to the story that takes place when he was young. Much like *Stand by Me*, this voice-over deepened both the story and its theme.

The Story Voice-Over

In a few films, a character tells us the story, or at least leads us into the story. This voice usually comes from a relatively unimportant character whose mission is simply to start the story, not to reveal his or her own character. In some films, a storyteller—perhaps a mother or a grandfather—reads a bedtime story to a child. In the opening scene of *The Princess Bride*, a young boy is sick in bed, playing a video game. His grandfather, a minor character, comes in to read a book to him.

GRANDFATHER

"Buttercup was raised on a small farm in the
country of Florin…"

The Mission begins with the first person voice-over of a priest writing about the troubles at his mission, thereby starting the story. He is not a main character, so his function is not to tell us about himself, but simply to introduce the story.

In *The Age of Innocence*, we never learn who the narrator is. She's not a character. Is she the book's author?

In *The Illusionist*, a voice-over combined with a flashback allows Inspector Uhl to tell us what he has discovered about Edward and now reports to Crown Prince Leopold:

INSPECTOR UHL

In fact, we know all about his life….

And the story then flashes back to Edward walking down a road, where he meets a magician, as Uhl continues to narrate this important meeting.

The inspector then narrates the meeting between the Duchess and Edward:

INSPECTOR UHL (O.S.)

And then he met her…
and they were forbidden to see each other…
But soon, they were doing just
that. Over the next few years, they
could always find a way to be together.

But the two young lovers are then separated, which is seen in flashback.

INSPECTOR UHL (O.S.)

What happens next remains a
mystery. We do know that he
traveled the world...
and he began to perform his magic
in public...
that he changed his name to
Eisenheim...
and then almost fifteen years
later, he appeared in Vienna.

And the story then proceeds as we see the story of Eisenheim, his magic, and his love for Sophie.

The story voice-over is usually less effective than the character V.O., since film, by the very nature of the medium, is supposed to *show* us a story rather than *tell* us a story. In many situations, a story V.O. simply tells us what could be shown. And although a story voice-over might give us information that helps us understand a story better, if we don't see it, we don't believe it.

What's the Problem with Voice-Overs?

Voice-overs can easily become a crutch for a writer. A writer can fall into the habit of *talking about* events and people, rather than *showing* events and people through images and action. Of course, figuring out how to show events, show the emotions of the characters, and show the theme through visuals, is difficult. But it's the writer's job to search for those visuals and to make them clear and original.

In the film *Adaptation*, the Robert McKee character, who is teaching a screenwriting seminar, says, "God help you if you use voice-over, my friends. God help you. That's flaccid, sloppy writing. Any idiot can write a voice-over narration to explain the thoughts of a character." I would agree with that character in most cases. Writers love voice-overs because they can show off their beautiful use of words. But the device usually takes away from the impact of the action and the images.

Telling a story through voice-overs is particularly problematical when the voice describes what we're already seeing. In *The Age of Innocence*, there were a number of times when voice-overs described the very paintings, hallways, and large houses that the camera was showing us. We saw it—we didn't need to hear about it.

In *Bonfire of the Vanities*, the reporter, Peter Fallow, told us about what was happening, but we really wanted to see it. *Fight Club, The Royal Tenenbaums*, and *Vicky Cristina Barcelona* use many narrative voice-overs, interrupted by scenes of action and dialogue. This narrator character, who tells us the story, can often get in the way of our visceral experience of a film.

Film is a visual medium. We don't want anyone between us and the action. We come to the theater to watch the film's action as if we were standing on the street watching an exciting event take place just across the road from us. We aren't in danger, but we are involved and engaged and *experiencing* the action.

When used sparingly, voice-overs can be highly effective. However, I often challenge my writing clients to try to show, rather than talk about, action. If you must use voice-overs, use them sparingly and as meaningful juxtapositions to actions and images, as in *Notes from a Scandal* and *Michael Clayton*, or to help layer a story thematically, as in *Stand by Me*.

USING FLASHBACKS

A *flashback* is a scene or sequence of scenes that shows activities that took place at some time earlier than a film's present. It often represents a character's remembrance of past events. Flashbacks can be used subjectively to get inside a character's head or objectively to serve the story by showing some bit of backstory that the audience needs to know.

Flashbacks often play out the relationship of the past and the present. *Stand by Me,* which is about the past, flashes back to the past to help us better understand it. *Ordinary People* uses flashbacks to help Conrad Jarrett remember, and understand, the sailboat accident in which his brother drowned. *The Prince of Tides* moves back, through flashbacks, to a central incident in the life of Tom Wingo. *Beloved* uses flashbacks to recall a traumatic past incident.

Sometimes, almost an entire film is told as a flashback (e.g., *Citizen Kane*), which can make the film's beginning feel awkward: a character says, "I'm going to tell you a story about what happened to me" (or to some other person). We then flash back, the story is told, and, at the end, the character reappears to say, "And that's what happened." Such appearances by a character—to introduce and wrap up a lengthy flashback—may be said to "frame" a flashback.

I found the present-day frame of *The Green Mile* somewhat ungainly and unnecessary. I felt the same about the variation on this idea in *Saving Private Ryan. Titanic* used this idea to show what Rose Dewitt Bukatar had made of her life over all these years. In *Fight Club*, we begin in the present, as the protagonist sits with a gun in his mouth, being questioned by Tyler Durden. The movie than flashes back to the story of the protagonist and Tyler, and at the end, we're back in the opening scene.

Sometimes the use of flashbacks is both effective and essential. *Fried Green Tomatoes,* like *Stand by Me,* used both voice-overs and flashbacks, threading the voice-overs throughout and using the flashbacks to deepen our understanding of the present by showing its relationship to the past.

What Goes Wrong with Flashbacks?

Often, flashbacks are chiefly informational rather than dramatic. Although flashbacks can help establish a subjective POV, they generally are used to give information about a character's or a story element's backstory. Writers often explain their use of flashbacks by saying, "I wanted to give you further information about my character. The past seemed relevant to explain the present."

Flashbacks as a means to explain a character's motivation rarely work well. They put an emphasis on details rather than drama. They stress the inner psychology of a character rather than present actions that force present responses. They reveal character, but rarely do they *motivate* character. Motivation pushes a character *forward*. Flashbacks, by their nature, stop action or move a story *backward*. Real motivation happens in the present, not the past. A character's *final* motivation—the straw that broke the camel's back—may be the last in a series of events, but it happens now. It's in the present.

This is not to say, "Never use flashbacks!" Some flashbacks are necessary for thematic purposes or to serve the style of the film. The flashbacks in *The Illusionist* and *The Prestige* help clarify the many twists and turns in those films, as well as their illusions.

If I don't use flashbacks or expository speeches to explain my story, where do I start it? How do I find that beginning image that sets everything in motion? A good way to begin a story is to place the main character at a *crisis point*. At a crisis point, characters are particularly vulnerable to being thrust in new directions. They are ready for something new to unfold because, in some way, their old world (or old story) has been destroyed, and a new story is emerging. Whether it's a murder or a promotion or embarking on an adventure, a crisis point is a good beginning for a story.

The Flash Forward

Occasionally, a movie flashes forward to the future. Or, it might flash both backward and forward. There are flashes backward and forward in *Twelve Monkeys*, although, technically, the movie seems to move from present to past since it begins in the present. In *Y Tu Mamá También* there is a voice-over flash-forward when we're told what will happen on this road in the future.

INTERCUTTING SCENES

Intercutting is the direct juxtaposition of usually short moments from different scenes. For example, Scene One might show a girl at a desk, writing a letter to her sweetheart, Joe, who's in the Army. Scene Two might show Joe's heroic battle activities. By cutting back and forth between short moments from these very different scenes, they comment on each another and, thus, both become very poignant and dramatic.

In many films, the action moves back and forth between a series of characters and/or a series of incidents to build tension or help us understand the story from several different POVs. This also helps the writer build the action to a climax. We see this in most chase scenes: If, for example, the hero chases the villain in a car, we see the villian's car go around the corner, and then we immediately see the hero's car go around the same corner. Through repeated variations on this inter-cut, we see the chase car close in, until the villain takes an unexpected turn and gets away.

Sometimes the intercutting is used to build the scene and make sure that every story beat is clearly shown. *The Sting* builds much of its action this way. In the setup of one of its cons, for example, the film intercuts among the actions of Hooker, Lonnegan, and Twist. At the end of this intercutting we arrive at Henry Gondorff's private club—all set up for the con to go into effect.

```
EXT. STREET

Johnny Hooker hustles out across the street and into
the alley.

INT. DRUGSTORE
```

Doyle Lonnegan watches him through the window and then settles back in his seat to wait for the phone call.

OUTSIDE STORE

As Hooker descends the stairwell into the store, he gives Kid Twist the office. Twist turns away from the window and looks at his watch. 12:58.

CUT TO:

DRUGSTORE

Lonnegan waits by the phone, idly pinging a knife on the salt shaker. It's 1:40. A man enters the store and walks over to use the phone.

> LONNEGAN
> We're waitin' for a call.

The man looks at Lonnegan a beat, and then at his four goons. He decides maybe he'll make the call later.

CUT TO:

INT. THE STORE

Kid Twist turns as Billie enters the room with a piece of paper. Twist looks at it, then picks up the phone and begins to dial.

INT. DRUGSTORE

Lonnegan's getting impatient now and lights a cigarette. The phone rings. He answers it quickly and we hear:

> TWIST
> Bluenote at 6 to 1 on the nose.

The phone clicks off at the other end. Lonnegan hangs up and goes out the door, followed by his entourage.

EXT. STREET

We follow him across the street and into the alley, where he signals one of his bodyguards to check the place out.

Kid Twist pushes a button on his window sill, and a buzzer goes off inside the store. The previously inert figures there spring to life.

Lonnegan's bodyguard descends the stairwell and knocks at the door, where he's greeted by Hooker in the capacity of host. The bodyguard looks the place over and motions an okay to Lonnegan.

INT. THE STORE

As Lonnegan enters, we see the room for the first time in its entirety. Overnight it has been transformed into a swank private club, with bar, cigarette girls, upholstered furniture and chandeliers.

> SINGLETON
>
> Look at that. He's got four apes with him.

> GONDORFF
>
> That's what I like about these guys, J.J...
> They always got protection against things we'd
> never do to 'em.

In the last act of *The Godfather*, there is dramatic intercutting between a baptism and the killing of the enemies. In the last act of *The Godfather: Part 3*, there is dramatic intercutting between the opera and a series of murders. The last act of *The Fugitive* intercuts among the POVs of Richard, Charlie, and Sam.

The Dark Knight has exciting intercutting between The Joker, Batman, Commissioner Gordon, Harvey Dent, Rachel Dawes, Policemen, and The Joker's thugs as the clock ticks and we wonder who will be saved. The intercutting shows the Observation Room in Gotham Central, then to the Interrogation Room with Batman and The Joker, back to the Observation Room, to the street, to the basement apartment where Harvey Dent is kept, to the warehouse where Rachel is held captive, to the street, back to the interrogations room, to the Holding Area, and back and forth between the various locations, building tension and building the action to the final moment of the explosion of the warehouse, when it's clear that Rachel is killed but Harvey is saved.

The intercutting of scenes allows the writer to build up anticipation. The lovers are ready to meet—and we see them coming from two different directions. The chase is on—and we follow both chase cars. The antagonist is preparing to kill the protagonist, and we watch his preparations and watch the unwary protagonist, who has no idea of the danger and no idea of what is about to happen. Back and forth, as we see the inevitable coming together from two different strands of the story.

The Prestige has some interesting intercutting. Cutter tells how a bird appears and disappears in his illusion. As he explains how it's done, the movie suddenly cuts to this illusion being performed in front of an audience. The film then cuts back to the explanation, and then to the performance again, back and forth, telling us and showing us how the technique works.

APPLICATION

Questions to Ask Yourself about Your Script

Have I chosen POVs that work for my story? Do they need to be expanded? Or limited?

Am I running into any problems because of my POV choices? Does that mean changing a POV, or might it work to keep the current POV but simply find another way to deal with a particular challenge?

If I've used voice-overs, were they necessary? Could my story work just as well without that extra talk?

If I used flashbacks, are they intrinsic to my story? Do the flashbacks fit the style and the theme of my story, or are they merely cinematically interesting?

If I have omniscient POVs, have I created interesting transitions from one POV to another? Am I using these POVs to help the audience understand the broader story?

EXERCISES AND THINGS TO THINK ABOUT

(1) Watch the following films that are told mainly via a first person POV or a two-person POV but broaden their POVs for one or two scenes. Did the addition of POVs feel jarring? Here are the films: *Fight Club* (note changes to Marla's POV); *When Harry Met Sally* (note changes to their friends' POVs); *Changeling* (note changes described beginning page 91); *Resurrection* (note changes to the boyfriend's POV); *Everything Is Illuminated* (most of the film is told from a two-person POV, but there is also the scene where the grandfather remembers the massacre and we are suddenly in his POV); *Pulp Fiction,* (note when we move off of the main characters' POVs and then, in the middle, switch to the POV of a character who had been a minor character in Act One).You may also want to watch *Amadeus* to see how the subjective narrator character brought us into his POV, but how the film still left room to switch to other POVs from time to time.

(2) Watch films that have a very broad use of POVs (*Crash, Traffic, The Big Chill, Babel*). Are there times when the POVs were so broad that you lost interest in or identification with the characters and the story?

(3) As an exercise, write a scene that's implied in a film you know, but isn't shown since the POVs the writer chose to use didn't allow

for this scene. It might be an offscreen murder scene or an offscreen beginning of a romance or an offscreen traveling scene. Does expanding the POVs to include this scene help, or hinder, the story?

(4) Watch films that show intercutting—in chase scenes, work scenes, or love scenes (some examples: *The Fugitive, When Harry Met Sally, The International*). Could the intercut scenes still work without intercutting? Watch films that use voice-overs and flashbacks (e.g., *American Beauty, Duplicity, Stand by Me, Slumdog Millionaire*). Look at the structure of the flashbacks, and how they interweave. Could they be eliminated? How? Watch many different films to see whether the techniques they use—such as voice-overs, flashbacks, intercutting, expanding POV—were enlightening or confusing.

CHAPTER SIX

Creating the Scene

Scenes are a story's building blocks. Through action, images, and dialogue, a scene can advance a story, reveal character, explore an idea, and build visual context. A great scene will do all of these. A good scene will do more than one.

Many times writers have said to me, "I wrote that scene to reveal character." And that's all the scene is doing. But film is multi-dimensional. A scene can accomplish many purposes at the same time. Its background might show an image that expresses an idea. Its actions might reveal character. Its dialogue might advance the story. And the combination of all of these elements can explore a theme.

A great scene involves an audience emotionally. It can build tension or suspense or terror, and even cause physical changes in the audience, from sweaty palms to tears to faster heart rates.

Aristotle said that tragedy should engender pity and fear. And many of the best film scenes might awaken those emotions. But they'll also bring out other feelings—such as compassion, joy, anger, frustration, excitement, disappointment, and sadness.

THE IDEA OF THE SCENE

As you work on your scenes, remember why film is called "moving pictures." Although "writing" implies working with words, the screenwriter actually creates dialogue *and* images. This means that the writer creates scenes that contain directed movement, conflict, and emotions—all expressed through cinematic locations, dramatic actions, and dynamic character relationships.

Most film scenes are short—anywhere from a sentence or two to as many as three or four pages. Dialogue tends to be spare, moving back and forth between characters with just a few sentences for each speech. Since a script is usually limited to around 100 to 120 pages, every line of dialogue and every description needs to count.

Since they're going to be expressed by the director and actors, scenes need to *imply* colors and textures and relationships and feelings that can be brought to life by these other artists. Many details need to be conveyed in just a few well-chosen sentences to paint a picture of the characters and their actions, while not telling so much that you're actually doing the job of the cinematographer, director, actor, composer, and editor.

A good scene accomplishes a number of objectives:

(1) *It advances the story*, giving the information that's needed to follow the story. It might advance the story by giving clues in a mystery or developing a relationship in a love story or taking us on a journey in which each scene moves us closer to a final destination. In a good script, scenes take us in a direction, and a good proportion of those scenes move us closer to a film's climax. Think about how every scene, in one way or another, builds to a final showdown in such Westerns as *Shane*, *Gunfight at the O.K. Corral*, *Unforgiven*, *3:10 to Yuma* (both the original and the remake), and *Butch Cassidy and the Sundance Kid*, as well as such non-Westerns as *Saving Private Ryan*, *A History of Violence*, *Star Trek* (2009), *Angels & Demons*, *Rear Window*, *Bonnie and Clyde*, *12 Angry Men*, *Mr. & Mrs. Smith*, *Seabiscuit*, *Gladiator* (2000), and *Gangs of New York*. Think about how every scene, in one way or another, builds toward solving a mystery and getting the bad guy, in films such as *State of Play*, *The Fugitive*, *Zodiac*, *Rear Window*, *Dial M for Murder*, *All the President's Men*, *The Dark Knight*, and *Angels & Demons*.

A scene that advances a story anticipates the next scene. It implies that related action will follow in the next scene. This might mean that a clue planted in one scene is paid off in the next, or that two people meet in one scene and start developing a relationship in the next. One scene sets up and contains the seeds of the next; one scene flows into the next.

(2) *A scene reveals character.* Most character revelations occur in subplot scenes, but "A" story scenes can also reveal character by showing how someone makes decisions, what kind of actions a character chooses, and how he or she operates under pressure.

Character information in a "B" story scene can be paid off in an "A" story scene. Sometimes a scene might seem to be only about revealing character, yet it might also introduce some useful ability of the protagonist, as she approaches her goal.

Perhaps we see a protagonist taking part in a favorite sport—rock climbing, let's say. It seems at first as if this is just a character revelation scene, but later we see that the protagonist needs this skill in order to rescue the MIAs or storm a fortress at the top of a cliff.

The best character revelation scenes don't choose character details by happenstance, but reveal character traits that will pay off in some other part of the script. So the character details that you give your character in one scene, such as a love of computer games (*WarGames*); an ability to imitate different voices (*Mrs. Doubtfire*); swimming for exercise which later pays off when the person has to rescue someone under water (*Angels & Demons*); knowledge about permanent waves (*Legally Blonde*) or about cars (*My Cousin Vinnie*); or a love of reading (*The Reader*) or of playing the piano (*The Piano*), are not simply there for character revelation, but act also to advance the story and pay off at some other point in the story.

(3) *A scene explores a theme.* Movies are about something. They may be about good and evil or about identity or integrity or greed or love or betrayal or any number of ideas that relate to the human condition. Scenes explore and expand upon an idea through the words that characters say, the actions they take, and the expressive images written into the script.

Sometimes the theme is simply stated. Sheriff Ed Tom Bell in *No Country for Old Men* delivers the theme in a voice-over:

```
            ED TOM BELL

The crime you see now … it's hard to even take
its measure. It's not that I'm afraid of it.
I always knew you had to be willing to die to
even do this job. But, I don't want to push my
chips forward and go out and meet something I
don't understand. A man would have to put his
soul at hazard. He'd have to say, "O.K., I'll
be part of this world."
```

And the film then explores this theme of evil, and the intersection of this policeman and the murderer.

Occasionally the theme is the opposite of what is said. In *The Graduate*, Benjamin is told that the answer to his future is "plastics." We know, and Benjamin knows, that the answer is almost anything but plastics.

Sometimes the theme is expressed through a character's decisions and reactions. A character chooses to try out for the school play or to dance or to participate in some artistic endeavor (*High School Musical, Dead Poets Society, Fame, Billy Elliot, Dirty Dancing*), or to overcome evil (*United 93, Passenger 57,* all the *Die Hard* films, and innumerable cop shows), and these decisions, actions, and reactions tell us about courage and the universal desire to express oneself and mankind's indomitable spirit.

(4) *A scene builds an image.* Writers need to include images in their scripts, and be conscious that those images mean something.

When chosen poorly, an image merely repeats rather than develops an idea. A stagnant or repetitive image of greed might depict a character counting his money in each scene, scene after scene.

But a good scene develops and expands an image. To *build* an image of greed, the writer might show a person willing to do anything to make money. The next scene might show the person buying expensive furnishings or jewelry. Another scene might show the guards, alarms, and dogs that protect the wealth. Later, a scene might show the greedy person putting money above his family, friends, and personal integrity.

In *A Christmas Carol*, a number of images convey the ideas of greed and frugality: Scrooge skimps on the coal in his office, refuses to celebrate Christmas, refuses to give to the poor, raises his prices, eats only his meager porridge, and heats only one room of his home.

Sometimes images carry a film's theme within a scene. These might be images that set a theme of community, as in the first scene in *Witness*: "Black-clad figures make their way down a lane," showing a community that is alike in values, dress, and lifestyle. In *Titanic* (1997) the theme of classism is shown by contrasting the accommodations of those in first class with those in steerage. In *Happy Feet,* in the midst of the cold of Antarctica we see the warmth and protection of the family. In *The Shawshank Redemption*, Brooks's crow, Jake, is an image of freedom. *Pan's Labyrinth* contrasts the real world with the fairy world. *Coraline* shows us two worlds—one on each side of the little door—and raises questions about which is better.

Ideally, a scene will advance the story, reveal character, explore a theme, and build an image. Rarely, however, will a scene actually reach this multifaceted ideal. Some scenes in a mystery might only advance the story and give some small character revelation. Some subplot scenes might not advance the story, but will concentrate on character and theme instead.

WHICH SCENES TO USE, AND WHERE TO PUT THEM

Any story contains an infinite number of potential scenes. Characters eat, sleep, get up in the morning, interact with each other, argue, make decisions, strategize future events, take part in leisure-time activities—the list is endless. How does a writer choose which ones to use?

To a great extent, you can trust your dramatic instincts. But there are some ideas to keep in mind as you create scenes.

Make sure that the beats of your "A" story are clear.

Every story *advances* its action through story beats. (See Chapter 2 for a discussion of "beats.") Although you may not show every beat, it's helpful to map out your needed beats (whether in an outline or a treatment) to make sure that your story adds up. In a murder mystery, there's the murder, the investigator taking the case, specific discoveries made along the way, and capturing the bad guy at the end. In a romantic comedy, there's often the meeting (sometimes called the "cute meet"), the moment of interest (or sometimes of disinterest that will change), the first date or first get-together, the developing attraction, the first kiss, and a movement toward some kind of togetherness at the end.

Make sure that the beats of your "B" stories—your subplots—are clear as well.

Outline the beats of your subplots so that all of their storylines make sense from beginning to end, and so each subplot intersects your "A" storyline—isn't free floating but has a relationship to your main plot. Make sure that your subplot doesn't have holes in it: Check all your scenes to make sure that they all contain the beats you need to tell your story.

Show, rather than talk about, the action.

Film is about action. It moves the audience forward toward a story's climax by literally moving forward through a series of filmed events (actions). Rather than talk about a murder or a promotion or a meeting between lovers, *show it.* As you outline your story, find those events that can create the most cinematically compelling moments, and put them onscreen in the most dramatic way.

Make static scenes interesting by adding action.

Even though a scene is about boring exposition, you can make something interesting happen in it. Sometimes you will need to show scenes that basically are static, such as driving in a car or sitting in a restaurant. Even these scenes, however, can be made intense, interesting, dramatic, and revelatory by adding some activity. Think of the eating scenes in *When Harry Met Sally, The Remains of the Day,* and *Tom Jones,* which made what could have been boring scenes fascinating.

Think of how often you see a scene that imparts valuable information while characters work in their gardens, shell peas, weed hydrangeas, fold their laundry, or brush their hair before bed. In *12 Angry Men* (1957), one juror polishes his glasses while giving us important information. In *Lost in Translation,* important exposition material about Bob Harris and his wife is conveyed while Harris sits in a huge sunken granite tub in a beautiful room. He's trying to relax, but his wife calls him on his cell phone. Tension is conveyed in opposition to his relaxing setting. Things clearly are not going well in their marriage, and his wife would just as soon he stay just where he is—Japan.

Use scenes to orient the audience to your film's setting and context.

Sometimes, you will need to add simple establishing scenes to let the audience know where they are, and/or the relationship of one onscreen element to another. Generally, an establishing scene is brief. It might show a car driving up to an apartment building to establish where a character lives, or it might establish a prison setting by showing a prison's exterior, followed by a short interior scene showing the arrangement of its cells. An establishing scene might show the height of a dam (*The Fugitive*) or length of a race (*Ben-Hur*), or the height of a tower (*Vertigo*). Without these little scenes, an audience can be disoriented easily. If you want to see films that don't have sufficient establishing scenes, watch *Mrs. Soffel* and the O.K. Corral gunfight in the film *My Darling Clementine*. In both these films, we often don't know where we are and don't know the physical proximity of various people and buildings (and horses).

Montages can give important information and show the passage of time.

A montage is a series of short consecutive scenes (shots, really) that generally combine in our mind's eye to give us a single piece of information. Generally, they are undeveloped scenes without dialogue, although some montages may contain one or two spoken lines.

We've all seen montages of characters falling in love—they have a candlelight dinner, walk on the beach hand-in-hand, kiss under a full moon, and finally make love passionately. Instead of spending an entire act showing the couple falling in love, a montage can show them falling in love over a period of but a few seconds, so that the film can spend more of its time developing other aspects of their relationship (What happens after they've fallen in love? What happens after they marry?). *Up* (2009) collapses a love and marriage into a montage of a few minutes, showing a couple's happy life—marrying, fixing up their clubhouse, growing older, dreaming of travel, attempting to have kids, and struggling with disease. *The Parent Trap* (1961) features a romantic montage that helps the audience know that two people were once happy together. Although these romantic montages are popular, and often overused, a montage can be about anything. It can be a series of scenes about finding a job, building a house (or a barn, as in *Witness*), moving to a new city, getting dressed, or investigating a crime.

A montage is often played against a song or some other piece of distinctive music. In *Toy Story 2,* Jessie's backstory is shown in a montage that plays under the song "When She Loved Me." In *The Sound of Music* there's the "Do-Re-Mi" montage showing the children learning to sing as they bicycle around the city.

Sometimes the music played under a montage defines the movie. In *Rocky*, the second act ends with the famous training montage that shows Rocky running up the steps of the Philadelphia Museum of Art—clearly ready for the fight.

Occasionally a montage has some short snippets of dialogue. In *A Few Good Men*, a montage that shows the legal team preparing for court has a few pieces of dialogue explaining certain procedures and policies. In *Ocean's Eleven* and *Ocean's Thirteen*, the team prepares for the take-down at the hotel while explaining each step.

In *The Sting*, a montage helps show the passage of time as preparations are made for the big sting:

MONTAGE SEQUENCE

Detailing the arrival of the other three members of Gondorff's "mob". Throughout Gondorff wears the fedora which is his trademark. We begin with –

A tall, good-looking man, Kid Twist, making his way through the railway station. Impeccably dressed and carrying a small suitcase, he scans the area carefully. Finally, he catches a glimpse of the thing he's been looking for. It's Gondorff, standing by a newsstand. Gondorff makes a quick snubbing motion on his nose as if flicking off a gnat. This is known among con men as the "office." Twist returns the sign with a barely discernible smile as he walks on by. Con Men rarely acknowledge each other openly in public, but it's obvious that these two are glad to see each other.

                                          CUT TO:

    INT. BARBER SHOP – DAY

Hooker is having his hair cut and his nails manicured. Gondorff gives instructions to the barber, as Hooker makes eyes at the MANICURIST. .

                                          CUT TO:

    INT. HABERDASHERY – DAY

Hooker is modeling a new suit in front of a mirror. He doesn't look too pleased, but Gondorff peels bills off his bankroll anyway.

                                          CUT TO:

    EXT. HOTEL – DAY

A pair of white spats stepping off a bus. We follow them into:

INT. HOTEL LOBBY

Where we tilt up to reveal J.J. Singleton, the
most flamboyant of the bunch. On his way to the
check-in desk, he silently exchanges the "office"
with Gondorff, who is sitting on a lounge reading the
paper.

CUT TO:

INT. APARTMENT - DAY

Hooker being shown into a small apartment room
by an old woman. It consists of a bed, a table and
a sink. Hooker nods his acceptance to the woman and
gives her a bill. He takes another look around the
room and decides to go out somewhere, but first he
wedges a small piece of paper between the door and
the jamb, about an inch off the floor.

CUT TO:

INT. A BIG METROPOLITAN BANK - DAY

We hold on a slight, bespectacled teller, Eddie
Niles, in the process of counting a large deposit.
Niles is all business; if he's ever smiled, no one's
seen it. He glances up for a second and sees Gondorff
"officing" him from across the bank. Without a word
he shoves the money he's been counting back into the
hands of a startled customer, abruptly closes up his
window, flips his identification tag on the manager's
desk and walks out of the bank.

CUT TO:

INT. AN UPSTAIRS ROOM OF THE CAROUSEL BUILDING -
NIGHT

Normally used as a storage room, it contains the
water heater, mops and brooms, old bed springs, etc.

> In the middle, a space has been cleared for a table,
> around which are seated Hooker, Gondorff, Niles,
> Singleton and Twist. Gondorff is in his T-shirt, but
> still wears his hat. Kid Twist is in a suit as usual.
> The room is illuminated by a single bare bulb hanging
> from the ceiling.

>   TWIST
>   (showing Hooker photographs of three men)
>   These are Combs' favorite torpedoes. Riley and
>   Coles.

And the script then moves back into scenes as the men further prepare for the con.

THE EXPOSITION SCENE

Sometimes an audience simply must receive uninteresting information if it is to understand a particular story. Even in these situations, you can use a number of techniques to avoid writing a boring scene.

(1) Put it under the opening credits.

Sometimes important exposition material is tucked under the opening credits, in order to start off the audience with information that's key to understanding the story. In *Quiz Show*, the credit sequence shows how the questions and answers for the $64,000 question are stored, guarded and transported. As a result, we have what we need to understand the corruption of the process when we later see it. At the beginning of *The Color of Money*, the audience has to understand the game of pool, so the basic rules are conveyed under the credits. At the beginning of *Junior Bonner*, the audience needs to understand the world of rodeo bull riding, so the credit sequence shows the intricacies of the sport and its competitors' lifestyles.

(2) Whenever possible, use visuals.

In *Titanic*, we need to understand why this ship was an "unsinkable" marvel. We also need to understand the problems it encountered. In the film's present-day opening frame of the story, a computer-generated model shows how the ship was constructed and why and how it broke apart.

In *Raiders of the Lost Ark*, Indiana Jones shows a visual of the ark, taken from an old, leather-bound book, to add interest to the scene in which he explains the mythology of the ark.

In *The Matrix*, instead of merely talking to Neo, Morpheus explains the dream world and the real world to him by taking him (and the audience, of course) on a visual journey that shows the unbelievable state the world is in.

(3) Scatter the exposition, instead of delivering it all at once.

Most long passages of exposition are, by their nature, boring. Therefore, try sneaking a line or two of this information into many places throughout your script, rather than lumping it all into one scene.

Titanic had to get across a great deal of information about the ship and its lifeboats, various decks, and various classes as well as data about the formation and danger of icebergs. To do this, snippets of information were sifted into many scenes. The Captain talks about the ship's boilers in a short scene over tea. Rose asks the ship's builder about the lifeboats in another scene. The Captain receives information about the icebergs in one line of dialogue. All of this is backed with a great many establishing shots to provide us with what we needed to know.

(4) Whenever possible, let interesting characters deliver uninteresting information.

Make a character interesting enough and that person will hold us in a scene while delivering even somewhat boring exposition.

In the beginning frame of *Titanic*, the computer-generated model is talked about by a burly, bearded character with a yellow smiley face on his T-shirt. He speaks with great excitement and with his own personal sound effects happily added as the computer-generated Titanic dramatically goes down.

In *Ratatouille*, the rat gives information about cooking and the famous chef gives insights into how a four-star restaurant runs. In the

Harry Potter films, Hermione, who loves homework and reads extensively, often provides important facts and backstory, connecting the other characters' dots for the audience.

Sometimes several contrasting characters might give the information. In *Raiders of the Lost Ark,* two government men—one fat, one skinny; one with a tie, one with a bow tie; one skeptical, one not— give Jones information about Ravenwood and the lost ark.

(5) Whenever possible, add emotions to your information's delivery.

In *The Reader,* some of the information about the church tragedy, in which people were locked in and burned alive, became emotional for us because we saw some of those hearing about it responding emotionally (but Hannah had no response whatsoever).

In *Raiders of the Lost Ark,* Jones and Professor Brody become very excited when they hear that the Nazis have discovered Tanis, the ark's resting place. Their excitement and enthusiasm is contagious, spreading into the audience.

In the third Indiana Jones movie, *The Last Crusade,* the interests and fears of the father and his son are contrasted. One fears rats, the other snakes. One kills people and destroys property to save relics while hardly blinking, yet the other finds these adventures terrifying at first, and later exhilarating.

(6) Add conflict to make the scene more dramatic.

In *Pirates of the Caribbean: The Curse of the Black Pearl,* Elizabeth explains "the code of parlay" as pirates, ready to shoot her, hold her captive. Amid this conflict, Elizabeth gives exposition:

> ELIZABETH
>
> Parlay. I invoke the right of parlay. According to the Code of the brethren, set down by the pirates Morgan and Bartholomew, you have to take me to your Captain.

(7) Deliver exposition through dialogue between characters.

Many times, a writer adds interest to boring information by having it delivered as dialogue rather than monologue. Sometimes one character asks a question and another answers it. Sometimes several characters add new information. In *Raider's of the Lost Ark,* Indiana Jones is told, "The Nazis have discovered Tanis." The Government men reply, "What exactly is Tanis?," and Indiana Jones tells them. In *Fargo,* Marge asks a couple of hookers to describe a suspect. One of them replies, "He was funny-looking. More'n most people even." In *Doubt,* Sister Aloysius begins to plant the idea about doubt in Sister James's mind by asking her:

> SISTER ALOYSIUS
>
> This past Sunday. What do you think that sermon was about? …
>
> SISTER JAMES
>
> Well, Doubt…
>
> SISTER ALOYSIUS
>
> Why? … Well, sermons come from somewhere, don't they? Is Father Flynn in Doubt? …

The idea of doubt is raised and will be further explored.

WHERE TO START THE SCENE? WHERE TO END THE SCENE?

Some scenes begin too early. As a result, they lag, they dawdle, and they don't seem to have a clear focus. They don't know where they're going or how to get there.

Some scenes begin too late. As a result, they either don't give the audience all the important information needed to understand the scene, or they don't allow adequate time to build tension, conflict, and/or suspense.

In order to decide where to start a scene, first decide where to end it. What is the point of the scene? What is its focus? Why include the scene? What's the most important information the audience needs to get from the scene? Where is it heading? This goal will occur at the end of the scene.

A scene might be about a character getting the job, with the hiring as the point of the scene. A scene might build to a murder, with provocations along the way. It might be about a detective finding important information.

Now, where to begin? What does the audience need to know in order to understand the scene? That's the scene's setup. A scene might have to establish an office or a corporate headquarters or a small high school in a rural town or the outside of a chicken ranch.

Now that you have a beginning and an ending, what is the development of the scene? What events are *necessary* to take us from the setup to the climax of the scene? Where are the turns and movement that lend interest and excitement to the scene?

Always keep in mind that one scene needs to link up with the next. How does one scene lead to another?

Think about the scene's action. Many writers will think in terms of a scene's information, and their scenes will become chatty (telling instead of showing). But if you think about a scene's action, that scene will automatically get energy. Things will start happening. It will contain events that force reactions and decisions and new actions.

Maybe a scene of yours shows people talking at a dinner party. It might talk about, rather than show, what's important. If you rethink that scene in terms of *what* is happening, you may decide to start the scene by showing the people meeting and reacting to each other. Or maybe you'll decide that the scene is about a conflict and confrontation that happens between two guests, which leads to some action. (One guest leaves in disgust? An argument becomes heated, and someone throws a wine glass?) Thinking about the action in the scene—even a relatively static scene—will help it along its way to becoming dramatic, emotional, and dynamic.

CONTRASTING SCENES

Strong contrasts from one scene to the next can create vivid images and truly emotional reactions in the audience.

For instance, you might contrast scenes through the use of light and dark. The first scene is THE PARK—DAY. The next scene might be THE STREET—NIGHT.

Scenes might contrast through moods. An intimate, passionate lovemaking scene might contrast with an argument in the park. A violent scene might play off of a light, comedic scene. In *Fatal Attraction,* Alex and Dan are in bed together when Alex asks if he's up for something energetic. CUT TO: Dancing at a loud, frenzied club.

Contrast can be had by varying long and short scenes, visual and dialogue scenes, and interior and exterior scenes.

The pacing of scenes can change from one to the next. For example, a slow-paced scene of a cop getting ready for bed is followed by a car chase scene as that cop is called into action.

Subject matter can be contrasted from scene to scene. You might move from a violent murder scene to a quiet scene inside a church. Or a family scene about an argument might contrast with another family scene that's peaceful and tranquil. (Many of Woody Allen's films have good contrasting scenes between different types of family relationships.)

Contrasting subject matter can be further enhanced through inter-cutting (see "Intercutting Scenes" in Chapter 5). In *Schindler's List,* a wedding scene in the concentration camp is intercut with a scene of Schindler kissing a woman in the club, which is intercut with a scene of the Commandant beating Helen, the maid he has taken into his home. In *Cabaret* there is a similar scene, as a beating outside in the alley is echoed by the music, noise, and laughter inside the cabaret. As mentioned earlier in this book, *The Godfather, The Godfather: Part II*, and *The Godfather: Part III* offer exceptional examples of effective intercutting.

WHAT GOES WRONG WITH SCENES?

Scenes that work well do not exist in isolation. They are part of a sequence that moves a story forward toward its climax. When films don't work well, the problem often lies with scenes that may be complete in themselves but are not well connected to other scenes. If its scenes do not flow well, and are not well connected with its story and with other scenes, a two-hour film can feel like a four-hour film. Compare your experiences of watching the three-hour films of *Schindler's List*, *Dances with Wolves*, and *JFK* versus your experiences of watching the long films *The Last Emperor*, *Hope and Glory*, *The Unbearable Lightness of Being*, and *Short Cuts*. These last four films have their own brilliance, but they may feel long because rather than being part of scene sequences that give the films momentum, many of the scenes are more static and descriptive. When scenes stay on track, build, and have direction, a film involves you and moves you without consciousness of time.

Sometimes scenes don't work because there is little momentum or dramatic build within the individual scene. Instead of building to make a particular point, the scene is flat, static, simply descriptive. The scenes might show a cop driving down the street, a woman writing in her journal, and a man at work, followed by the cop working in the office, the woman leaving for work, the man coming home. Although there's room in every film for some of these merely expositional character scenes, if they overbalance the story-driven scenes that move a story forward, the film will feel static. If you like the characters, you might be patient with a story that lacks buildup and drive. If you don't like the characters, however, a ninety-minute film can feel like a three-hour film.

Many writers leave out a scene's emotional content. Most good scenes show a shift of emotion during the scene; perhaps a character moves from positive to a negative emotional state, or vice versa. If a scene has such shifts, it won't be static. It will have both movement and the opportunity for audience empathy.

In the movie *New in Town*, there are some good emotional shifts that move the scenes forward. In one scene, Blanche is talking to Lucy, her boss, who's calling from Miami, where she's on a business trip. Lucy asks Blanche for some information from a file in her desk. Blanche, eager to help, starts the scene from a positive emotional stance. But, while looking through the desk, she discovers a list of possible terminations, with her own name second from the top. With this discovery her emotional state changes, and the story takes an emotional dip, thereby keeping the simple scene moving.

If you combine emotional shifts with strong images, your whole film will become sturdier and deeper, and audiences will identify with both its story and characters.

APPLICATION

Questions to Ask Yourself about Your Script

Do all of my scenes have a reason for being in my story?

Do the majority of my scenes move my story forward toward its climax?

Have I structured most of my individual scenes so that they have a direction? A sense of going somewhere? A point to make?

Is my entrance into each scene made at the latest possible point, or am I giving unnecessary information before my scenes actually start?

Do I get out of each scene after I've made my point, rather than continuing to hang around with nothing more to be said?

Have I remembered that scenes are about images? Have I remembered to play the image, to play the conflict, to play the emotions, rather than simply playing the information?

Are the relationships among my scenes—particularly one to the next—interesting? Are my scenes repetitive, flat, or boring?

Will an audience be entertained by each individual scene in my script?

EXERCISES AND THINGS TO THINK ABOUT

(1) Watch the montages in *The Money Pit*, *Witness*, *Batman Returns*, *Schindler's List*, *The Deer Hunter*, *Casablanca*, *Home Alone*, *The Royal Tenenbaums*, *The Graduate*, *Forrest Gump*, *Close Encounters of the Third Kind*, *The Sound of Music*, *Rocky*, and *Ocean's Thirteen*. Are they all necessary? How do they move their stories forward by using montage?

(2) Watch the scene sequences in *The Fugitive*, *The French Connection*, and *Fatal Attraction*. Do the scene sequences have clear three-act structures? Time them to see how long they are, and how they're shaped.

(3) Watch a few of your favorite films. How do they use scene transitions? Are there contrasting scenes? Are there exposition scenes? Do these scenes work well, or do you find little thought has been given to the content of the scenes and the movement from scene to scene?

Film creates a visual rhythm. It achieves its rhythm partly through the movement within scenes, and partly by the interplay of one scene with another.

* * * * *

If your scenes are working, you are well on your way to creating a script with momentum and clarity. Now you want to create a script that not only moves, but is also cohesive.

CHAPTER SEVEN

Creating a Cohesive Script

Whether listening to a piece of music, looking at a painting, or watching a movie, we tend to want an experience that feels unified and cohesive. Different art forms attain cohesiveness in different ways. Music tends to use recurring motifs, rhythms, and harmonies to set up expectations that will be either thwarted (for tension) or fulfilled (for repose). Through repetition it builds tension and expectation and simply lets us know that we're still listening to the same piece. A single instrument might thread its way throughout a piece, playing many variations on a melody, or the sound of one instrument might be used to contrast with the sound of another.

In painting, cohesion may derive from a color or shape or texture that may repeat itself across a single canvas or throughout a series of paintings. And a painting's contrasts and repetitions of elements may direct our eyes in very specific ways across and around a canvas. Architecture achieves cohesiveness through repeated and contrasting patterns of windows, arches, and two- and three-dimensional shapes, and through the use of light.

A film gains cohesiveness through the use of foreshadowing (and payoff), recurring motifs, repetition, and contrast.

Foreshadowing

In film, *foreshadowing* is the use of visual or audio material (an object or image or word or sound or piece of dialogue) to hint at and build the audience's expectations for specific future events. All of us have watched murder mysteries in which the camera zooms in on a letter opener that is later used as a murder weapon (a benign object is now ominous). This is an obvious use of foreshadowing and payoff.

We often see foreshadowing and payoff in mysteries in which the audience needs help following a series of complex clues. We also see it in comedies, where jokes need to be set up (drop a banana peel on the sidewalk and...).

Near the beginning of the *Star Wars* trilogy, significant information is given about Luke Skywalker's father. This information is paid off later when we discover that his father is Darth Vader.

In Act One of *Pirates of the Caribbean: Curse of the Black Pearl*, Elizabeth Swann invokes the Right of Parlay, asking for the pirates to follow their own code of conduct. Later, Jack Sparrow invokes Parlay as well. What was set up in Elizabeth's scene is paid off in Jack's scene. In this same film, it's mentioned that Barbossa left Jack on an island with a pistol but only one shot (foreshadow). Later in the story, that one shot is used (payoff).

In *Pulp Fiction,* Vincent's frequent trips to the bathroom are set up, and then paid off when he's there rather than in the restaurant, when the robbery takes place.

Some good foreshadowings and payoffs are found in *Back to the Future.*

```
                    DR. BROWN

    If my calculations are correct, when this car
    hits 88 miles an hour, you're gonna see some
    serious shit.
```

And it works just as he says it will. At 88 miles per hour.

Sometimes foreshadowing works cleverly when an object or piece of information is set up in one context and paid off in another. This subtle kind of foreshadowing gives us information that at first seems unimportant, but later pays off when we understand its significance. *Witness* uses subtle foreshadowing: Samuel guides John Book on a tour around the farm, showing him the water wheel and the silo. John asks, "What's up there?" and Samuel replies, "Corn," thereby setting up the corn in the silo that will be used to kill Detective Fergie in Act Three. But immediately after his reply, Samuel takes the focus off the corn by picking up a kitten and asking John if he wants to pet it. The scene seems to be a farm travelogue, but it is really about setting up the corn in the silo.

In *Back to the Future*, notice how the important information about the clock tower is presented. At the beginning of the film, while Marty and Jennifer discuss their plans to get together for a weekend, a "clock tower activist" gives them a flier, screaming, "Save the clock tower! Save the clock tower!" The flier mentions the date and the time when the clock stopped ticking—the moment, years ago, when it was hit by lightning. Jennifer takes the flier and uses it to write down her phone number and a message to Marty: "I love you!" Later (but in the past via time travel), when Jennifer's loving message becomes the reason why it's so urgent that Marty return to the future, the flier is paid off.

```
                    MARTY

     But I can't be stuck here. Don't you
     understand, Doc? I have a life in 1985! I've
     gotta get back! My girl friend's waiting for
     me . . . See what she wrote here?
```

Marty pulls out the clock tower flier and, as he turns it over, realizes that it has specific information about *when* the lightning will strike the tower. He can now harness the lightning's energy to return to the future.

In this same film, Dr. Brown (in 1985) mentions the historic date of November 5, 1955:

```
                    DR. BROWN

     That was the day I invented time travel ... I
     was standing on the edge of my toilet, hanging
     a clock ... I slipped and hit my head on the
     sink and when I came to, I had a revelation
     ... a vision . . . It's taken me almost thirty
```

> years and my entire family fortune to fulfill
> the vision of that day.

Later, when Marty arrives at Dr. Brown's door in 1955 with an incredible tale about Brown's new time-travel machine of 1985, he notices the Band-Aid on Brown's forehead and convinces the doctor that he's telling the truth about knowing him in 1985.

> MARTY
>
> Dr. Brown... That bruise on your head. I know
> how you got it! It happened this morning! You
> fell off your toilet and hit your head on the
> sink! And then you came up with the idea of
> the Flux Capacitor, which is the heart of the
> time machine!

Sometimes foreshadowings and payoffs are used simply to give a sense of integration to a script without necessarily being essential to its story. In *Back to the Future*, for instance, we see the 1985 campaign to elect Goldie Wilson mayor. And back in 1955, we see how Marty planted the political idea in Wilson's mind.

> WILSON
>
> I'm gonna make something of myself.
>
> MARTY
>
> That's right, he's gonna be Mayor someday.
>
> WILSON
>
> Mayor . . . That's a good idea! I could run
> for Mayor!

In this film, Lorraine's brother Joey is foreshadowed in Act One, and paid off—with humor—in Act Two. In the present (in Act One), Lorraine has prepared a cake, hoping to welcome her brother home from prison. Unfortunately, poor Joey didn't make parole again. In the past (in Act Two) we learn why.

LORRAINE'S MOTHER

```
Little Joey loves being in his [play] pen. He
actually cries when we take him out, so we
leave him in there all the time ... it seems
to make him happy.
```

Even the seemingly unimportant information that the young George liked to write science fiction stories gets paid off in *Back to the Future*'s resolution, when we see that he's just published his first book.

Notice that, in all these examples, whatever is needed to make a story work at its end is planted somewhere in its beginning.

Recurring Motifs

Whereas foreshadowing and payoff usually relate to the story, motifs tend to be more thematic. A *motif* is a recurring image or bit of dialogue or sound that is used throughout a film to deepen its story and add texture to its theme. Motifs need at least three repetitions to work, and they work best when they continue throughout an entire film, helping the audience focus on certain elements.

One of the most recognizable motifs in film history is one of sound: *dum-dum-dum-dum*—the shark music in *Jaws*. This music, which is used whenever the shark comes near, is set up in the first three minutes of the film. The audience quickly learns to recognize it as a signal that the shark is about to strike, so their tension is ratcheted up whenever they hear it. The one time the motif is not used during a shark attack occurs when the shark makes its first assault on Quint, Matt, and Martin. This intensifies the audience's fright, because the attack is so unexpected.

Witness gains cohesiveness through a recurring grain motif. The changes in the use of grain throughout the film symbolize changes that both John Book and the community undergo throughout the film. These grain images either reinforce the simplicity and gentleness of this community or gain added dramatic power through contrast.

At the beginning, we see the Amish walking through the grain to a funeral. They are a farming community that lives in harmony with the earth, as shown by the image of them emerging from the tall grain as they walk to the house. During the funeral scene, bread is placed on the table. Here the grain has been transformed, but it remains natural, wholesome, nurturing. In the city, Rachel and John Book break bread together by eating a hot dog and bun at a fast-food restaurant. Here the grain has been corrupted, processed, changed from its healthy, natural state—just as Rachel and Samuel have been corrupted by the city and the murder. In Act Two, Rachel hides John's bullets in the flour, showing that violence and domestic tranquility are now tied through John's presence in the community. And in Act Three, the grain in the silo becomes a weapon of death. It is the ultimate symbol of the violence that has come to this peaceful community.

Repetition and Contrast

Repetition can come via images, dialogue, character traits, sound, or through the combined use of all these elements to keep an audience focused on an idea. For instance, if you are doing a story about an alcoholic man, you might show him drinking. You might show him sleeping off a hangover. You might show his home filled with empty wine bottles. You might show him staggering down a street or fishing for money to buy beer or sobbing in despair about his alcoholism.

Contrast sets up two things (objects, places, people, or ideas) for an audience to compare. Like repetition, contrast helps to keep an audience focused, since it requires that they remember something from past that they now must evaluate against something new.

In *Gone With the Wind,* the first and second parts of the film contrast pre- and postwar living. We see the contrasts of Twelve Oaks, before and after; Tara, before and after; Mr. O'Hara, before and after; and Scarlett—before and after.

City life and small town life are often contrasted in films. In *New in Town,* life in big, sunny, bustling Miami, Florida, is contrasted with small town life in Minnesota in the winter.

Contrasts allow the writer to play opposites and to help the audience make connections by showing the differences between one part of the story and another. A contrast throws information into high relief, making us notice it more because we've been introduced to its opposite.

You might contrast characters, perhaps pairing up two vastly different kinds of people in a detective story, such as Reggie Howard and Jack Cates in *48 Hours*. You might contrast a man's wife and his mistress, such as brunette Beth (the wife) and blond Alex (the mistress) in *Fatal Attraction*. In *Star Trek*, Kirk and Spock regularly contrast human emotion with emotionless reason.

PROBLEMS IN UNIFYING A SCRIPT

The process of rewriting often works against creating a unified script. Many rewrite discussions fail to keep in mind the script as a whole. If a director wants to rework a murder scene, he or she must realize that changing the payoff demands finding a whole new approach to foreshadowing in an earlier scene. Once, I arrived at a meeting that began with the writer-director and producer informing me that they had decided to add a murder in the first scene. They didn't realize that it would change the storyline from then on. After twelve hours of trying to make it work without losing the excellent scenes that followed, we decided not to do it.

Problems in unifying a script are particularly prevalent in mystery and espionage stories. Some executives refuse to buy these scripts, believing that the public isn't interested since they generally don't do well at the box office. Actually, many of us love a good puzzle, but few are satisfying because clues are missing, or information isn't set up and paid off in ways that keep us with the story. Think about *Gorky Park*, *The Little Drummer Girl*, and *The Osterman Weekend*, all of which did less-than-satisfactory business. In spite of some exciting action and intriguing storylines, all of these movies had problems with clarity of information. Insufficient foreshadowing and payoff contributed to their lack of success.

Dramas, comedies, Westerns, and science fiction films also need clarity in the way they present information. *The Mission* received some criticism for an unclear setup and payoff regarding its geography. Sometimes it was difficult to get up the mountain, sometimes it was relatively easy. The foreshadowing of the difficulty in Act One and the payoff during the battle scenes in Act Three didn't completely mesh.

The same criticism was given to *Full Metal Jacket* and *The Color of Money*. Many critics felt that some of the twists at the end did not connect with the setups at the beginning. And we've all seen innumerable detective stories and mysteries that lost us somewhere along the way because the clues didn't quite fit together.

Unifying the script is one of the most difficult rewrite jobs. It demands great attention to detail, a thorough analysis, and constant attention to the script as a whole. But there are innumerable payoffs for this attention in critical and box-office success and Academy Awards.

APPLICATION

Questions to Ask Yourself about Your Script

Many times writers don't know that they have the beginnings of motifs in their scripts, or that some things that are paid off can be further foreshadowed for greater dramatic punch and unity. Working with these elements demands that you do a thorough check of how they function in your story. The rewriting process is a good time to begin to build up and weave these elements into a script.

When you begin rewriting, first make sure that everything you've foreshadowed is paid off and everything that's paid off is foreshadowed. If you've already done several rewrites, you may discover that some foreshadowing might have been dropped from the script as you moved from one rewrite to the next. Or what you thought was paid off never was—except in your mind's eye. Carefully follow through every thread, or your script will have loose ends.

Look for motifs that can be expanded. To do this, you might find it helpful to look through the physical objects you've used in the script. Could the use of any of these be expanded upon to create a recurring motif? Or there might be some sound that's an integral part of your story which needs to be created as a motif. In a mystery, the sound of squeaky shoes might work both as a motif and as foreshadowing and payoff. In a space story, it might be recurring music, such as was used in *Close Encounters of the Third Kind*, to communicate with the aliens.

Ask yourself:

> Is everything I've paid off foreshadowed in my script? Is everything I've foreshadowed paid off in the script?

> Have I found original ways to foreshadow and pay off information? Have I changed functions, or disguised foreshadowing information, or used humor to set up and pay off information?

> Have I created or implied motifs that the director could use to integrate the script visually? Have I thought through my script visually, repeating images that will give it a sense of cohesiveness?

> Have I contrasted scenes, characters, actions, and images to give my script more dramatic texture and punch?

> Have I done at least one rewrite during which I tried to see the script as a whole, rather than focus on its individual parts?

EXERCISES AND THINGS TO THINK ABOUT

(1) Watch a favorite mystery, perhaps a Hitchcock film, to see how foreshadowing and payoff are worked out. Look also at both the visual and the sound motifs. Which motifs are thematic and which add tension to my story? What examples of foreshadowing and payoff can I recall from other films?

(2) You may want to re-watch *Back to the Future*, since it is filled with clever uses of foreshadowing and payoff. See how many are unexpected because they are introduced in one way and paid off in another.

(3) Look at the use of contrasts in some of your favorite films. Look for repetitions. Look for motifs. How are they used? Are they effective?

* * * * *

Part of the joy of rewriting is the opportunity to expand on themes and images by threading them throughout your script. But in order to find potential images that can add dimension to your story and theme, it becomes necessary to explore the thematic lines of a script. Ask yourself, "What does it really mean, and how can I build meanings through dramatic images?"

The next chapter begins to explore how one clarifies and executes the theme behind a story.

CHAPTER EIGHT

Making It Commercial

No matter how good a writer you are, no matter what your track record is, and no matter how good your script is, all producers and executives will ask you one question: "Is it commercial?"

Everyone has different ideas about what makes a script commercial. Many producers think that it's a matter of packaging: "Get the right actors, and it will be commercial." Many of them say, "If we get Julia Roberts or Tom Cruise or Russell Crowe or Reese Witherspoon, it'll be commercial." However, every one of these actors has had box-office failures.

Many people think that a commercial script depends on commercial subject matter. They look for trends and try to capitalize on the "in" subject. The wild success of the fantasy film trilogy *The Lord of the Rings* seemed to imply that everyone wanted to go see fantasy a few years ago, but box-office statistics show that plenty of fantasy films didn't do well at that time. *The Golden Compass* had an estimated budget of $180 million but brought in about $70 million at American theaters. *Eragon*, based on the popular children's books, brought in $75 million in the states after costing $100 million to make.

With the success of 2002's *Chicago* (budget $45 million, gross $170.6 million), *High School Musical 3* (budget $11 million, gross more than $251 million), and *Mamma Mia!* (budget $52 million, worldwide gross more than $602 million), musicals seemed to be popular again. But many musicals have failed: *Moulin Rouge!*, which cost $52.5 million and brought in only $57.4 million in the United

States, and *A Chorus Line,* which was a huge hit on stage but a huge commercial failure as a film.

The Passion of the Christ made everyone think that Christian films were "in" in 2004, though producer/director Mel Gibson struggled to find a willing distributor. Aided by an unusual and aggressive marketing campaign, it garnered more prerelease ticket sales than any other film in history. It is also the highest-grossing R-rated film, the highest-grossing religious film, and the highest-grossing subtitled foreign-language film. It cost an estimated $30 million to make and made over $370 million just in the United States. Although some religious films have done quite well (*Fireproof* and *Facing the Giants*), others, such as the Rapture-based *Left Behind* and *The Rapture*, have fared poorly.

Some recent Westerns have done well, such as *Dances with Wolves* and *Unforgiven* (1992), but *Heaven's Gate*, with its big production costs, bankrupted United Artists in 1980 and eliminated the Western genre for years. In 2007, *3:10 to Yuma* (a remake of the classic 1957 movie) cost $55 million and took in only $70 million worldwide. In 2008, *Appaloosa* cost $20 million and grossed only $27 million worldwide.

Adapting a best-selling novel for the screen is often a good road to commercial success. Many films that started out as best-selling books went on to win Academy Awards and become commercial blockbusters (e.g., *The Lord of the Rings, The Godfather,* and *One Flew over the Cuckoo's Nest*). But *The Bonfire of the Vanities,* based on the best seller of the same name, was a box-office disaster (budget $47 million, gross $15.7 million), as was *Beloved,* based on Toni Morrison's acclaimed novel of the same name and starring Oprah Winfrey and Danny Glover (budget $53 million, gross $23 million). *The Namesake,* based on Pulitzer Prize winner Jhumpa Lahiri's novel of the same name, cost $9 million and made only $13.5 million in American theaters—not a very impressive profit by Hollywood, or even Bollywood, standards, especially considering the international acclaim of its director, Mira Nair, and its stars, Tabu and Irrfan Khan.

And what about sequels? The success of *Rocky II* through *V* seemed to point toward sequels as sure moneymakers. The *Die Hard* series of films has done well, as have the very profitable *High School Musical 2* and *3*, the Harry Potter series, and the *Ocean's* series. But what about *Jaws 3-D*? Furthermore, sequels can be very difficult to write. *Rambo: First Blood II* came out years after *First Blood*, and it took seventeen rewrites before it had a workable storyline.

Regardless of the successes mentioned above, rarely do sequels fare as well at the box office as the original films. Generally, a sequel lacks the charm, clarity, and originality of the first film. And sequels often don't work because the protagonist's arc has already been played out in the first film. This puts the writer in the tough position of trying to stay true to a spent character while finding some new emotional arc for him or her that is as compelling as the one in the first film.

What about remakes? Some have done well. *Heaven Can Wait* (1978), a remake of *Here Comes Mr. Jordan* (1941), was commercially and critically successful and was nominated for nine Academy Awards. Some remakes do well at the box office (such as *King Kong* in 2005) but don't have the impact or influence of the original. Some, such as the remake of *Stella Dallas* (1990), based on the 1925 and 1937 films, and *Always* (1989), based on *A Man Called Joe* (1943), lose much in their translation to a contemporary setting. For many, the question about remakes is always, "Why?" Why remake *Psycho* (1990) or *Fame* (2009) or *Stella Dallas* when the earlier version was so good? Just because the original was successful does not mean the remake will have critical or commercial success.

For every neat theory about success, there exist numerous examples that disprove it. However, there *are* certain elements that seem to contribute decisively to the success of a film and are not dependent on the writer's close personal friendship with Julia Roberts or Tom Cruise.

THE THREE ELEMENTS NECESSARY FOR COMMERCIAL SUCCESS

Commercial success is almost never dependent on any single element. However, three elements seem to significantly contribute to a script's commercial success: (1) solid script structure, (2) creativity, and (3) strong marketability. If a script doesn't have one of these elements, there's a good chance that it will not sell, and even if it does sell, it won't do well at the box office.

I discussed story structure in the first six chapters. If a story isn't tight and well structured, if it doesn't make sense, it will have a difficult time succeeding commercially and critically. Certainly we've all seen films without solid story structure that were sold and then produced—a few of these even did well at the box office. But such exceptions are very rare. Most of the big critical and commercial successes, such as *Juno, The Dark Knight,* and *The Lord of the Rings,* have well-structured stories. Good structure has been proven again and again as essential to a film's success.

Structure, by itself, means little without creative writers. When producers ask whether a script is creative, they usually mean, Is it fresh? Is it original? Is it different? Is it unique?" They can also mean, Does it have a *hook* or a *kicker* or *spin?* Is it compelling? Am I grabbed by its premise? Producers wonder, "Why would someone go to see this movie?" In answering this question, they look for a conflict or problem that is resolved in the script. They ask, "Will the audience identify with the characters, relate to the problems, and cheer on the transformations and solutions the characters encounter?" They sometimes use the term "relate-ability" to try to get at the elusive element that pulls together the audience and the characters.

Sometimes it's difficult to predict how well an audience will identify with a film's characters, since the most predictable problems and solutions can be derivative and uninteresting. Many of the most successful commercial films are based on an original premise that is well executed and a problem that seems unusual. There were no precedents for films such as *Slumdog Millionaire*, *Chicago*, *The Lord of the Rings*, and *WALL-E*, and there have been no successful copies.

But creativity, by itself, will not make a script sell (or a film succeed at the box office). It needs elements that can help market it and capture an audience.

Marketability might be thought of as those elements that make people want to invest in a film and that make it *look* like it has a reasonable chance of success. Certainly a script directed by Ron Howard or Oliver Stone or Michael Mann or James Brooks has a better chance of being made than one directed by an unknown, first-time director. A film produced by Todd Black or Brian Grazer or Harvey Weinstein already has an important element in its favor. If Meryl Streep, Morgan Freeman, Brad Pitt, Kate Winslet, or Reese Witherspoon are interested in your script, you have a huge addition to its marketability.

But marketability and salability are not limited to just *packaging* the project (putting together a script with above-the-line talent), and they need not be vague words based on the whim of an executive. Some marketability and salability elements can be defined and explained clearly. They are the underlying concepts that make people want to go see a movie. These elements can be developed and focused in your script to make it more commercial.

HOW TO FIND CONNECTIONS WITH AN AUDIENCE

Generally, people go to a film because there is something in it that speaks to them. They identify in some way with both its characters and its story. They connect with it. Audience connection is the key to marketability. Understanding the specific ways that people connect with a film can help you bring out and make the most of the commercial elements in your script.

The Universal Appeal of the Idea

Most successful films express a clear *theme*—some underlying idea that tells us something about the human condition and, one hopes, has universal audience appeal. The theme, often the reason why a writer wrote a script, is an idea that hovers over and simmers within a story and causes audiences to identify with a story's characters and situations. A theme conveys the meaning of a story's events—what the writer believes about why things happen and what we can learn from them. A theme is about cause and effect and the meaning of life. It might be about the meaning of something we've experienced—the chance to have a better life no matter what one's circumstances (*Slumdog Millionaire*), our integrity and the integrity of our society and confronting the corruption and resistance that stands in the way (*Erin Brockovich, The Insider, Michael Clayton*), the need to resolve the past and the present (*Mystic River*), or the need to realize our potential (*Little Miss Sunshine, The Visitor*).

Many times a theme can be expressed very simply. One of the most prevalent ideas in many successful films is that of the *triumph of the underdog*: *Rocky, The Karate Kid, Slumdog Millionaire, Billy Elliot, Working Girl, Pretty Woman, Shrek, The Wrestler,* and *Seabiscuit*. This idea is very strong and appealing to audiences because all of us want to overcome adverse circumstances. By watching the success of an onscreen underdog, we triumph vicariously.

Revenge is another theme that has universal significance. Have you ever felt like getting back at someone? *Die Hard: With a Vengeance, V for Vendetta,* the *Bourne* films, *Braveheart, Man on Fire, The Italian Job, Fatal Attraction,* and *Gladiator* (2000) speak to our universal desire to get back at someone who has done us wrong. Did you feel betrayed and angered by the unenthusiastic reception many of the Vietnam War vets faced? *First Blood* makes revenge simple—and takes care of all the bad guys, too.

Another universal theme is *triumph of the human spirit*. This theme was used very successfully in the films *Rain Man, Dead Poets Society, The Pursuit of Happyness, Places in the Heart, Milk,* and *Schindler's List*.

Why do we watch films about rich people outsmarting other rich people to get richer? Because *greed* is a common feeling. We've all felt it at some time, along with envy, jealousy, lust, and the more socially acceptable emotion "the desire to have it all." *The Thomas Crown Affair, Ocean's Twelve, Wall Street* and even *The Sting* speak to these feelings.

Some themes seem particularly relevant to certain age groups. If you know the demographics of your intended audience, you can capitalize on themes that will appeal to them. For instance, about fifty percent of today's moviegoers are between the ages of twelve and twenty-nine. That's why many coming-of-age stories or stories about the pressures and issues faced by this age group are popular. *Juno, Lars and the Real Girl, Stand by Me, Diner* (1982), *Risky Business* (1983), *Almost Famous* (2000), *American Graffiti, The Breakfast Club*, and *The Princess Diaries* speak to identity issues that often confront teenagers and young adults.

Other themes that can make connections with audiences include *integrity*, as shown in *Erin Brockovich, Michael Clayton*, and *Jerry Maguire*; *resolution*, as shown in *Magnolia, Big Fish*, and *The Royal Tenenbaums*; and *redemption* (perhaps a person saving or redeeming their reputation), as shown in *Flash of Genius, The Verdict*, and *Cruel Intentions*.

You can see that all of these themes have to do with psychological and emotional states, or life processes such as "coming of age" and "finding one's identity." Many good writers are well versed in human psychology. They observe. They read. They interpret. They study the human animal in order to figure out what it does and why it does it. The more descriptive they can be, the more accurately they can portray us, the more likely we are to want to watch their characters on the screen.

Finding Commercial Appeal through Trends

Most successful films have a theme that connects with the audience. Many films, however, also connect with an audience because their release timing is serendipitous.

One of the most famous examples is *The China Syndrome*, which premiered March 16, 1979, just days before the Three Mile Island nuclear power plant disaster (March 29). This nuclear accident in

Pennsylvania, and the fears it created about the possibility of similar accidents across the country, helped the film succeed. A few years later, *WarGames* premiered at about the same time that we were inundated with news stories about kids who could tap into computers that were supposed to be secure. *The Insider* came along in 1999, when various stories of corrupt business practice appeared regularly in the newspaper, as they continue to do today. *State of Play* (the 2009 film) seems pulled right out of today's headlines about overly powerful, corrupt defense contractors working for the United States in the Middle East.

Some films successfully capitalize on news stories well after the actual events that inspired them, by playing into the public's lingering fears and prejudices: *World Trade Center* and *United 93* arrived five years after the twin towers attack, and *Munich* arrived thirty-three years after the tragic Olympic games it was based on. *Taken* played into a general fear of terrorism and distrust of foreigners that our "War on Terror" created in certain segments of the population.

Not all current-event and hot-button-issue films find success. *Not Without My Daughter*, which was set in Iran and released right after the start of the first Gulf War, died almost immediately at the box office. *A Mighty Heart*, set in Pakistan when we had ongoing military operations there, failed to connect with viewers in spite of its major star, Angelina Jolie.

Since films take several years to write, sell, make, and release, it seems miraculous that any movie can capture a social trend except by powerful foresight. To understand how this might happen, think about how some artists tend to be ahead of their times. They tap into the beginning stages of intellectual subcurrents and cultural trends and find expression for movements that might still be locked in the subconscious of the rest of the population. They have their collective ear to the ground, and sometimes notice things that are ready to happen—months, or years, before others.

In the early 1980s, certain pockets of America's population placed an emphasis on so-called traditional family values. This found mainstream expression through such television sitcoms as *Family Ties*. In the mid- and late eighties, many baby boomers were struggling with raising children, and this cultural trend was reflected in such television sitcoms as *The Cosby Show, Growing Pains, Roseanne,* and *Married ...with Children,* and in such feature films as *Baby Boom, Look Who's Talking, For Keeps, Three Men and a Baby, Raising Arizona,* and *She's Having a Baby.* In the 1990s, new themes emerged in popular entertainment: the difficulties encountered by twenty-somethings *(Reality Bites* and *Free Enterprise),* the issues that confront thirty-somethings *(thirtysomething,* and *Sex and the City),* the problems of forty-somethings *(Grand Canyon),* and the desire to heal old wounds individually *(Gran Torino)* and in the national consciousness *(Heaven & Earth).*

As we stepped into the twenty-first century, another crop of movie themes sprang up to capture our consciousness. Some movies capitalized well on the age-old dangers of greed *(Michael Clayton* and *There Will Be Blood).* Some dealt successfully with our ambiguous relationship with violence *(Capote, A History of Violence,* and 2004's *Crash).* And some worked with such hot-button issues as our dependence on oil *(Syriana),* gun violence *(Babel),* and political machinations *(Persepolis, The Sum of All Fears,* and *Charlie Wilson's War).* Ecology themes have played out in a number of films *(Erin Brockovich, Michael Clayton, The Day after Tomorrow,* and *WALL-E).* Of course, trendy subject matter/themes don't guarantee box-office success, but they do begin to create *potential* audience connections, because certain ideas are already in the wind.

Most successful films that depend in some way on trends and topicality make the most of these commercial connections by emphasizing a personal side of a story.

Making It Personal

Connecting with an audience in a personal way can be achieved by two modes of writing, descriptive and prescriptive. *Descriptive* tells the audience "how it is." *Prescriptive* gives the audience the writer's take on "how it should be." A film can capitalize on either or both of these modes.

Descriptive writing accurately and realistically depicts a character, and how that character will act and react within a particular situation. We've all seen films in which a character's reactions seem so extraordinarily "true." We identify with the "truth" of that character, and we wonder whether we would act, and react, in much the same way. Sometimes we hope we would, sometimes we hope we wouldn't. When watching *Juno*, we wonder what we would do in Juno's place. Similarly, we wonder how we'd solve the moral dilemma presented in *In the Bedroom*. We wonder what the Queen (in *The Queen*) should do. We want to solve the tragedy shown in *Hotel Rwanda*. We wonder how we'd fare if we were a character in *Blood Diamond* or *Dangerous Beauty*.

These movies give us insights into humanity. They deeply and accurately describe people and situations. And they achieve commercial success because they echo the audience's experiences.

Prescriptive films show us our ideals. Many of these are "hero" films. The hero rarely feels fear or uncertainty or lack of confidence, acting instead as we hope we would act. As a result, we live vicariously through him or her, all the while knowing the character is not real. We get lost in the character and in the film, wanting them to be reality.

The James Bond films, the *Die Hard* films, *Con Air, The Rock, 300*, and *Tropic Thunder* prescribe heroic behaviors we might wish we were capable of, if they were not physically and psychologically impossible.

Both descriptive and prescriptive writing have three important elements: the physical, the psychological, and the emotional. In working with specific characters, it's possible to deepen your descriptive dimensions by "physicalizing" your character, by asking yourself, "What would my character really look like in this situation?" If he's a fifteen-year-old boy in love for the first time, he might blush, he might be awkward, he might wear "geeky" glasses, he might try an "in" hairstyle that doesn't quite work. Psychologically he might lack confidence, or he might try to imitate the football hero because he's unsure of his own good qualities. Emotionally, he might get angry and irritable, or want to be left alone, or even laugh too much.

If you're writing a prescriptive film about the class leader or the football hero, he'd probably be strong, tall, and good-looking, the kind of guy who always looks terrific no matter what he wears. Psychologically he'd probably be very confident and without a care in the world. Emotionally he'd probably be as steady as a rock, impervious to pain and fear.

Many films connect with audiences on both the descriptive and prescriptive levels. You can do this by creating some descriptive and some prescriptive characters or a transformational arc for the main character that moves from the descriptive to the prescriptive, from uncertainty to the heroic. (This is another reason why "underdog triumphs" films are so popular.)

Most characters who have to achieve a goal also have to go through a personal process, which can be depicted by moving from the descriptive to the prescriptive mode. *Rocky, Working Girl, My Big Fat Greek Wedding*, the Harry Potter films, *The Princess Diaries, Pretty Woman*, and *The Devil Wears Prada* have characters who have to become more confident, more skilled, more clever, or perhaps more beautiful or handsome in order to succeed. Not only do these films have a universal and understandable theme, but they *connect* us to a character's personal transformation.

Exploring Social Issues

Many movie themes explore social issues. Those that tend to work best personalize the issues in some way. In *Juno*, the social issue of teenage pregnancy is shown affecting the individual, Juno, as she confronts becoming a teenage parent. The social issue of gay rights shows both its political and personal sides in *Milk* and *Philadelphia*, as well as the television movie *An Early Frost*. *Munich* and *A History of Violence* explore the social issues of violence—how society and the individual handle it, its effect on the individual, and the moral dilemma it raises about confronting evil. *Erin Brockovich* confronts the problem of pollution—its economic and personal costs and the justifications put forth for its continuation. *Silkwood*, which has a similar theme, confronts nuclear irresponsibility. *Norma Rae* deals with the issue of workers' rights.

Many writers find it difficult to fully explore particular social issues since they usually have strong viewpoints about them. They're for an issue or against it. But to give an issue drama in a film, it needs to be understood, analyzed, and considered in its many dimensions. This usually means giving some screen time to a point of view that the writer may not hold.

This doesn't mean that the writer's point of view can't be expressed. A writer who stands in the middle, without any point of view, doesn't offer much to the discussion of an issue. Writers who are far to one side of an issue risk alienating many in their potential audience. Exploring many facets of an issue allows the audience to arrive at its conclusions (along with you, the writer). This is more engaging for the audience than being preached to.

The more controversial your subject matter, the more difficult it can be to sell your story. It's a producer's job to take note of subject matter that can cause division within a film's core audience. *Vera Drake* would probably never become a Hollywood film, since its stance on abortion is clear, and the controversy over this red flag issue engenders great anger on both sides. One movie is not going to solve such a problem, so many producers will just avoid the subject.

Juno, however, was a successful Hollywood film partly because it did not tackle the issue of abortion, but rather that of teenage pregnancy from the personal side. It delicately looked at the issue from the viewpoint of the girl and her boyfriend and the viewpoint of a woman who wanted a baby but was unable to have one. It avoided the part of the issue that was so controversial, and instead connected us with the characters' personal concerns—keeping our focus on the human dilemma, not the social issue. Pro-lifers could say, "She kept the baby," and feel the film affirmed their side of the issue. Pro-choice advocates could say, "She made an informed choice, and that's the point." Both could connect with the personal exploration of the social issue.

Most of Hollywood's social-issue films deal with issues on which there is some sort of common agreement. We can root for Erin Brockovich because we all wish that polluters would stop polluting and making people ill. The issue engages our basic sense of justice, and we root for the underdog who confronts evil with integrity.

A film is not meant to be a sermon or essay or lecture, and its nuances are not so much the nuances of an idea, but the nuances of human frailty, human cost, and human possibilities. We see how social problems affect the individual. It is not an abstraction of the problem, but an insight into how the problem affects the human subject of a drama. Generally, the more pointed the approach to stories about ideas, the less human those stories' characters become. We enjoy a story because of its humanity, not because of its particular take on a pressing social problem. The proper study of drama is humankind, so social issues never exist by themselves in some abstract philosophical universe, in a vacuum, but are always put in human terms. Ideas might tantalize our heads, but characters move our hearts.

CONNECTING THROUGH THE STAKES

It's not unusual to hear a producer or executive ask a writer, "But what's at stake?" If the protagonist's jeopardy is unclear, if there's no reason to care about the character, then the audience will be unable to see connections between their experiences and those of the character.

Survival stakes are the most basic. They can be thought of as what we need to do to survive in our world. We need to be safe, to have enough to eat and drink, and to have a roof over our heads. Many films put these basic needs in jeopardy in order to stir the audience's most primal level of identification and concern with their characters.

Some films, particularly action-adventure and detective films, are all about survival stakes. The protagonist has to go to considerable lengths to overcome the threat of imminent death. James Bond is constantly in life-and-death situations. *Castaway* makes us care about survival and reconnecting with the rest of the world. Many B movies gain huge audiences because they play for life-and-death stakes, and make them seem very personal. Cameron Poe in *Con Air* is constantly in danger from the plane crashing, explosions, and gunfire, and everyone else seems to be in imminent danger as well. Many hijacking and women-in-jeopardy films are successful because we identify with their basic life-and-death situations.

A great deal of drama speaks to an individual's will to survive, because it is the one basic drive that we all understand intimately. Films that address this drive tend to work well because they are essentially dramatic. The conflict is always clear—and there's plenty of motivation.

Most of us identify with the need to love and be loved. We yearn for love, and we look for the person who will fulfill us, our soul mate. Romantic comedies, of course, deal with this need, but most films of any genre have a love story subplot that dimensionalizes characters who may otherwise be solely action driven. A love subplot gives them a personal side, rather than defining them solely in terms of the storyline's needs. *Lars and the Real Girl*, *Vicky Cristina Barcelona*, *High Fidelity*, *Must Love Dogs*, *Meet the Parents*, and *Sweet Home Alabama* address this basic need in different ways.

The longing for love can uncover other aspects of a character. These might include the desire for family (*Juno*, *Shane*, *On Golden Pond*, and *Gladiator*) or the desire to be part of a larger community of like-minded people (*Lars and the Real Girl*, *Babette's Feast*, *Milk*, and *E.T.*). There's a reason why so many sitcoms deal with family: We all can identify with the desire for love, warmth, and acceptance. And there's a reason why so many television drama series have subplots about the love life and family life of their characters: Love, in all its guises, is one of our most basic drives.

A variation of the love need is the strong friendship. A love subplot was edited out of *Michael Clayton* in order to put a spotlight on the friendship between Michael and Arthur. Love in this film is about loyalty to one's good friend.

Sometimes our integrity and our sense of wanting to be admired and respected for our skills and contributions become the focus of the story. Many films deal with the yearning to make something of ourselves. *A Beautiful Mind* looks at how a brilliant thinker overcomes tremendous obstacles to realize his talents. *Milk* explores one man's desire for equal rights and to follow his political desires.

This can include the desire to do something great or to be part of something artistic and creative that makes life more beautiful. We want to express ourselves, to communicate who we are, and to actualize our talents, skills, and abilities. Writers certainly understand this, and many films about struggling writers, composers, and athletes have been successful because we root for these people to succeed.

This desire is not just about being rewarded and achieving recognition. It relates to our desire to express ourselves, whether or not one is recognized or rewarded. It's one thing to paint in hopes of becoming famous or winning an award; it's quite another thing to paint because we *have* to. These needs can pertain to people in all fields, not just artists or athletes. A comedian *has* to be funny. A doctor *has* to heal. An aviator *has* to fly. These people come alive when they are doing what they *have* to do. And that drive, when we see it in a film, is always worth rooting for. The movies *Pollock*, *The Agony and the Ecstasy*, *Sideways*, *Adaptation*, *Million Dollar Baby*, *The Pianist*, *American Beauty*, *Walk the Line*, and *Synecdoche, New York* speak to this need.

This particular need is often difficult to convey since it's often the most abstract. However, it is a recognizable need, and most of us can cheer on a character who confronts all the internal and external resistance to greatness.

Raising the Stakes

A writer raises the stakes in a film by including more than one stake in it. Most movies will have personal stakes as well as relationship stakes, survival stakes, and maybe even stakes related to success and achievement.

Even in a film considered a good B movie, such as *Con Air*, there are not only survival stakes but also wagers on the protagonist's future life, his relationship with his wife, and whether he can get the bunny to his daughter for her birthday—a major personal stake.

In *Slumdog Millionaire*, relationship stakes exist between Jamal and his girlfriend, Latika, and Jamal and his brother Salim. There also are social-issue stakes because Jamal is, in a sense, the representative of all those living in poverty. If he wins the money, there's an opportunity to anticipate a future as something more than a slumdog.

In *Changeling*, the story begins with personal stakes. The film then expands to show us that the personal conflict involves other families and, eventually, society as a whole. In this film, however, once this social issue is resolved, the personal issue still remains—even after the end credits roll.

The more stakes you gamble with in your story, the more opportunity you have for hooking an audience and giving them something universal to connect with in your film.

You can also raise the stakes throughout your story by keeping the protagonist's goal out of reach, making it seem throughout the story as if that character will never achieve it. If the audience identifies with the importance of that goal and are concerned that the protagonist may not achieve it, they will vicariously journey with that character, creating a strong emotional connection with him or her along the way. This means that you must create strong second acts in which you explore the goal's obstacles and the protagonist's determination.

The more we experience a character's deeply personal desire to achieve a goal, the more we can connect with that person. This means raising the protagonist's personal stakes by playing the emotions that are connected with any journey toward achieving one's needs: anger, fear, joy, uncertainty, despair, and hope. The more emotional range you give a character in his or her search, the more understandable and sympathetic that character will be to the audience. Many films show *only* the action necessary to achieve the protagonist's goal. As a result, the audience feels distanced from the character and the character's jeopardy. By playing emotions as well as actions, you make the stakes larger and more personal, and the audience is better able to identify with them.

COMMUNICATING THE THEME

Once you know what you want to say, you need to know how to say it. Writers can communicate themes through the story events that they choose to show, through the choices their characters make, through dialogue, and through images.

Events have meaning, and they communicate what you, the writer, believe about why things happen in life. Deciding that a character gets robbed and mugged because he happens to be in the wrong place at the wrong time might communicate your idea that life is haphazard and nonsensical. Choosing characters who respond compassionately to each other can communicate that you believe that the world is a loving and caring place. Showing characters whose lives continually meet and intersect may communicate your idea about fate and destiny and our intrinsic interconnectedness with each other. As a writer, you are always making choices about the direction of your story. Every choice you make has meaning and the potential to communicate your ideas about life.

Your theme can be communicated through decisions that your characters make. The fact that a character chooses to fight the bad guy can show courage or a sense of justice. Characters who refuse to run away when the going gets tough embody the theme of integrity. Characters who decide to change their lives embody themes of transformation and growth. Themes of corruption, greed, cowardice, and disillusionment can easily be expressed dramatically through the actions of characters.

One of the most important methods for communicating theme focuses on the images chosen by the writer, and later by the director. Since film is a visual medium, the images that you create can give many levels of meaning to your story. You might use images of light and dark to show good and evil, or small versus large spaces to show oppression versus freedom. You might create a lot of color, to show it's a colorful, happy world that your characters inhabit. You might show lots of snow and cold to express how cold-hearted people can be (*Fargo*) or images of heat to express their passion (*Body Heat*). Or you might show love and happiness through the sunny sea-blues of *Mamma Mia!*

Although the director's job is to create a visualization of a script's images, it's the writer's job to create a cinematic script that can be translated into powerful visuals.

A theme is least interesting when it's communicated through talky dialogue, when it's said rather than expressed through more dramatic means. But in most movies there will be at least a few spoken lines that express the theme. It's important that this dialogue show up as only a line or two here and there, and not as a long lecture.

Shrek offers a good example of the different ways that a theme can be communicated. Its main theme is, "Don't judge by appearances." (*Beauty and the Beast* shares this theme, although each story works it out in a different way.)

Shrek's theme is communicated first through its characters. Shrek is not a good-looking ogre. He's big and doughy and his teeth are in need of a good orthodontist. He has funny ears, he's a strange color, and he has a few edges that need to be ironed out with the help of a good woman. He lives in a swamp, and just wants to be left alone. But he's courageous and strong and generally kind. He is a good contrast to the self-involved, manipulative, egocentric prince. Shrek, the character, *shows* the film's theme by proving that even the strangest looking ogre has a beauty within, but he also has some lines of dialogue here and there that talk about the theme:

SHREK

There's a lot more to ogres than people think.
Onions have layers. Ogres have layers.

Later, Shrek says, "Sometimes things are more than they appear."

Shrek complains that "they [the world] judge me before they even know me."

Not only is Shrek outside the beautiful mode, Fiona is also. Although during the day she's just lovely, at night it's another story. She turns into an ogre herself—big, fleshy, and overweight—the perfect match for Shrek. And clearly she and Shrek make a better pair as we root for her not to marry the prince.

The theme runs throughout the story. It is Shrek, not the prince, who does all the courageous acts of derring-do. He battles the dragon, rescues the princess, and eventually fights for his true love.

The movie's theme is also expressed visually. There is contrast between the visual context of Shrek's world and the prince's world. At the end, when magic happens at sunset, we expect Fiona to turn into her beautiful self because of love's first kiss, but she instead becomes her true self—an ogre who is perfectly matched to Shrek. The sparkly fireworks that surround her at this moment provide an unexpected image, but one that underlines the theme: When you love and accept yourself, there will be light, and possibly fireworks.

Some movies communicate a theme by having a character say the opposite of what the writer really wants to say. Sometimes this may take the form of a song that expresses a character's view of life. In *The Lion King*, Simba and Timon and Pumbaa sing the song "Hakuna Matata," which has the lyric "…no worries for the rest of your days," showing that they don't want any responsibility; they just want to be happy. The movie's theme, however, is responsibility and not running away from your past, and as the story evolves, we see more actions and dialogue about responsibility as Simba learns the lesson.

In *High School Musical*, the students sing a song called "Stick to the Status Quo," which has the lyric "Keep things as they are, stick to the stuff you know." But the film is really saying the opposite. A song called "Breaking Free," which expresses the theme more directly, is sung later.

THE PROBLEMS OF MAKING IT COMMERCIAL

"Commercial" is, of course, easier to understand after a film is a hit than before it's released. Many executives and producers feel that commerciality is subjective. Sometimes all they can say is, "I know it when I see it." Yet, obviously they don't, or there wouldn't be big box-office flops.

I do not mean to suggest that what makes something commercial is just a matter of research, analysis, and psyching out the audience.

Studio research departments have shown that this is not the case, since often their research "proved" that no one would go see *Star Wars* and that *E.T.* had little appeal.

Since no one is sure what makes something commercial, there often is an unfortunate unwillingness to think about a script's commercial elements at all. Sometimes this leads executives to turn over the responsibility for commercializing a script to the director, writer, and actors, hoping that somehow they'll know enough about what they're doing to pull off a commercial success. Sometimes this leads writers to say, "I just want to express myself," thereby giving no consideration to whether they're communicating with audiences. Sometimes it leads writers to bypass their own feelings and intuitions, which can offer clues about how audiences will respond. After all, the writer is the first audience, so the writer needs to be hooked on the project before attempting to engage anyone else.

Ultimately, "commercial" has much to do with one's own sense of connection to a project. If you feel passionately about a story, if there's some profound connection that you personally make with its subject matter and characters and journey, then you have made a start at finding what's "commercial" about it.

In the final analysis, the executives who say, "It's all subjective," are partially correct. It begins with our personal connections to the story and with communicating the feelings and excitement that make us want to share that special story. It then moves to recognizing those audience connections that combine the personal and the universal.

APPLICATION

Questions to Ask Yourself about Your Script

Finding your script's connections with an audience is often difficult. Such commercial aspects are not always clear. Often the theme is unclear or underdeveloped. Sometimes there are several themes that conflict with each other, and the job of rewriting becomes deciding what you really want to say. Think about all the big and universal ideas that seem to relate to your story. Then, as you become clearer about your theme, ask yourself:

> Can I state my theme in one line? Does my story serve my theme, and does my theme serve my story?
>
> Is my theme expressed through character and action, rather than just through dialogue? Do my images help clarify my theme? Have I stayed away from having a character "deliver a message" to the audience?
>
> Have I been willing to give up a small theme if it conflicts with the main theme of my story?
>
> Have I thought through my personal connections to the theme? Have I considered ways that the audience might respond, given their anticipated demographics?

EXERCISES AND THINGS TO THINK ABOUT

(1) Watch a film that you consider to be thematically rich. Watch a film that's been a huge box-office hit. In what ways are their themes universal? List all the ways that their themes are communicated.

(2) Think of films you've seen that have the same universal theme(s): the underdog triumphs, integrity, the value of community, finding identity, overcoming peer pressure, and/or the triumph of the human spirit. How is each film that explores the same theme similar? How is each one different? In these films, what methods were used to connect with the audience?

(3) Watch *The Dead Girl* and *Roshomon* to see how their themes are similar, but with different nuances depending on who is telling the story.

Once you find connections between your audience and your material and your story and your theme, there is another area to explore: the relationship between your visuals and your dialogue.

CHAPTER NINE
Balancing Images and Dialogue

Many writers are drawn to writing because they like words. They like the ring and the rhythms of words and phrases. They enjoy finding the right word to lend nuance and style and insight to their work. They like writing because they like the way that words tell a story, convey ideas, reveal character.

But when writers turn to the specific craft of screenwriting, they soon discover that they have to learn a whole new way of telling stories—telling them through short spurts of dialogue and images. They can't describe to their audience what a character is feeling or thinking. This inner world needs to be cinematically dramatized, shown by actors and by actions and images. In filmmaking, the eye is paramount: If an actor says something that contradicts what we see, we'll believe what we see on the screen, not what is said.

A script is a blueprint for a story that will be conveyed through action and visual details, including colors and costumes and sets. It is by no means a finished product. The writer has a vital part to play, but so does everyone else involved with making a film. It all starts with the writer, but it never ends there. The writer serves the art of film, not just the art of wordplay.

When producers look at a page from a script, they don't want to see too much dialogue or too much description. They like to see "a lot of white" on the page, meaning no big, dense paragraphs, but little clusters of dialogue and small splotches of description. Producers look for a few lines of dialogue, followed by a few lines of description, followed by a few lines of dialogue, followed by a few lines of description. Generally, dialogue is one to three sentences long. Description is usually a short paragraph, or maybe two. Writers can be greatly helped in finding the best dialogue/description balance by reading great scripts to see how great writers balance these two.

If a script contains many paragraphs describing what the audience will see, producers know it's overwritten. The director, art director, set designer, and costume designer need the writer's good hints about what the movie will look like, but it's their job to *create* a film's visual aspects.

If producers see long speeches that go on for pages and pages, they know the writer doesn't trust the actors and the director, and doesn't know it's the writer's job to get across emotions and attitudes and even backstory information without having the characters talk too much about it.

WHAT DOES IT LOOK LIKE?

Since its birth, the art of motion pictures has relied on images, not on dialogue. Silent films communicated their stories well with the aid of occasional lines of dialogue written across the screen. As the train bore down on the heroine in *The Perils of Pauline*, perhaps she cried out, "Help!," but chances are good that we would've gotten the picture if she had said nothing. As Charlie Chaplin gave a flower to the beautiful blind girl, he didn't have to say anything. Clearly, he was in love, and she was most thankful for his kindness. To make a film cinematic, and attractive to directors and audiences, writers must learn to use images and actions to get across their stories. This may mean a drastic rethinking of what writers are writing about.

Writers learn to write for movies by getting out of their apartments or homes or lofts or mansions and noticing the world around them. What is dramatically interesting about their surroundings? What kind of a movie would fit in this kind of context? What details make a setting cinematic? Is it the rush-rush of people as they scatter to their jobs in New York or San Francisco or Houston? Is it how they get to their jobs—by ferries, subways, congested freeways, country roads—that is cinematically visual?

Screenwriters should tune in to *the look of a place*. This isn't a matter of what they *think* it will look like if they haven't been there, it's a matter of what it really looks like because they've *seen* the place and memorized the small, specific details that differentiate it from everywhere else. Accuracy is an important part of visualizing environments. Writers must not presume that every place is similar, and they can't just make up a real place's visual details.

I have worked on many scripts where the airport in Madrid is described exactly like the airport in Los Angeles, and the cars people drive in Moscow are described the same as the ones people drive in New York. This is simply wrong. Every city—with its buildings and people and culture—is unique. Madrid isn't Los Angeles; Moscow isn't New York. Each town, city, geographic region, country, and continent is unlike any other, and each has important visual details that differentiate it from all others.

Visuals are not arbitrary but carefully planned out. Many writers keep notebooks and file folders of visuals they notice in their day-to-day activities and travels, ready for when an appropriate script idea presents itself. In this way, they soon become good observers of a place's telling details.

Once a writer understands a character's world, that character can be introduced doing something in that location, interacting with that environment. A character might be writing a letter at an Early American desk or chopping up a salad in an all-chrome kitchen or hanging a theater poster. If a writer simply describes a detail without letting that detail interact with a character, a great opportunity to give depth and dimension to that character, and to a locale, has been missed.

Adding your Imagination

Once a writer knows an environment's visual details, it still takes *imagination* to make those visuals fit within a particular story. It's through their imaginations that writers decide what they'll add to an environment, without contradicting its uniquely important visual details. Add more shadows and darkness? Perhaps set the scene at night? Perhaps set it in the back of a church or factory or tenement building? Perhaps a writer wants to show something uplifting in spite of an environment's poverty, so he or she adds a small candle glimmering with hope on a table or a brother who plays a joyful tune on his worn-out guitar. There might be a fancy apartment, but how does the character decorate it? With Toulouse-Lautrec posters or antique Chinese furniture or chrome and glass and white everywhere? White sofas? White dinnerware? White statuettes on the glass corner tables?

The screenwriter doesn't need to plan visuals down to their every detail (unless those details are essential to a basic sense of a place's style, or essential to the story), but a script that offers some hints about how its visuals determine character can make a director and art director take notice and get excited about the story's visual potential, and about the visual world they'll create on the screen.

Creating Cinematic Metaphors

Although the language of images may seem foreign to many of us, we intrinsically understand it better than we might think. Images can have a thematic meaning that goes well beyond a simple description of something that has color and visual interest.

If someone asked you to do a film about conformity, you could probably think of many images that express the idea without having to talk about it. You might think of uniforms—at school, in the military, or as accepted forms of dress among peers. You might think of people walking in step—soldiers marching together or a marching band or simply three friends crossing the street together in step. Perhaps everyone orders hamburgers at the restaurant because that's just what people do. Maybe the father orders for the whole family or group, without consulting anyone. Maybe all the characters' homes are little ticky-tacky houses on the hillside. Perhaps everyone drives the same kind of car, and wears the same type of clothes.

To get more creative with this image, a writer might find amusing images that illustrate the idea that everyone is far too much the same. One of my favorite images of this sort comes from the 2004 remake of *The Stepford Wives*. After Joanna Eberhart has been supposedly transitioned to a Stepford wife, she comes around a corner in the grocery store and passes a display of many-colored egg cartons perfectly stacked up—the yellow cartons in one stack, the turquoise blue in another, the pink in another. Each in its proper place. Eggs, a symbol of new life and new possibilities, have been changed into eggs as an image of everyone who is now neatly stacked up, wound up, and perfectly aligned.

If you need to find images of new life and new love, your mind might first think of dawn—with the sun rising, the flowers blooming, the birds singing. We all know what that means. We've seen it a thousand times. It's a cliché. As a *creative* writer, you want to go past clichés to images that are understandable but fresh. You might think of the image in *The English Patient* when Kip has lit small candles leading from the villa where Hana stays to the place where he stays. She sees them and follows them—into his arms. It is a magical and original image that sets the stage for the beginning of their love affair. Or you might think of the images of chocolate in *Chocolat*—particularly how the mayor's transformation is proven when he lies in the window, surrounded by chocolate, his former rigidity lost.

These visuals support the theme and underscore what the film is about and what challenges the character is confronting at any given time in the story. The creative writer tries to render ideas into images that will not only tell the story, but communicate the film's overall theme.

CHOOSING AND USING DIALOGUE

There is always important story information that cannot be conveyed just by looking at visuals. Characters talk, and they need to reveal themselves and move a story forward through what they say.

Dialogue has a number of functions. It gives basic information that the audience needs to know in order to understand a story and its characters. One of dialogue's most basic functions is to communicate who people are, and to introduce them so that the audience knows who's the protagonist, who's the antagonist, and who are the major and supporting characters.

It is certainly clear, but boring, to have characters introduced in a formal way: "Bob, this is Mary. Mary, this is Bob." So characters will often just call one another by name: "Bob, over here!" "Hi, Mary, can you join us?" Characters might wear name tags (if a story takes place at a conference or convention) or have signs on their office doors (although their names still need to be mentioned), or receive a letter with their name clearly shown on it. A good writer becomes adept at all the different ways to let us know who the characters are so their names are quickly set in our minds.

In *Little Miss Sunshine,* all the characters in the family have to be introduced fairly quickly. They are introduced in a variety of ways:

```
                    SHERYL

          Hey, Frank.


                    FRANK

          Sheryl.

          ...


                    SHERYL
                  (to Frank)

          We have you with Dwayne.
          Dwayne, Hi, Uncle Frank's here.
```

...

                    SHERYL

Olive? Dinner time!

...

                    RICHARD

              (on telephone)

Richard Harvey for Stan Grossman.

...

                    GRANDPA

              (walks in)

What is this?! Chicken…Every day it's the
chicken!..

                    RICHARD

Dad.. Dad…Dad…Dad!

In *The Royal Tenenbaums*, after we're given a quick backstory
of the family's previous glory, we're introduced to the present-day
Tenenbaums through a montage of each individual in a different
vulnerable process—shaving, trying on new hats, at a hair salon,
etc. During this, each character and actor is labeled like a name tag:
"Gwyneth Paltrow as Margot Tenenbaum," "Bill Murray as Raleigh
St. Clair," "Luke Wilson as Richie Tenenbaum."

Sometimes the introductions are reinforced by visuals. In *The
Illusionist* we hear the name of Eisenheim, which is reinforced by a
large poster hanging outside the theater.

Dialogue Clarifies a Character's Function

We need to know what characters do, and how they figure into a story.
When doing this, writers need to be careful that they don't create what

I call "date dialogue," such as, "Hi, my name is Judy, I live in the Bronx but work as a receptionist in the children's wing at Columbia University Medical Center. What's your name?"

We need to know who the characters are—their occupations, what they're doing, why they're doing it, and how and why they do what they do in your story. Sometimes a character's function in a cop show is understood simply because the character wears or flashes a badge. Nothing needs to be said. Sometimes seeing that a character is clearly in authority at a crime scene tells us everything we need to know.

It's relatively easy to introduce teachers (they're at the front of a classroom) or students (they're sitting at desks or opening lockers) or clerks (they're behind a counter) or models (they're walking down a runway). But some characters have unusual professions that have to be understood in order to understand the story. Robert Langdon, a character in both *The Da Vinci Code* and *Angels & Demons*, is a symbologist.

His occupation is evidenced by his talk with Swiss Guard Commander Richter about *La Purga*—revenge—and how the symbol of the cross was used.

RICHTER

La Purga?

ROBERT LANGDON

Oh geez, you guys don't even read your own
history do you? 1668, the church kidnapped
four Illuminati scientists and branded each one
of them on the chest with the symbol of the
cross. To "purge" them of their sins and they
executed them, threw their bodies in the street
as a warning to others to stop questioning
church ruling on scientific matters. They
radicalized them. The Purga created a darker,
more violent Illuminati, one bent on ... on
retribution.

In *Michael Clayton*, Clayton describes his specialty as a lawyer:

> MICHAEL CLAYTON
>
> ```
> There's no play here. There's no angle. There's
> no champagne room. I'm not a miracle worker,
> I'm a janitor. The math on this is simple. The
> smaller the mess the easier it is for me to
> clean up.
> ```

In *Pineapple Express*, the focus on Dale moves from his clothes color to his job description, giving important information about his job.

> SAUL
>
> ```
> What's up with the suit?
> ```
>
> DALE DENTON
>
> ```
> Oh, I'm a process server, so I have to wear a
> suit.
> ```
>
> SAUL
>
> ```
> Wow, you're a servant? Like a butler? A
> chauffeur?
> ```
>
> DALE DENTON
>
> ```
> No, no. What? No, I'm not like ...
> ```
>
> SAUL
>
> ```
> Shine shoes?
> ```
>
> DALE DENTON
>
> ```
> I'm a process server! I like…
> ```
>
> SAUL
>
> ```
> Oh, process.
> ```

> DALE DENTON
>
> I work for a company that's like hired by
> lawyers to like hand out legal documents and
> subpoenas to people who don't want them so I
> gotta wear, like, disguises sometimes, just to
> make them admit that they are themselves so I
> can serve them the … the papers.

Sometimes a character's introduction belies what we see. Whichever bit of information comes first is usually what we will believe. In *The Sting*, Henry Gondorff is talked about before we meet him:

> COLEMAN
>
> I got a guy named Henry Gondorff I want you to
> look up. There ain't a better insideman alive.
> He'll teach ya everything ya gotta know.

We then meet him as Hooker meets him—living in the back of a carousel:

INT. CAROUSEL - DAY

Hooker walks past the now motionless carousel to the
room in the back and knocks on the door. No answer.
He gives the door a little push and it swings open.

INT. GONDORFF'S ROOM - DAY

The room is small and cluttered, containing a bed,
a sink, and a bathroom; all covered by a layer of
books, dirty clothes and beer bottles. Lying on the
floor, wedged between the bed and the wall, fully
dressed, but completely passed out, is the one and
only Henry Gondorff.

> HOOKER
>
> (to himself)

The great Henry Gondorff.

We might be surprised at his drunken and disheveled appearance, but the audience now is not sure whether to believe Coleman or to believe what it sees. But we're quite willing to see how these contradictions will unfold.

Creating Important Story Information

There is also basic information we need to know about the story. This might be background about a murder case that the detective is trying to solve—where it took place, who they think did it, what the modus operandi of the perpetrator is, and what else is known at this point. It might be information about a disease, so we understand how dangerous it is and how few alternatives there are for a cure. Or information about the competition that the underdog really wants to win. Or information about whose family is important, and why they don't want their son marrying the girl from the other side of the tracks.

In *Se7en*, the detectives have to figure out that the murders they're investigating are related to the seven deadly sins. As Detective Somerset and artist William McCracken look at pictures in a book, the clues begin to add up.

```
                    SOMERSET (O.S.)
     The seven deadly sins.


                    WILLIAM (O.S.)
     That's what these murders remind me of. Paintings like
     these.


                         (points)

     Gluttony ... greed ...


                    SOMERSET (O.S.)
     Envy, wrath, pride, lust and sloth. Seven deadly sins.


                    WILLIAM
     Amen, brother.
```

Dialogue Reveals a Character's Sound

Individuals have very specific voices. Often the rhythm and even the pitch of their speech is distinctive. Sometimes it's the words they use. Sometimes it's their dialect. Sometimes it's their grammar, or the way they never complete sentences or only talk in short sentences with an occasional grunt (such as Yoda in the *Star Wars* films). People simply sound different. In many scripts, however, all characters sound the same, regardless of their occupation, socioeconomic class, education, or place of origin. They talk in complete sentences, with a subject followed by the predicate with a verb in between. "I'm going to the store now." "We need to catch the criminal." "She's a very beautiful girl!"

Great dialogue gives us the flavor of a character and of his or her place of origin and profession. In Colorado, where I now live, people often say, "See what I'm saying?" and, "You're good to go." In Hollywood, people "do" lunch and "take" a meeting.

In fairytales, we might notice a sort of fairytale-speak. In *Shrek,* Fiona says to Shrek:

FIONA

This be-eth our first meeting - you should
sweep me off my feet out yonder window and
down a rope onto your valiant steed.

Later, Fiona says, "I pray that you take this favor as a token of my gratitude."

In *Enchanted,* another fairytale, we find a focus on the optimistic (fairytale) attitude that everything is supposed to be nice and end happily:

PRINCE EDWARD

Fear not, fair maiden. I am here.

PRINCESS GISELLE

I've been wandering very far and long tonight
and I'm afraid no one's been very nice to me…
I'm certain that Edward is already searching
for me… he'll take me home and the two of us
will share in true love's kiss.

Characters show their cultural background through the lilt or pounding of their dialogue. In *The Curious Case of Benjamin Button*, there are a variety of different character voices:

Ngunda Oti says: "You'll see, little man, plenty of times you be alone. You different like us, it's gonna be that way."

Benjamin Button says: "Momma? Momma? Some days, I feel different than the day before."

And Queenie replies in a different type of voice: "Everyone feels different about themselves one way or another, but we all goin' the same way."

Some movie dialogue establishes a location's flavor. Both *New in Town* and *Fargo* use a type of Minnesota dialect that has a Scandinavian lilt to it.

In *Fargo*, Officer Gary Olson says, "Hiya, Norm. How ya doin', Margie? How's the fricassee?"

Marge replies, "Pretty darn good, ya want some?"

Jean Lundegaard says to her husband, Jerry, "Hiya, hon! Welcome back! How was Fargo?" Jerry replies, "Yah, real good now."

Mr. Mohra explains about the guy he met that was going crazy out at the lake: "And then he calls me a jerk, and says the last guy who thought he was a jerk was dead now. So I don't say nothin' and he says, 'What do ya think about that?' So I says, 'Well, that don't sound like too good a deal for him, then.'"

Writers learn to listen for these small turns of phrase and speech patterns and word choices. They often keep journals in which they jot down these sounds whenever they hear them. Language is rhythm, and if a writer can capture a character's speech rhythms, not only will that deepen and better define that character, but it will also create dialogue that is easy for the right actor for the role to say.

Adding the Senses to the Dialogue

Dialogue is music that can awaken the senses. Adding visual metaphors to dialogue enriches a script's language, and encourages the audience to bring more thought and emotion to their understanding of a character.

Many people naturally speak in metaphors. They might use color in their language, saying they feel "blue" or they're "in the pink." Someone might say, "Don't fence me in," but we understand that nobody is literally putting a fence around that person. She's simply asking for more room to work or play, more latitude for her dealings, and less interference from others.

When someone says he went through a "baptism by fire," he's saying that he passed through a period of struggle and torment. When someone refers to a problem as "my cross to bear," that person means that the problem is a heavy mental or spiritual burden.

Any of the senses can be incorporated into the dialogue. A spy might say, "I smell a rat," as he recognizes that someone might be betraying him. Perhaps a character says she feels a "touch of mink," meaning that she feels elegant. A character might say, "Cue the violins," if somebody's behavior is too maudlin or sentimental. Even taste might figure into dialogue, as a character says "the whole deal leaves a bad taste in my mouth."

Using Similes

A writer can enrich dialogue by using similes. Forrest Gump tells us,

"Life is like a box of chocolates."

Thugs say, "You're acting like a chump."

Boxing announcers say, "He went down like a ton of bricks."

The poet Robert Burns said, "My love is a like a red, red rose."

Agent Smith in *The Matrix Revolutions* says, "I remember chasing you is like chasing a ghost."

Creating Subtext

Characters are defined as much by what they don't say as by what they do say. They keep secrets from others and from themselves. And they often hide their true meanings beneath their words.

Subtext is a thought or idea that is not directly or overtly expressed. In a screenplay, it might be a character's thought that belies what the character says or does.

In real life, subtext can be confusing and frustrating. We want people to mean what they say. We want a straight answer. But others sometimes don't know the truth, or don't want to tell us the truth. We often know that someone is holding a grudge against us, even though that person won't admit it. When we ask what's wrong, we get the reply, "Nothin'," or, "There's no problem," or, "I'm fine," but we know what's meant: "I really have issues with you," or, "You are really a jerk," or, "I'm so angry at you I could scream." Sometimes a character says, "I don't care…" when that may not be true at all. Overly daring people might say, "It was easy," after they almost get killed doing a difficult job.

Sometimes subtext is about misinterpretation. A gal might say to a guy, "Do you like that china?" And he might respond, "Sure, it's fine." She thinks he means, "We have so much in common. We should get married," but what he really means is "We're never going to buy china together so I don't care either way."

Coming up with subtext is one of the most difficult skills in dialogue writing. But it is through subtext that a character becomes richer and deeper. Through subtext in a character's dialogue we begin to feel the emotions beneath the words, what image a character is trying to sustain, and what truth keeps peeking out.

In *Unforgiven,* The Kid puts on a brave front as a killer throughout most of the film. But when he finally kills someone, he begins to fall apart. He first tells Will Munny:

```
                    THE KID

   I was even scared a little…
```

But it's clear to the audience, and the other characters, that he was scared a lot.

He tries to keep up his bluster for a while, but then breaks down:

```
                    THE KID

   It don't seem real… how he ain't gonna never
   breathe again, ever…
```

The Kid is shaking, becoming hysterical. And the truth about him comes out from underneath the words.

When writing subtext, you must understand what is going on emotionally and intellectually behind the cloak of a character's words, and then suggest it with images or actions. Imply that not is all as it might seem on the surface.

Sometimes this might require you to add a word or phrase that cues the actor about how a line should be delivered. For example

> THE CHARACTER
>
> (seething)
>
> Yes, everything is just fine!

Sometimes the writer might clarify a character's subtext through a sentence of description. In *Schindler's List*, during his lunch hour, Stern tells Schindler there's a machinist who would like to thank him for his job.

The description gives clues about the subtext: "Schindler gives his accountant a long-suffering look."

Stern asks Mr. Löwenstein to come in, which he does, thanking Schindler over and over again. On the surface, Schindler seems perfectly polite, but underneath his politeness he's embarrassed by his effusiveness and uncomfortable with this encounter.

> SCHINDLER
>
> You're welcome. I'm sure you're doing a great job.

Schindler shakes the man's hand perfunctorily and tells Stern with a look, "Okay, that's enough, get him out of here."

The man continues to thank Schindler and tell him he's a good man. Schindler continues to be polite but keeps giving Stern a look that says, "Get this guy out of here." The subtext is written into the description, and the actor's job is to communicate it.

WHAT GOES WRONG WITH IMAGES AND DIALOGUE?

Working with images and dialogue is usually a learned skill. Just as musicians develop an ear for pitch and harmony, so do writers develop an ear for dialogue and an eye for uniquely appropriate images.

Inexperienced writers who haven't done their homework often believe that everything looks the same and sounds the same. So they fail to add images and dialogue that give us insight into their characters and locations.

Most good writers read their dialogue out loud; they want to make sure that all their characters don't sound the same, and they want to make sure that the words aren't easily garbled or confusing or simply impossible to say.

An audience doesn't know the difference between "hole" and "whole" or "aloud" and "allowed" except by context. A writer needs to look out for homophones (words that sound the same but aren't).

Writers also need to watch out for sentences and words that have obscure meanings. Technical words need to be phrased in such a way that they're understandable, or backed up with some visuals for us to understand them. Many times writers have done good research, but they haven't translated the words into everyday language. We've heard "over and out" and "10-4" enough in movies that we understand their meanings.

In *Star Trek* (2009), Spock mentions the theory of transwarp beaming. Scotty helps us understand what that is and puts it into a context that we understand by explaining how you beam a beagle from one planet to another.

SPOCK

You are, in fact, the Mr. Scott who postulated the theory of transwarp beaming?

SCOTTY

That's what I'm talkin' about! Had a little debate with my instructor on relativistic

> physics and how it pertains to subspace
> travel. He seemed to think that the range
> of transporting something like a... like a
> grapefruit was limited to about one hundred
> miles. I told him that I could not only beam
> a grapefruit from one planet to the adjacent
> planet in the same system – which is easy, by
> the way – I could do it with a life form. So,
> I tested it out on Admiral Archer's prized
> beagle.

Ultimately, learning to create meaningful visuals and great dialogue is a matter of using the writer's keen powers of observation—being alert and tuned into everything that goes on around you and listening closely to everyone around you.

APPLICATION

Questions to Ask Yourself about Your Script

Fixing visuals and dialogue usually occurs in a late rewrite, often after the story and characters have been worked out. It's part of the process of honing and tweaking and smoothing out and nuancing a script. It's not unusual to hear a great writer say, "I changed that phrase ten (or twenty or thirty) times before I felt I got it right."

> Look through your script and see how many scenes contain strong images. Are you creating too many scenes that take place in vague apartments or unexciting restaurants? What can you do to make these scenes and/or these places more cinematically interesting?
>
> Do characters state or allude to your theme? Have you kept such statements short?
>
> Do you have any cinematic metaphors? If not, what is your theme? Can you render your theme into any visuals?
>
> Read your dialogue out loud. Do all your characters sound the same? Start working through your characters'

dialogue to find ways to give them unique voices. If necessary, do more research, listening to the speech patterns, accents, and dialects of people who are somewhat like your characters.

EXERCISES AND THINGS TO THINK ABOUT

(1) Read a script that you find on the Internet. Then, take out the character names, and see if you can tell who is speaking just by the sound of the dialogue.

(2) Read scripts about characters with unusual professions (e.g., *Angels & Demons, Star Trek, Michael Clayton*). How are these characters introduced? What dialogue gives us information about their work? Are any places in the scripts overly talky?

(3) Read a script that you think has great dialogue. What techniques does the writer use to make it interesting and extraordinary? (If you're unsure about a script to use, consider *As Good as It Gets, Schindler's List, Amadeus,* or *Juno.*)

CHAPTER TEN

From Motivation to Goal:
Finding Your Character's Spine

Most stories are relatively simple. They can be told in a few words: "E.T. gets caught on Earth and then goes home." "A shark threatens a resort town over the 4th of July." "A murder is committed and a cop is assigned to find the criminal." "Politicians are corrupt, and a journalist exposes the truth."

Stories become complex through the influence of characters. Characters impinge on a story, give it dimension, and move it in new directions. Characters make a story compelling. Through a character's idiosyncrasies and willfulness, a story changes.

The main character influences a story because that individual is motivated to achieve a *goal*. This goal gives the story direction.

It's not unusual for a producer to ask a writer, "What does this character want?" If a desire, or need, or yearning, isn't *driving* the main character through the story, the audience can (and usually will) disconnect. If the character doesn't want something badly enough to go to considerable lengths to get it, then the audience won't want it either. If the character doesn't care, the audience won't care.

At the beginning of a story, something motivates the main character to go after a particular goal. The character then takes certain actions to achieve it. And at the end of most films, the goal is attained.

Just as a storyline has a spine that is determined by its setup, turning points, and climax, characters also have spines. A character's spine is determined by his or her *motivation, goal,* and *actions* taken in achieving that goal. Characters need all three of these elements to clearly define who they are, what they want, why they want it, and what they're willing to do to get it.

If any one of these elements is missing, the character's spine becomes confused and unfocused. That person has no direction. We're unclear who to root for and why we're rooting for someone at all.

Motivation

All of us have watched films in which we didn't know why the characters did what they did. We've seen films where the hero goes to considerable lengths to save his country, yet we never see any evidence that his country means anything to him.

We've seen films where characters seem irritated, get angry, or fall in love for no apparent reason. In these cases, their motivations are weak and unclear. If we don't know *why* a character is doing something, the story loses momentum and we lose interest.

Motivation pushes a character forward. It's a catalyst at the beginning of a story that forces a main character to get involved. Like any catalyst, motivation can be expressed physically, through dialogue, or through a situation.

A physical action will always give a story the most push. This is one reason why crime stories are often very clear. They often begin with a physical action that immediately catapults a character into the plot, forcing that character's involvement in what's to take place.

A physical action can include any number of possibilities. If a boy collapses on a baseball field during a game, other characters will be forced to react in any number of ways to get him medical treatment. If a terrorist arms a bomb or captures a band of hostages, those actions will be a strong beginning for a film. They will force a reaction.

Sometimes a story uses a combination of physical events and dialogue to build up a *situation,* so we sense what's pushing the character. In *Michael Clayton,* the protagonist is motivated through his own financial struggles, the manic behavior of his friend and colleague, his family's erratic situation, and his son's interest in the *Realm and Conquest* book's universe. However, we get the most grounded sense of the conflict's urgency through Arthur's attempted explanation for his behavior, and the behavior itself: taking off his clothes and running naked through the parking lot during a $3 billion class-action lawsuit.

Although motivation is set up in Act One, sometimes a climactic action is so strong that further motivation has to be laid in throughout the film. In *Gran Torino*, Walt Kowalski's climactic action that results in his death could not have happened without a variety of motivational factors. We learn that he is sick, probably without much time to live. This is shown through action, when we see him cough up blood. We then see his developing connection with his neighbors, specifically his developing care for Thao. His motivation is reinforced by pieces of information about his backstory: He is a vet, he loves his car, and he wants a safe and peaceful neighborhood. We then see further motivation from the threatening gang that raises his ire. His motivation is embedded in his character, he is not one to sit back and watch his world spin out of control.

Sometimes stories rely too much on a character *explaining* a motivation rather than *showing* it. This happens when there is no action to push that character into the story. If we don't see any motivating actions, characters have to explain why they're involved. This, of course, works in novels but is rarely effective in film. If we can't clearly *see* what motivates a character's entrance into the story, chances are that no amount of explaining is going to help us.

In many scripts, writers emphasize a character's backstory as that individual's chief motivator. This requires that characters have long expository speeches about their pasts as the causes of their present actions. They might discuss their backgrounds and psychological tics, giving us information about where they grew up, with long tales of their early lives and their parents. They might talk about the influences of other characters on their lives at an early age, discussing favorite aunts or villainous uncles. They might talk about the trouble they had two (or fifteen) years ago, explaining at length how that causes them to do things in the present.

These kinds of speeches usually bog down a script. Sometimes what they talk about isn't relevant to the issue at hand. Sometimes they even fail to show an important *present motivation*. Many times a writer believes that these speeches reveal character, but character is best revealed through actions that advance the story. Scenes that *only* reveal character fail to give a character a necessary motivational push. And since film is image-oriented rather than talk-oriented, anything that tells rather than shows diminishes a scene's dramatic power.

Motivation needs to be clear and focused. It should be expressed through action, not talk. It should catapult the main character into the story. Motivation propels a character. A goal gives direction to that propulsion.

The Goal

As a result of his or her motivation, a protagonist is heading somewhere. There is something that the character wants. Just as motivation pushes a character forward in a specific direction, a goal *pulls* a character toward a climax.

The protagonist's goal is an essential part of drama. Without a clear goal for its main character, a story will wander and become hopelessly confused.

The protagonist's goal is achieved at the story's climax.

But not just any goal will do. To function well, a goal requires three elements.

1) Great *risk*. Something important must be at stake. The audience must be convinced that a great deal will be lost if the main character does not gain the goal. We need to clearly understand the goal and understand that achieving it is essential for the character's well-being, and perhaps for the future life of our planet. If we don't believe in the necessity of the protagonist's goal, we won't be able to root for that character.

2) Direct *conflict*. A strong protagonist's goal should directly conflict with the antagonist's goal. This conflict sets the context for your entire story and strengthens the main character, because that person now has an opponent who will see to it that the protagonist's goal is not easily attained.

3) Character *transformation*. The goal should be sufficiently demanding and difficult to achieve that the protagonist must undergo changes while striving to attain it. In some way the protagonist will be transformed and will gain extra personality dimensions in the process. This character may discover courage or resourcefulness or determination. Achieving the goal without some kind of character change cannot be possible.

Sometimes the protagonist very directly states a goal. It might be established in the setup. Perhaps a flier announces a competition or a tryout, and the protagonist decides to go for it (*The Karate Kid, High School Musical*). Perhaps a crime is committed, and the police are on the case immediately. Perhaps someone discovers they're ill and states early in Act One that they'll "lick this thing!"

Sometimes an idea is introduced in Act One, but the protagonist doesn't really state the goal until the first turning point. In *The Royal Tenenbaums,* Royal states his goal at the first turning point: "I got six weeks to set things right with you and I aim to do it, if you give me a chance." The Second Act then shows how he tries to set things right with his family.

At the first turning point of *The Fugitive*, Marshal Sam Gerard states the goal of his team: "Our fugitive's name is Dr. Richard Kimble. Go get him." And Act Two focuses on what the team does to get him.

In *Iron Man,* Tony Stark has an awakening from his playboy lifestyle after he escapes from an Afghan rebel prison and learns that his company, Stark Enterprises, has been supplying arms to anti-American terrorist groups. The escape is Act One. Act Two finds him working against arming the terrorists.

> TONY STARK
>
> Now that I'm trying to protect the people I've put in harm's way, you're going to walk out?
>
> VIRGINIA PEPPER POTTS
>
> You're going to kill yourself, Tony. I'm not going to be a part of it.
>
> TONY STARK
>
> I just finally know what I have to do. And I know in my heart that it's right.

In many cases, a goal that guides the protagonist throughout a story is explicitly stated, like a mission statement, but a writer can imply a goal too. It's not always necessary to state a goal explicitly, as long as the audience is clear about what the goal is.

Action

The method by which a character achieves a goal demonstrates that character's strength and sincerity. People who claim they want something but won't *do* anything to get it are not sincere. They lack credibility. So a character has to take actions in pursuit of a goal. The stronger the actions and the stronger the barriers to achieving that goal, the stronger that character will seem.

Naturally, obstacles and actions come in many different forms. Actions can range from investigating and capturing a criminal (most crime stories) to tearing down and rebuilding a society (*Gone With the Wind*) to trying to get a better job or finish a project (*Working Girl, Big*) to finding a cure for or getting healed of a physical or mental disease (*Lorenzo's Oil, Awakenings, Sibyl, The Three Faces of Eve, One Flew Over the Cuckoo's Nest*) to setting up and executing a heist (*Ocean's Eleven, Twelve,* and *Thirteen*).

In all of the films mentioned above, the motivations are clear, the actions are strong, and the goals are sufficiently compelling to pull the main characters forward toward their objectives.

CHARACTER SPINE PROBLEMS

Unclear motivation, or lack of motivation, is one of the most common script problems. We've all seen many films during which we keep asking ourselves, "Why is he doing that? Why doesn't he do this instead?"

In some love stories, the two people clearly don't like each other at first and then, *suddenly*, seem to fall in love for no good reason. If the love story is to be compelling we must believe its characters' *motivations*.

Sometimes a motivation needs to be repeated more than once for audiences to catch it. Many times, motivations are clear only when they're expressed through action, image, *and* dialogue.

Motivational information can be difficult to incorporate into a film. Setting up a story and introducing a character while creating a dramatic opening image demands careful integration of many elements. Character motivation often gets shortchanged in the process. It's difficult to know how much backstory and how much exposition is necessary for an audience to get with a story. Beginning writers tend to include too much. Veteran screenwriters sometimes err on the other side, leaving out an image or a piece of dialogue that might have made all the difference.

Sometimes a goal isn't clear. We wonder what the protagonist really wants.

Occasionally a film has a passive character who doesn't interact with the story, or fight back. This kind of character does not engage in sufficient action to achieve a goal. This sort of character might be workable for part of a film, especially if it's a story about someone who gets *caught* in a story, but if a main character remains passive for most of a film, we lose interest. If a main character doesn't care enough to exert the effort needed to achieve his or her goal, we don't care about that character. Somewhere by the midpoint of the script (if not before), the protagonist has to begin acting upon the story rather than being victimized by it.

APPLICATION

The first job of a character rewrite is to make sure that you've created a strong character spine. In many scripts, too much information simply covers up a character's clear motivation, action, and goal. Uncovering and clarifying this spine is a process of tearing down some beats and building up others.

If you feel that your script is bogged down by too much talk and not enough action, you might want to begin your character rewrite by removing all the expository scenes. Look for places where characters are explaining themselves. Look for any section of dialogue where characters have long speeches that give psychological sketches about the backstory. Take those out of the script.

Now look at the beats that are left in the story. Is there a clear catalyst that motivates your main character into the story? If not, see if you can create a crisis point that will force your character into action. Find a visual way to show that crisis point.

Consider the actions that remain. With the removal of some of your exposition, perhaps there are too few actions left. If so, look back to the expository passages you removed to see if any actions are discussed or implied that could be played out by your characters. If so, substitute new action beats for the expository dialogue you've removed.

Look at your protagonist's goal. Is it set up in Act One? Is it clear? When the main character reaches that goal, do we know the story is finished? Are the climax and the goal the same (which is almost always true)? Do all of your plot and subplot lines have clear goals? Are all of them resolved toward the end of the script?

Once you have focused on your story's images and actions, look back at everything you removed. Within those expository passages, there might be pertinent information that needs to be in the script. If these are long speeches, see if you can reduce the pertinent information to a sentence or two. Rather than placing it all in one scene, thereby creating a talky scene that will slow down your story, cut it up into small expository sentences that can be sparingly salted throughout your script, particularly in Acts One and Two.

By uncovering the spine of your story and its protagonist through removing expository dialogue, it should be easy to see what's slowing down your story and what's essential to its clarity and movement.

Questions to Ask Yourself about Your Script

Is my main character motivated by action or talk? Is there a clear moment when that character enters into the story? Why does my protagonist begin to act?

What is my main character's goal? Is it sufficiently compelling to propel that character through three acts?

Is my main character active or passive in achieving that goal? Does the action meet the needs of the story? If it's an action-adventure script, do I use strong, dramatic actions? If it's a relationship script, do I find subtle ways to employ action?

Can I clearly discuss my protagonist's spine in a few words? Is it clear how this character's spine intersects with the spine of the story?

EXERCISES AND THINGS TO THINK ABOUT

(1) Consider some of your favorite movie characters. What are their motivations, goals, and actions? How are they expressed? Do these three elements flow logically?

(2) Think of a story in which there isn't sufficient action to fit the goal. Do you find the story believable?

(3) Analyze an action movie. How willful are its characters? What variety of actions do they take to reach their goals?

Many scripts, particularly by beginning writers, are bogged down with excess information. Once this information is removed, a script often picks up energy immediately, and what may have seemed like a dead script might start exhibiting signs of life and vitality.

Motivation, goal, and action will give drive and direction to a protagonist and to a script. But, as we'll see in the next chapter, the lifeblood of drama is conflict.

CHAPTER ELEVEN

Finding the Conflict

It's not unusual for a movie executive to tell a screenwriter, "Make it strong!" or "It needs more punch!" or "It's flat!" What the executive usually means is, "It lacks conflict!"

Conflict is the basis of drama. A novel can be "interior" and "soft," a poem can be flowery and appreciative, but drama needs grit, punch, and fight. That's true whether it's an action-adventure, a comedy-romance, a warm sitcom, or a sci-fi fantasy. Drama doesn't focus on characters playing nicely with each other. In good drama, characters enter into dynamic relationships that emphasize their differences. They confront, scrap, argue, and try to force their point of view on people who don't see things in the same way.

Conflict happens when two characters—the protagonist and the antagonist—maintain mutually exclusive goals. The cop wants to catch the criminal; the criminal doesn't want to be caught. The young woman wants to win the piano contest, but so does the young man, and there's only one first prize. One character will win, and one will lose. During the course of the story, we watch the protagonist and antagonist battle to achieve their opposing goals. Other characters usually come into conflict with them too. Conflicts are not meant to go easy.

Conflicts come in many sizes and shapes. Some conflicts are better material for cinematic drama than others. Whether they are fights, arguments, car chases, or clear differences in attitude, good scripts have a wide range of conflicts and play more than one type of conflict throughout a story.

Six types of conflicts are found in stories: *inner, relational, social, situational, cosmic,* and *us versus them.* In a screenplay, some of these are more workable than others. Some are simply better suited to the dramatic form.

Inner Conflict

When characters are unsure of themselves or their action or even what they want, they suffer from *inner conflict.* Inner conflict works well in novels, where a character can confide in the reader, sharing insecurities and uncertainties. It tends, however, to be somewhat problematical in film. Onscreen conflict works best when it's externalized, when it's portrayed through actions.

Sometimes screenplays use a voice-over or an expository statement to express inner conflict. Sometimes characters express inner conflicts by confiding their feelings to someone else. Unless these devices are used carefully, they can easily make a screenplay talky and too interior for most audiences.

Sometimes characters show their inner conflicts through quiet, reflective scenes that show them brooding, brewing something inside of them. There's a wonderful scene in *As Good as It Gets* in which Melvin looks out the window, clearly thinking about something, clearly struggling with some idea. This scene is part of a group of action-reaction scenes. First, Melvin helps Carol get Spence to the hospital. Melvin knows that Spence has various physical problems. Then, Melvin *thinks* about it. Although thinking is difficult to show in film, and inner conflict is difficult to externalize for film, we clearly get a sense that Melvin has some inner struggle going on. Although we don't know exactly what Melvin is thinking, the next scene clues us in. It shows Melvin asking his publisher to do something for him. She agrees, although we don't yet know what she's agreed to. In the following scene, we learn that Melvin asked his publisher if her husband, a doctor, would help Spence. Melvin will pay all expenses.

We can imagine Melvin's interior dialogue as he struggles with two sides of himself, dealing with his internal conflict: "I have the money to help Spence, but do I really want to get involved? If I get involved, will my publisher help out? Do I really want to have to ask her?" In lesser hands than James L. Brooks and Mark Andrus, the writers of *As Good as It Gets,* Melvin's internal conflict might have been the subject of all sorts of discussion. But by simply sequencing the scenes the way they did, the writers made Melvin's internal conflict clear.

Often, we understand inner conflict in drama because it's projected outward onto someone else. The scene might begin with a character struggling with uncertainty or anger, but as soon as someone comes into view, the character projects these onto whoever is around. Now the fight is "relational" rather than simply internal.

We often see this in real life: A husband who has lost his job comes home and screams at his wife or kicks his dog. His inner conflict is projected onto someone or something else.

Or a woman might not be sure her boyfriend really loves her. So she picks a fight to test him, and all her insecurity gets projected onto him. Her inner conflict has become relational.

Here we see a key to portraying inner conflict: *Project it outward onto a person or an object.* By projecting it outward, the conflict becomes relational. As a result, the conflict becomes more dynamic. We can now see it rather than hear about it.

Relational Conflict

A *relational conflict* is a dynamic encounter between two strong-willed, diametrically opposed people. Most film conflicts are relational because it's the strongest and most dramatic form of conflict. As two people simply have a go at it, conflict builds, develops, and eventually reaches some kind of dynamic conclusion—a shootout, an explosion, a fistfight, or simply someone leaving the room in a huff. It isn't pretty. It isn't nice. But it *is* dramatic.

In *Frost/Nixon* the relational conflict is, of course, between David Frost and Richard Nixon. In *Milk,* it really gets down to Harvey Milk versus Dan White. Other, larger relationships are explored, but the main conflict is the Milk-White relationship.

Societal Conflict

Many Movies-of-the-Week and feature films deal with a conflict between an individual and a group. The group might be a bureaucracy, a government, a gang, a corporation, an army, or a family. Think of the many films that pit a person against a large system: In *Star Wars*, Luke, Princess Leia, and Han Solo stand against the evil empire. In *Valkyrie*, individuals oppose an evil government. In *Jaws*, Marty takes a stand against the town fathers. In *Little Miss Sunshine*, Olive stands against the pageant officials. In *Erin Brockovich*, a woman stands against a corporation. Whenever a film's theme has to do with justice or corruption or oppression, chances are good that the conflict is societal.

Whenever a conflict occurs between a person and a group, it's in danger of becoming too abstract. It's difficult to get blisteringly angry at The Government, or The Military, or The Corporation; the conflict is too vague. Conflict needs to be concrete. If we can't see it, it's not concrete. Although a screen conflict might start with a person opposing a group, it works best when it shows just one person representing each side of an issue.

In most societal conflicts, one or two people usually represent the larger group. In *Gone With the Wind*, the Civil War gets in the way of Scarlett's attaining her goals (because the war might kill her beloved, Ashley Wilkes), but specific people personalize her societal conflicts: Rhett Butler won't give Scarlett money to save Tara; the Atlanta charity bazaar won't let her dance; a Yankee soldier tries to steal her valuables. Each of these little conflicts gives greater dimension to the larger conflict. And each little conflict focuses on the relationship between two people, treating societal conflicts like relational conflicts.

Situational Conflict

In the 1970s, disaster films were very popular. In these movies, characters had to confront life-and-death situations. The disasters were varied: an earthquake (*Earthquake*), a fire in a skyscraper (*The Towering Inferno*), and a capsized ocean liner (*The Poseidon Adventure*). That decade also brought us the disasters in *Avalanche*, *Flood!*, and *The Hindenburg*.

In the 1990s, filmgoers were treated to another spate of disaster films: *Twister* (1996), *Dante's Peak*, *Volcano*, *Poseidon* (a remake of *The Poseidon Adventure*), and *Armageddon*.

Airplane disasters are perennial favorites: *Airport*, *Airport 1975*, *Airport '77*, *The Concorde: Airport '79*, *Snakes on a Plane*, and *Flightplan*. Another disaster favorite finds space aliens visiting Earth: *E.T.*, *The War of the Worlds* (1953 and its 2005 remake), *The Day the Earth Stood Still* (1951 and its 2008 remake), and *Independence Day*.

When a person battles a natural disaster, it's usually an unequal battle. So, although such situations in themselves create tension and suspense, screenwriters will choose to convey much of a situational conflict relationally. A disaster situation becomes a pressure cooker as one person with one idea about what to do comes into conflict with another person who has another idea about what to do. Relational conflicts develop as characters disagree about how best to survive. Within each scene, different points of view emerge. Some characters panic, others become leaders who try to persuade the group to follow them.

Situational conflicts can be further individualized and made relational if family members struggle with one another, perhaps about leaving behind a dying relative, perhaps about children who must choose to disobey their parents if they're to survive. In these intense situations, old family conflicts might emerge to be screamed out and fought about.

Without these relational conflicts, situational conflict would be difficult to sustain for any length of time. We can only fight so long against a hurricane, a blizzard, a fire, or a sinking ship. Like other forms of conflict, situational conflict needs to be made personal and relational to keep us involved.

Cosmic Conflict

On very rare occasions, conflict occurs between a character and a cosmic force—God or the Devil. The conflict is supernatural, although sometimes God or Satan might appear in human form, as in *The Devil and Daniel Webster* (or its 1941 precursor based on the same story, *All that Money Can Buy*). The conflict is relational rather than cosmic in this story because it's essentially a conflict between two human beings.

King Lear (the play as well as any number of films based on it) rages against these supernatural powers. Salieri in *Amadeus* declares war on God for creating the brilliant Mozart. Job (both the Biblical story and Oskar Kokoschka's play of the same name) questions and argues with the cosmic force.

But in each of these examples, conflict is *projected* onto a human being. Salieri might be angry at God, but he takes it out on Mozart. King Lear might rage against cosmic injustice, but the immediate cause of his problems are his two daughters, who plot against him. And Job has as many arguments with his friends as he has with God.

For a cosmic conflict to unfold clearly for a film audience, the main character must project his problems with a supernatural force onto some human being (who just happens to be in the way).

Us versus Them Conflict

When I taught in Russia in the early 1990s, one of the writers in my class said, "You forgot one type of conflict—us versus them." There is, of course, plenty of this type of conflict that occurs in life and in films: Nazis or fascists or communists or socialists or anarchists against proponents of democracy or other forms of government; the Republicans versus the Democrats; the union versus greedy corporate types; feminists versus male chauvinists. Regardless of which side you're on, it's always the good guys versus the bad guys.

To dramatically convey the us-versus-them conflict in a film, each group should have a representative so the conflict becomes relational, focusing on the relationship between the protagonist and the antagonist. In *Erin Brockovich*, the fight might seem to be between the group that wants justice and the greedy polluters, but it becomes Erin versus the corporation, with specific characters representing the corporation. In *Defiance* (2008), the conflict might really be between the Jews and the Nazis, but it still gets down to individuals versus representatives of the opposing group. In *A Few Good Men*, the conflict might be between the people who want to cover up a crime and those who want to expose it, but the movie's most dramatic scenes show one person pitted against another, one representing the "us" (with whom the audience identifies) and the other representing the "them" (who need to be defeated).

RESOLVING CONFLICT

In many films, conflicts are not resolvable without somebody getting hurt. In real life, however, many people learn how to handle conflict. They learn to discuss it. They learn to give a little. Sometimes they simply agree to disagree and let it go at that.

Many believe that a certain amount of learning occurs as we watch films (although psychologists disagree about how much, and what kinds of people are most apt to learn from films). And most people seem to agree that movies have the potential to teach us behaviors and attitudes.

Natural Born Killers was watched repeatedly by the Columbine High School murderers. Many children begged for a pet Dalmatian after watching *101 Dalmatians* (animated version, 1961; live-action version, 1996). Some people left their uninspiring jobs and started doing what they really wanted to do after watching *Dead Poets Society.* Underdogs have been inspired to work harder after watching *National Velvet, Rocky,* and *The Karate Kid.* Some young women have become more determined to get ahead in their careers after watching *Working Girl.*

The ways that conflicts are usually resolved in films (through fist-fights, explosions, and a whole lot of killings) may be limited and unrepresentative of the ways we resolve conflicts in real life. So some writers have wondered if there might not be new (yet dramatically fulfilling) ways to resolve conflicts in films. They wonder about the possibility of resolving movie conflicts differently and allowing them to lead to win-win conclusions.

I first began to explore this idea in 1995, when I went to the United Nations Fourth World Conference on Women. I attended a seminar there by a woman who was using film to show alternative ways to resolve conflict. I then began to search for my own list of alternative ways for working with conflict, but discovered that very few films used them. Three that seemed to show good alternatives were *Strictly Ballroom, Howards End,* and *To Kill a Mockingbird* (1962). All have scenes that show nonviolent conflict resolutions that don't compromise the conflicts themselves. I began to look carefully at how they did this.

In *To Kill a Mockingbird,* Atticus Finch sits nightwatch outside the jail as a mob comes by to pull out Tom Robinson and lynch him. But this scene suddenly moves in an unexpected direction as three children enter the scene and gather around Atticus, who tries to shoo them home. Then, just as the tension begins to peak, Atticus's daughter, Scout, sees someone in the mob she recognizes, Mr. Cunningham. Being a polite child, she begins speaking nicely to him and talks about his son, who's in her class at school. Mr. Cunningham doesn't know what to do, except to respond politely as well. As a result, the conflict is diffused and the mob leaves.

A similar situation develops in *Strictly Ballroom.* Scott comes to Fran's home to apologize for blowing her off and seemingly choosing another dance partner. Fran tries to get him to go home. We expect, based on previous hints, that Fran's dancing is a secret she keeps from her family, and that her father might be abusive to her if he found out. But her father hears them talking, and confronts Scott. He asks them about their dancing, and asks to see their dance. The tension builds as we expect there will be big problems for Fran. Instead, we discover her father is a dancer himself—in fact, a pretty good one—as is her grandmother. Grandma recognizes that Scott needs some lessons in rhythm, and the scene moves in a new direction as she and Fran's father teach the young couple a way of dancing that comes from the heart, not just from the feet.

In both of these instances, tension is built up and then someone changes the direction of the scene. Someone humanizes the situation, rather than objectifies it. As a result, the conflict is resolved in a different way. Rather than building to blows, it moves toward a reconciliation or dissipation.

Howards End resolves the conflict between Margaret and her fiancé, Henry, as Margaret insists on airing the problem about Henry's affair of some years before and then letting him know, "It's not going to trouble us."

PROBLEMS WITH CONFLICT

Sometimes there are too many conflicts, so it's unclear what the main issue is. Sometimes there are too many antagonists, so the main character seems unfocused to the audience. Sometimes the main conflict changes from one section of the script to the next. And sometimes a story simply lacks conflict. It might have interesting and watchable scenes, but it doesn't have a compelling throughline to give it cohesiveness.

Problems in conflict are particularly prevalent when translating a novel into a screenplay. Most novels are narratives that take us into the psychology of their characters. We learn how they think and feel. We see how they grapple with issues. And we get insight into their insecurities and obsessions and concerns. This makes for interesting reading, but it can cause problems when making the jump from novel to script.

In many novels there is a significant amount of inner conflict that won't play well on the screen. If a book is of an epic nature, it may have too many conflicts. Sometimes a novel's major conflict is not workable for a film because it's too abstract or too intellectual or not of sufficient interest to mass audiences.

APPLICATION

When you define your main conflict, try to clearly express the goals of both the antagonist and the protagonist in terms that reveal *why* they're in conflict.

In working out a conflict, find ways to express it in strong visual and emotional terms. In the Stanislavski method of acting, actors are taught to phrase their roles' objectives (momentary/immediate goals) and superobjective (primary/overall goal) in terms that are actable and *dramatic*. For instance, if a scene's objective scene is about getting information, an actor might first phrase this goal as, "I want to try to get information." But that's weak and will not result in a dramatic action. So the actor might rephrase this goal as, "I want to squeeze every ounce of information out of him, no matter what it takes." This will lead to a much stronger scene.

Once you've clearly established the goals for your protagonist and antagonist, and phrased them so that we can clearly see why they conflict with each other, begin looking at your other characters. You can shade much of the conflict within scenes by smaller conflicts between your supporting characters and your main characters. If your antagonist is a Mafia boss, his bodyguard might not agree with him in every scene. Perhaps the two argue over how to handle another thug (one wants to kill him, and the other just wants information). Or the Mafia boss and his valet might disagree about what suit he should wear.

Questions to Ask Yourself about Your Script

Who is my protagonist? Who is my antagonist? What is their conflict? Is it relational? Societal? Situational? Cosmic? Have I expressed most of the conflict relationally?

How is the conflict expressed? Do I use images and action as well as dialogue to show conflict?

Have I created small conflicts among other characters to add extra "punch" to some scenes?

Does one overall conflict define my story's issue? Does it relate to both my storyline and my protagonist's spine?

EXERCISES AND THINGS TO THINK ABOUT

(1) Watch a film and identify all its different conflicts. What's its major conflict? What conflicts are used to shade individual scenes? Does the main conflict get resolved?

(2) Look at *To Kill a Mockingbird, Howards End*, and *Strictly Ballroom*, each of which have scenes that resolve conflicts in humanizing terms. Can you think of other films that do this? If so, see if you can analyze how their humanized resolutions work.

(3) In the next few films you watch, keep an eye on their minor characters. Can you imagine ways to add conflict to these films by creating small conflicts among their main characters and their minor characters? (You might enjoy watching the taxi scene in *Broadcast News* to see the conflict over how to get from one place to another.)

Although only one conflict should be the center of the story from beginning to end, remember to use small conflicts throughout each scene. These will give your story interest, punch, and dimensionality.

CHAPTER TWELVE

Creating Multidimensional and Transformational Characters

W e've all seen one-dimensional characters. They're stereotypes. They can usually be described in one or two words: the dumb blonde, the macho detective, the muscle-bound lifeguard, the voluptuous model. We've all seen many character stereotypes: the weeping widow who is all emotion, the pontificating scholar who is all philosophy, the rescuing hero who is all action.

Sometimes these characters have only a small role in a story and act as window dressing for the set. But sometimes they end up as a story's main characters, limiting the film because of their limited dimensions. James Bond is, in most films, a stereotype—the hero. He's defined by action. We know little about his attitudes, except that he likes to sleep with attractive women. His emotional life is irrelevant and almost nonexistent. You don't see Bond cry, show fear, show insecurity, get angry, or be anything other than cool. (Recently, however, there has been some attempt to dimensionalize him a bit, as new actors have added to the role's legacy.)

Well-drawn characters are broad, fleshed out. We can see different (sometimes even conflicting) sides of them. We observe how they act. We understand how they think. And we understand (perhaps even feel) their emotional makeup.

There are a number of different ways of describing a character's dimensions. Some describe them in terms of a character's physiology (appearance) and psychology (internal drives) and sociology (reactions to and interactions with others). Some describe a character's dimensions in terms of a kind of résumé: education, socioeconomic background, cultural background, strengths and weaknesses, and experience. Both approaches can be helpful.

I describe a character's dimensions in terms of *thinking*, *acting*, and *feeling*. A character has an intellectual life, an active life, and an emotional life.

Each of these categories can be further divided. *Thinking* consists of a character's philosophy, values, attitudes, and points of view. *Acting* consists of a character's actions as well as the decisions that lead to actions. And *feeling* includes the character's emotional makeup and emotional responses. With any well-drawn character, one of these categories might be more prominent than another, but each of them contribute to creating a multidimensional character.

On the Surface: The Character's Look

Although a character's look depends to a great extent on casting, a character's description in the script gives producers and casting directors ideas about who might play the part, and gives actors an opportunity to decide if they're attracted to a role. A character who is described purely by looks—"a sexy blonde, twenty-something" or "a ruggedly handsome man"—is more dependent on physical training and what the costumer and makeup person does than on anything the actor brings to the part. (Even the most ordinary person looks pretty good after working with a trainer and a great makeup artist.)

When describing a character in your script, think of more than just looks. Try to include something *actable*—give the actor something to do—in your description, so that the role might attract a great actor in search of a great part.

Daniel Day-Lewis is often noted as one of the best actors of our time. He's been drawn to a broad variety of multidimensional roles:

from mob leader Bill the Butcher in *Gangs of New York* to oil tycoon Daniel Plainview in *There Will Be Blood*, from quadriplegic Christy Brown in *My Left Foot* to former IRA member Danny Flynn in *The Boxer*, from wrongly convicted Gerry Conlon in *In the Name of the Father* to 17th-century New Englander John Proctor, who was accused of witchcraft, in *The Crucible*. All of these roles went far beyond asking the actor to simply be an attractive man.

As Good as It Gets, with its strong roles of Melvin, Simon, and Carol, attracted Academy Award–caliber actors by giving them multiple emotions, actions, and reactions to play. These included Melvin's obsessions with germs and locking doors and his increasing willingness to become a better man.

Thinking: Philosophy and Attitudes

Philosophy is the most difficult character dimension for writers to write and for actors to portray. Characters who are defined too much by their philosophies become abstract, talky, preachy, and usually *boring.* Yet every multidimensional character has a philosophy. All characters believe in something: perhaps in religion, women's rights, gay liberation, God, mother, and/or apple pie. That belief will find dramatic form in the character's actions, what that character does. A character who believes in gay liberation might march for civil rights and be quite vocal about the cause.

A character's philosophy often can be expressed best through that individual's *attitude* toward life. All well-written characters take a stance toward life. They might be cynical or positive or happy-go-lucky or aggressive. They might have a healthy outlook, they might be neurotic. They might be confident, they might be insecure. They might look at life through rose-colored glasses and miss the reality and seriousness of a situation. They might look at life through gray-colored glasses and never see the good in anyone or any situation. Their attitudes will determine their decisions and actions.

We usually know the truth about a character through attitude and action rather than through a stated philosophy. If philosophy and action conflict, we have a hypocrite. If I tell you, "I love humanity," and then proceed to keep everyone at a distance and go out of my way to make other people's lives miserable, obviously my attitude and actions *define* me, and my philosophy is nothing but empty words.

An attitude is more *actable* than a philosophy. It is more easily expressed through action. It's not difficult to show compassion or love or receptivity or cynicism through actions. But the danger in depicting both philosophy and attitude for the screenwriter is the temptation to have characters talk about these dimensions rather than act on them.

Sometimes characters simply have to talk about their attitudes and philosophies. If this is absolutely necessary, keep it short and then move away from it. Long speeches are fine for pulpits, but not for the movie screen. (There are, of course, exceptions to this. Reverend Briegleb in *Changeling* gave an important sermon about the corruption of the Los Angeles Police Department, but it was by no means a long sermon. It was just long enough to get the writer's point across.)

A character's philosophy is best stated in a line or two. When Jack Dawson in *Titanic* (1997) expresses his philosophy, he first says what he believes:

```
                    JACK

    I love waking up in the morning not knowing
    what's gonna happen or, who I'm gonna meet,
    where I'm gonna wind up. .. I figure life's a
    gift and I don't intend on wasting it.
```

And then he *acts out his philosophy* by taking Rose dancing and showing her his zest for life.

The first lines of *Crash* (2004) are about an attitude toward the city of Los Angeles as Graham relays his thoughts on the presumed safety, and vulnerability, of L.A.'s population, and how they keep everyone at bay until they crash.

GRAHAM

> It's the sense of touch. … In L.A., nobody
> touches you… I think we miss that touch so
> much, that we crash into each other, just so
> we can feel something.

Maya in *Sideways* expresses her attitudes toward life by raving about pinot noir, but she's really talking about herself.

MAYA

> I like how wine continues to evolve, like if I
> opened a bottle of wine today it would taste
> different than if I'd opened it on any other
> day, because a bottle of wine is actually
> alive. And it's constantly evolving and gaining
> complexity.

The character Christopher McCandless in the film *Into the Wild* (based on Jon Krakauer's book about the real McCandless) has an attitude toward life: He believes in the importance of testing ourselves.

CHRISTOPHER

> ... I also know how important it is in life
> not necessarily to be strong but to feel
> strong. To measure yourself at least once.
> To find yourself at least once in the most
> ancient of human conditions. Facing the blind
> death stone alone, with nothing to help you
> but your hands and your own head.

John Keating in *Dead Poets Society* tells his students: "Carpe diem, seize the day, boys, make your lives extraordinary… You are here… that the powerful play goes on and you may contribute a verse. What will your verse be?"

And Benjamin Button (*The Curious Case of Benjamin Button*) writes in a letter to his daughter, "For what it's worth, it's never too late…to be whoever you want to be… You can change or stay the same, there are no rules to this thing."

Acting: Decisions and Actions

A novel might focus on feelings and attitudes and beliefs. In a screenplay the focus needs to be on action. This action has two parts: the decision to act and the act itself.

When we watch films, we usually see only the action. Yet it's the *decision to act* that helps us understand how a character's mind works. The moment of decision—whether to pull the trigger, whether to say "yes" to an assignment, whether to commit to a relationship—is usually a strong moment of character revelation.

Decisions must lead to specific actions. It's the job of the protagonist to drive a story forward through actions. The protagonist can search, investigate, uncover, outwit, plan, transform (others and themselves), create, manipulate, avenge, and/or fix a wrong. Whatever the action, it's important that it drive the story forward, take a number of beats to execute, and affect the outcome of the story.

Some stories require that their main characters start off as passive characters. The story happens *to them*, and they are pushed in certain directions by the story. But in such stories the main character still must take over at some point. Somewhere, and certainly before the middle of the story, the protagonist needs to begin pushing back, to begin making the story happen, rather than being forever at its mercy.

In *Titanic,* Rose begins to make decisions about her life and her identity, and begins rebelling against the hand dealt her by her station in life. In *Gran Torino,* Walt Kowalski begins to come out of his shell and interact and engage with his neighbors, even putting himself on the line for them. In *Sideways,* Miles is criticized for being passive and a complainer, but he begins to engage again with life, as he first engages with Maya and then, by the end, takes action to see her again. In *Little Miss Sunshine*, it seems that everyone gives up on the pageant, but Richard resolves to make sure they get to the pageant and makes unusual decisions to carry out their original goal.

Feeling: Emotional Life and Emotional Responses

Emotions often get left out of stories, or they're limited to tears and anger and little else. Yet characters have emotional lives that define them just as their attitudes define them. A cynical attitude might result in despair or depression or withdrawal from life. So a cynical character might be sulky, bitter, or angry. A character with a positive attitude might smile or laugh a lot or be cute. He or she is optimistic, accessible, and outgoing. As a result of inaccessible emotions, a character might be hardhearted or hostile or vengeful.

Some characters have a broad emotional palette. They're comfortable showing emotions and their dialogue expresses their feelings. They might talk about being devastated or despairing or depressed or despondent, or maybe even delighted.

Some psychologists say that all emotions can be divided into the categories sad, mad, glad, hurt, and scared. Those who are sad might range from clinically depressed to just a little bit down. Those who are mad might be enraged or slightly irritated. The glad people might be ecstatic or mildly amused. Those who are hurt might be deeply, deeply offended or simply feeling a little edgy over something they heard. And those who are scared might be terrified or just a little bit nervous. Characters like The Joker in *The Dark Knight*, the emotional gorilla King Kong, and Tess McGill in *Working Girl* have very broad emotional palettes. And they wear their many emotions on their sleeves, readily showing happiness, sadness, frustration, determination, anger, and anxiety—little is left hidden.

Even characters who aren't emotional types will become emotional if pushed hard enough or far enough. The death of someone close to them will usually let the dam of emotions burst in even in the most stoic individuals. A close call with death, or a threat of bodily harm, can rattle the calmest people.

Extraordinary situations bring out extraordinary emotional responses. A character who is usually happy may become angry at an injustice that's been done. A despairing character may be touched by love and a whole new world of emotional responses will emerge.

In *There Will Be Blood,* Daniel Plainview, who has seemed in control, comes to terms with his life and shows a broad emotional palette as he confesses to Eli Sunday that he's a sinner and that he's sorry. In *Doubt,* Sister Beauvier is adamantly self-righteous, yet we begin to see her doubts as her emotional responses expand. In *Revolutionary Road,* emotions are tightly contained, but we begin to see these edges fray as emotions are pushed by frustration.

Just as many films leave out the story beat in which the protagonist decides to act, they also often leave out the beat that shows the emotional response to that action. Sometimes we see characters who are touched by an event or action, but we don't see the emotional responses that would make them understandable to the audience. How characters feel creates sympathy in the audience. It creates identification with the characters. Emotions pull us into a story. We vicariously experience a character's journey through various emotions.

The Dimensional Chain

These dimensions—thinking, acting, and feeling—create a chain that helps define a character, move a story forward, and arouse audience empathy, A character's philosophy creates certain attitudes toward life. These attitudes force decisions that create actions. These actions spring from the character's emotional life, which helps predispose him or her to do certain things and not do others. By connecting the dimensions, the story flows, and we're able to identify with its characters, and to feel with them.

PROBLEMS IN CREATING MULTI-DIMENSIONAL CHARACTERS

Creating multidimensional characters is not easy. There are many traps and pitfalls. Sometimes writers give in to the temptation to look to other films, rather than to life, for the source of their characters. I have read more than one script that describes a character as a "Harrison Ford type as he appeared in *Raiders of the Lost Ark*" or "a James Bond type as played by Pierce Brosnan."

Creating dimensional characters demands observance of real life. The best writers seem to be constantly noticing small details and character traits and listening for character speech rhythms. They make a commitment to moving beyond stereotypes and expanding their own understanding of people. They have a respect for their characters, giving them freedom to find a broad range of thoughts, actions, and emotions.

THE TRANSFORMATIONAL ARC

Character development is essential to a good story. As a character moves from motivation to goal, something needs to happen to the character in the process. A well-drawn character gains something by participation in a story, and a story gains something from a character's involvement.

Producers often ask, "How does the protagonist change and grow?" They recognize that a strong story with strong characters has the potential to transform the protagonist. Not every film needs a transformational arc, although many of the best films will show at least the protagonist becoming transformed in the process of living out the story. Supporting characters are also often transformed.

In many cases, a character's transformation is an *external* change. In most sports films or competition films, the protagonist will learn or improve a skill that will pay off at the end. Learning the skill will usually take a good teacher or coach, determination, and hours of practice.

Not every transformation needs to be external. Sometimes there is only an *internal* change—a change of heart or attitude. In *The Fugitive,* the transformation of Marshal Sam Gerard is one of attitude. Over the course of the film we see him shift from "I don't care whether Richard Kimble is innocent or not" to caring about and respecting Kimble, leading to him knowing, by the end, that Kimble is innocent.

In love stories, characters might shift from an unwillingness to commit to a desire to settle down (*Wedding Crashers*). Sometimes young characters change from a lack of confidence to confidence and high self-esteem (the *Home Alone* films).

In *Schindler's List*, the shift from materialism to humanity happens very much under the surface, as Oskar Schindler slowly shifts his attitudes about Amon Goeth, the Germans, the Jews, and himself. By the end of the film, a profound transformation has happened as he cries, "I could've got more out . . . I didn't do enough!"

To transform, characters need help. They receive it from the story and from other characters. Sometimes one character is a catalyst for change in other characters.

This influence by other characters usually doesn't take place because one character gives advice, or lectures another about what to do. Catalytic characters work by example. If someone needs to learn commitment, a committed character's actions show how commitment works and what it looks like.

In many films there are both external and internal changes. If someone needs to learn a skill (external change), there's usually a teacher or a parent or a coach who not only teaches the skill, but teaches something about attitudes and strategies and approaches (internal change). Often, a value is learned along with a skill.

It takes time to transform a main character. It doesn't happen in a few pages. It usually takes a script's entire three acts to create a believable transformation. It's a beat-by-beat process, slowly building up the transformation through many moments that show many gradual changes. We see how the decisions that a character makes change throughout the story. We see new emotional responses to new situations. And we see a character learn new actions as a result of interactions with other characters.

Most stories need at least five or seven story beats to create even a small transformation. Most of the time it takes more. *Tootsie* and *As Good as It Gets*—two strong transformational films—each have about thirty-five transformational beats. In both, not only does the protagonist (Michael or Melvin, respectively) transform, but supporting characters change as well. Julie and Sandy both transform in *Tootsie*. In *As Good as It Gets*, the child, Spence, has an external transformation as he gets physically better; Simon transforms his attitude toward art throughout Act Two, gaining self-confidence; and Frank, the art dealer, transforms his attitude toward Melvin. Carol doesn't transform, because she doesn't need to. She's the stable center that influences the others.

A transformational arc showing a character's shifts and how these shifts happen can be mapped out much like the structural arc of a plot or subplot.

A good film with multiple transformations is *Billy Elliot*.

ACT ONE/SETUP: Establishes that Billy loves music and movement. During the credits, he jumps on a trampoline. He plays his brother's records and plays the piano. He is supposed to take boxing lessons, but he sees the ballet class at the other end of the hall and becomes fascinated. This fascination begins his transformation. The ballet teacher, Mrs. Wilkinson, subtly brings him into the class.

ACT ONE DEVELOPMENT: Billy watches a Fred Astaire movie. He continues to go to ballet class. He shows an increasing commitment to dance by hiding his ballet shoes from his father, stealing a book on ballet from the library and studying it, and practicing at home when he's alone. During a montage, he learns to focus while doing a pirouette, and finally gets it! He is improving as a dancer, but his father discovers that he's not attending boxing class. At twenty-five minutes into the film his father sees him in ballet class, and thus begin the conflict and resulting obstacles that will be the focus of Act Two.

ACT TWO: Billy's father takes him out of ballet class. Billy stands up for himself and stands up to his father, and gets a beating as a result. The stakes of going after what he wants—against his father's wishes—are raised. Billy, though, finds an ally in his teacher. He goes to her home and she mentions the possibility of auditioning to get into the Royal Ballet School. She tells him he'll have to work hard, but she thinks it's possible.

Three important turning points are clustered together, led off by the first turning point. The first (at twenty-two minutes) shows Billy having a breakthrough and being very happy about his ability to focus on his pirouette. The second is a reversal, which occurs when his father sees him and takes him out of class (at twenty-five minutes into the film), making it seem as if he'll have to give up his dancing. The third turning point occurs (at thirty-five minutes into the film) when the teacher suggests a new idea: auditioning for the Royal Ballet School.

During Act Two, the teacher suggests a way around his family's resistance—working with Billy privately. He agrees to this plan. He begins to get ideas for the dance he'll perform for the audition. Things seem to be going well, but at the midpoint Billy tells his teacher he can't do it. He then has a vision of his mother, who's dead, which is a catalyst for him to continue with his practice.

Billy misses his audition, and the teacher confronts the father. Billy dances his frustration, beginning to incorporate emotion into his dancing—externalizing his feelings through dance.

The father finds Billy at the dance gym with his gay friend, Michael. In response, Billy dances his defiance, letting his father know who he is. The dance works on three levels: Billy stands up for his identity, shows defiance of his father, and also shows his hopes of some approval or recognition of his talent. The father leaves, and at a turning point that shows the father's transformation, asks the teacher how much it would cost for Billy to audition. He sells his wife's jewelry to give his son the opportunity.

The second turning point contains two beats: Billy's father deciding to help him and the two leaving for London (at seventy-nine minutes into the film).

By the second turning point, most of the transformational beats have been accomplished. The father supports his son. Billy has his opportunity and is committed to it. Even his brother has come around to some extent, and Grandma is supportive of Billy as well.

Act Three now has to prove that the transformation is complete and that Billy is capable. It needs to prove that this investment by him and his family (and the audience) will pay off. Billy auditions but at first seems tongue-tied about clarifying why he loves to dance. When, at the climax, he's finally able to talk about his love of dance, he's told that he got in. He moves to London. The film then flashes forward to Billy at age twenty-five, the lead in a performance of *Swan Lake*, proving that he made it.

The transformational arc shows Billy's external changes, his improvements as a dancer, and his internal changes, which allow him to stand up to his father, his community, and the take-for-granted identity that comes from the mining town. In the first half of Act Two, Billy caves in by not going to dance class, presuming that he has to give it up and that he can't do it. In the second half, Billy begins to assert his own identity and realizes his talent and his love of dance.

Billy's transformation is possible because of the influences of his teacher, his friends Michael and Debbie, and his father. He and his father actually effect each other's transformation. Other positive and negative influences also figure into Billy's changes: The Fred Astaire film convinces Billy that it's possible to be a great male dancer; the negatives of the life he doesn't want (the miner's life) influence him, as well as his father and his teacher, to seek other possibilities for his future. Set against his dancing, his contrasting environment also becomes a transformational influence.

APPLICATION

When reworking a main character, it's often helpful to begin with a transformational arc. Begin by looking at the skills and characteristics your character needs in order to attain the desired objective.

Think through how your character will acquire them. What will the story demand? How will other characters help your main characters achieve the desired objective?

Ask yourself: Is there evidence of my main character's philosophy within my story? Is it expressed through actions rather than through talk? Will an audience clearly see my protagonist's attitudes? Will an audience know how my protagonist feels about others and about the situation that character is in? Does this character's attitudes lead to certain actions?

If you want a character to be sympathetic, try to broaden that character's emotional palette. Think of a broad range of emotions. Is the character peeved, frustrated, or irritated? Delighted, ecstatic, or gleeful? Frozen with fear or having an adrenalin rush because of a situation's dangers?

Become a great observer of people's emotional states, and become cognizant of how broad emotions can be. Find ways to expand emotions beyond the usual fear, anger, and passion.

Look at your characters' actions. Are they playing an active or passive role in the story? Do their actions help move the story as well as help define them as characters? Some characters like to putter. Others knit, read, or collect small objects. Some characters have nervous habits. Others have idiosyncrasies, such as "manicuring" everything they come in contact with, whether removing dust or polishing doorknobs or filing nails. These action details will help expand and reveal your characters while still focusing on the necessary actions to advance the story.

Questions to Ask Yourself about Your Script

Have I gotten stuck in stereotypes? Have I defined certain characters through one dimension rather than creating multidimensional characters?

What is my protagonist's transformational arc? Have I given my character enough time to change? Is the change credible?

What influences help my main characters change? Do I have a catalytic character? Is there a love relationship? Does the story force change?

Will an audience clearly see via images and actions how the influences of the story and other characters created my protagonist's transformation? Does this transformation express both my theme and my story?

EXERCISES AND THINGS TO THINK ABOUT

(1) Watch a film for which an actor has won an Academy Award. How many dimensions do you notice that are part of the award-winning character?

(2) Map out the transformational beats for a character who has a strong transformation arc, such as Melvin in *As Good as It Gets*, Rocky in *Rocky*, David Larusso in *The Karate Kid*, Michael Dorsey in *Tootsie*, or the protagonist in one of your favorite films. How many are there? How many people had to help this transformation?

(3) Look at a film where a character *might* have gone through a very strong transformation but doesn't seem to. Some possible films include *The Fugitive* (Richard Kimble's character), perhaps *Slumdog Millionaire* (consider a stronger transformational arc), *The Reader*, or perhaps *Valkyrie*. All of these films have strong events that could have pushed very strong transformations. What might these transformations have looked like if they had happened?

Paying attention to dimensionality and transformation will help you create characters that audiences are not likely to forget. And by emphasizing these elements, you will also enhance audience identification and commercial viability.

CHAPTER THIRTEEN
Character Functions

Many scripts seem muddy and bogged down. Sometimes this is the result of an inconsistent or unstructured story. Often, however, it's a character problem: There are too many characters. They seem to wander aimlessly or repeat what others are already doing. They begin to run into each other and confuse the story. We don't know whom to follow.

With literature, a reader can page back and forth to keep track of who's who and what's what (though most authors try to keep from confusing their readers). But because of their inherent temporal nature, films, stage plays, and television and radio shows can't offer their audiences this luxury.

In a two- to three-hour film, there are only a certain number of characters we can absorb. Too many overwhelm us. Like watching a three-ring circus, we don't know where to focus our attention. Generally, a film can only support six or seven major characters who demand our attention. In most cases we see three to five. This might include the protagonist, the antagonist, the love interest, and perhaps several strong supporting characters. In ensemble pieces like *The Magnificent Seven*, *The Seven Samurai* (1954), *Magnolia*, *The Women* (1939), *The Lord of the Rings*, *The Royal Tenenbaums*, or even *Crash* (2004) or *Traffic* (2000), only five to seven characters are really central to the story. Even *The Magnificent Seven* didn't focus on *all* seven characters.

This leads to the question, who to cut? Screenwriters always have favorite characters, characters who are unique and memorable.

Unfortunately, "favorite" is not a workable criterion for "Who to keep?" Generally, when it comes to cutting characters, it is essential to look at character functions.

Every character in a film should have an essential role to play, something specific to contribute to the production. Everyone should have a reason for being in the story. A character might give a clue to a detective or be a love interest or add wisdom or depth to the story or add stature to a main character (as a bodyguard, assistant, etc.).

Characters often perform more than one function. A character might be a love interest, a catalyst, *and* a confidant. However, in most cases, several characters will not perform the same function. If several characters serve the same function, the effect of each character is dissipated. Five detectives doing the work of one detective-protagonist only diminishes the importance of the one. It's not necessary for three people to give the same information. Five love interests are too many if fewer will make the same point. Repeating the same type of character can keep the writer from having sufficient onscreen time to round out any one character.

We might divide character functions into five categories: main characters, supporting characters, characters who add dimension, thematic characters, and mass-and-weight characters.

MAIN CHARACTERS

Main characters "do" the action. They're the ones responsible for moving a story along. It's their story and they're its focus. They provide the main conflict and are sufficiently interesting to keep us intrigued for two or three hours.

The Protagonist

A script's main character is the *protagonist*. This is who the story is about. This is the person we're expected to follow, to root for, to empathize with, and to care about. We want the protagonist to win, to reach the goal, to achieve the dream. Usually, we see the story through his or her eyes.

Almost always, the protagonist is a positive figure, the hero of the story, like James Bond or Jason Bourne (in the *Bourne* series of films). She's Erin in *Erin Brockovich* or Rose in *Titanic*. He's John McClane in the *Die Hard* films, Benjamin Button in *The Curious Case of Benjamin Button*, or Atticus Finch in *To Kill a Mockingbird*. This does not mean that the main character is without flaws. The protagonist might have certain traits that we dislike or make certain decisions we disagree with, but the character commands our attention. The protagonist is eminently watchable. In most cases, we have no doubt who the protagonist is, and if the character is written well and performed well, we might go the film specifically because of the main character.

Occasionally, a protagonist is a negative character, as in *A Clockwork Orange, Taxi Driver, Thank You for Smoking, There Will Be Blood, Amadeus,* and *Gone With the Wind*. The whole genre of film noir is based on flawed protagonists who are often in equal measure both positive and negative. Such characters may not be sympathetic or empathetic. Nevertheless, they involve us. We see the story from their point of view.

The Antagonist

To attain dramatic conflict, every protagonist needs to be opposed by someone—the antagonist. In most cases this is the bad guy, the evil character, the villain who tries to keep the protagonist from reaching a goal. But the antagonist does not always need to be a negative character. The antagonist simply needs to provide the main character's opposition. In *Amadeus* the protagonist is Salieri, and the antagonist is Mozart, whom we undoubtedly like more than Salieri. In *Doubt* we see the story through the POV of Sister Aloysius Beauvier, the protagonist. But she's also the antagonist to Father Brendan Flynn, who doesn't want to be accused of misconduct with an altar boy. And Father Flynn is her antagonist. In *Enemy at the Gates* we see a similar use of the protagonist-antagonist duo: The rival snipers are each other's antagonists.

Sometimes the antagonist is a collection of people (main characters and/or supporting characters) who try to keep the protagonist from achieving a goal. It might be the townspeople in *Jaws* or the ghosts in *Ghostbusters* or one group of survivors pitted against another in *The Poseidon Adventure*. It might be the drug lords in *Traffic* or a group of policemen in *Crash* (2004) or the opposing team in a sports film (*Remember the Titans, The Replacements,* or *Any Given Sunday*).

The Love Interest

The protagonist often has a *love interest* who adds to the qualities we know about the main character, and usually adds something to the story as well. Sometimes the love interest helps the main character transform. Sometimes the love interest is a contrasting character or thematic character as well. In *Fight Club*, Marla provides a stable character for the narrator to try and hang on to. In *American Beauty*, the young cheerleader is a catalyst character who motivates Lester Burnham to exercise, to try to be more desirable, to think more deeply about what he wants out of life, and to get through his midlife crisis. In *Titanic*, Jack motivates Rose to embrace life and not just follow the rules. In *Pirates of the Caribbean*, Elizabeth Swan is the main object of desire for Will Turner. Jack Sparrow uses that to his advantage.

SUPPORTING ROLES

Protagonists cannot get through their stories alone. They need supporting characters to stand with them and against them. They need people who will listen, advise, help, push, pull, support, nurture, confront, and invigorate them.

The Catalyst Character

A catalyst character is any type of character—a main character, a supporting character, even a minor character—whose function is to *cause* events to happen and to *push* the protagonist into action. Mrs. Robinson in *The Graduate* causes the entire story to happen, even though she's a supporting character. In *Vicky Cristina Barcelona*, Juan Antonio is a catalyst who causes the girls to fall into and out of love. In *The Sixth Sense* the catalyst is a minor character—the young man who shoots Malcolm Crowe. In *Billy Elliot* the dance teacher starts the events moving. In *Jaws* the catalyst character is the shark.

Catalyst figures can be minor figures. In *The Fugitive* the man on the bus who starts to cough and then stabs the guard is a catalyst for the accident and, therefore, Richard Kimble's escape. A catalyst can be a minor character who delivers a clue to a detective that sends the detective off on a different path.

Sometimes a catalyst character forces the protagonist's transformation. In this case the catalyst might be a therapist, a parent, or a friend who confronts the protagonist, or the police who arrest the protagonist, or the judge who hands down a life-changing sentence.

Almost every story has catalyst figures. Every protagonist needs help in getting and keeping the story moving. When creating catalyst figures, it's important to make them active so that they catapult the story forward through action, not just through dialogue.

The Confidant

We often find the *confidant* in plays, particularly in those delightful eighteenth-century English comedies in which the maid is often the person to whom our heroine tells her deepest, darkest secrets. Our heroine confides in her confidante, telling her who she loves, her fears about their imminent meeting, her jealousies, and her concerns. She weeps with her confidante, laughs with her, and calls upon her for help in planning a strategy that will bring her into the arms of her own true love.

In films, the confidant is often a much less interesting character. This does not need to be the case, but, unfortunately, the confidant is usually thought of as the character in whom the protagonist verbally confides. And this makes talky scenes.

A confidant often is used as an excuse for giving information to the audience. As a result, scenes with a confidant often get bogged down, filled with long expository speeches, and used as an opportunity to tell everything that seems difficult to show dramatically.

But the confidant need not be dull. Think of the confidant as the person to whom the protagonist *reveals* herself or himself. This is a trustworthy character in whose presence a female protagonist can let her hair down, or a male protagonist can be vulnerable. The confidant can provide an opportunity for the protagonist to cry or laugh or be vulnerable, thus revealing other dimensions of the character.

Sometimes a confidant is a partner, even another protagonist. In *Butch Cassidy and the Sundance Kid*, *Brokeback Mountain*, and *Remember the Titans*, main characters are each other's confidants. In *The Silence of the Lambs*, Hannibal Lecter (besides fulfilling other roles) is a confidant of Clarice Starling, who tells him about seeing the spring lambs slaughtered and how it affected her.

In many television series, such as *The Office* and *Rescue Me*, as well as numerous doctor series and detective series, partners and work associates function as confidants when necessary, even though their main function may be to move the action forward.

Some actors are cast regularly as confidants. Joan Cusack, for example, often appears as the female friend with a soft shoulder to cry on, and always ready for a good laugh and good sharing (e.g., *Runaway Bride, High Fidelity*, and *Working Girl*).

CHARACTERS WHO ADD OTHER DIMENSIONS

If a story were simply linear, with the protagonist achieving his or her goal with just a little help from a catalyst or two, it quickly would lose your interest. There are always some characters who provide dimensionality for a story and its main characters. This, however, does not mean that these particular characters are dimensional, but that the film becomes more dimensional because of their presence.

The Comic Relief Character

We've all seen serious films with one funny character who provides comic relief. This character's function is to lighten up the story, to give the audience an opportunity to release tension. In *Star Wars* we get humor from R2-D2 and C-3PO, who always complains, "We're doomed," and from Chewbacca, who Princess Leia calls "a hairy carpet." In *Signs* Merrill Hess complements the tension with humorous lines.

If you've read much Shakespeare, you might remember that even in his most serious plays, there's usually some character who makes us laugh. The obvious example, of course, is Falstaff in *King Henry IV, Parts I and II*. In *Macbeth* there's the blabbering porter. In *Romeo and Juliet* there's The Nurse. In *King Lear* there's the Fool.

The Contrasting Character

A contrasting character helps define the protagonist (or sometimes a supporting character) simply by being different from that character. Sometimes this is done through different ethnic backgrounds: A Caucasian cop contrasts with a Native American cop and a Hispanic detective and an African-American Chief of Police. Sometimes tall characters contrast with short ones, or a fussily feminine girl contrasts with a tomboy, or a brave soul contrasts with a coward. If a story is about a homosexual, there might be a contrasting character who is heterosexual. If a story is about someone who is shady, there might be a contrasting character with great integrity (e.g., Carl Fox in *Wall Street*). Contrasting characters help us see a main character's subtle traits more clearly, while they expand a story's depth and texture.

Sometimes contrasting characters are major characters. Two contrasting characters might have close-to-equal roles. In *Brokeback Mountain*, Ennis Del Mar contrasts with Jack Twist. Although they're struggling through the same desires, they emotionally deal with them in different ways because they's come to different conclusions about their love. In *Frost/Nixon*, Frost's sense of fairness and integrity contrasts with the muddy boundaries of Nixon's ethics. In *Doubt*, Sister James has a sense of kindness and compassion that contrasts with Sister Beauvier's rigidity.

THEMATIC CHARACTERS

Four types of characters—balance characters, "voice of" characters, writer's point-of-view characters, and audience point-of-view characters—serve to convey and express a film's theme. Although one or two of these character types might be found in any kind of film, a film that focuses on its theme, such as *Crash* (2004) or *Syriana* or *Children of Men*, might contain several of these characters. In these films, the filmmaker has something definite to convey. The driving force behind making the film is not so much a fascination with the story or characters, but a fascination with an idea.

The Balance Character

In many thematically complex stories, one character is the *balance character*, the stable center who makes sure that the theme is not misrepresented or misinterpreted. If we're unsure about what the writer wants to say, we can look to this character who grounds the story, who lets us know what is important (what the writer is trying to say), and who provides a balance beam that can support other characters who might be less sure about where they stand.

In *Little Miss Sunshine*, Olive's mother grounds the story by letting us know what is really important. In *Spider-Man* it's Peter Parker's uncle; in *The Lion King* it's Simba's father; in *Titanic* it's Molly Brown. If we're unsure about the values a film is trying to convey, we look to this character.

Some films seem to require a balance character because they leave themselves open for misinterpretation. Films that deal with gay or lesbian issues sometimes need to balance their gay characters with some heterosexual roles. Otherwise the film might be in danger of being misinterpreted as being too myopic in its perspective. In *Philadelphia*, the wife provides this balance. She questions Joe's attitude toward gays.

Films in which minorities play important negative roles sometimes need to find balance in positive role models. *The Color Purple* was criticized for its one-dimensional male figures because it seemed to give an unbalanced picture of black men.

The "Voice of" Character

Some thematic characters bring breadth to a theme by showing it from different points of view, thereby helping to communicate the idea's complexity. These are *"voice of"* characters. In *Schindler's List,*

Itzhak Stern is a voice of clarity and insight, communicating the clearest perception of good and evil. In *Doubt*, Sister James is the voice of compassion. In *The Lion King*, Mufasa is the voice of wisdom or truth. In *Sense and Sensibility*, Elinor is the voice of sense and Marianne the voice of sensibility.

Be careful not to take the "voice of" designation literally. These are not meant to be talky characters. Instead, they convey their ideas through attitude, action, and—only occasionally—dialogue.

The Writer's Point of View Character

The writer comes to a script with a point of view. Most writers have strong philosophies, value systems, and beliefs, and often write because they want to inject their ideas and values into the world. Many writers want to change the world through what they write, through the stories they tell.

To make sure they get their personal takes on things clearly shown in their work, writers sometimes utilize a *writer's point-of-view character*. In a sense, this character is the writer's alter ego.

It's not always important for the audience to know who the writer's point-of-view character is. However, if you as the writer have something specific that you want to get across in your script, then choose a character you identify with—it might be a major character or a supporting character. It's often also a thematic character, since the writer's perspective is often a script's central idea. In *The Reader*, a thematic character who is probably also the writer's POV character is Professor Rohl, who is wise and ethical and grounds the story. In *Frost/Nixon* it is probably David Frost.

Sometimes this particular character becomes essential to the story. If you are working with a controversial or complex story in which there's not a clear right or wrong, there needs to be some help given to the audience so that they know how to think through and gain insight into your message.

I once worked on a feature film about war and violence. The writer *seemed* to take the position that violence was just fine and justified.

When I questioned him about his point of view, it became clear that what the story said about violence and what he really believed about violence were not the same. I encouraged him to think through his beliefs about the subject and to put his ideas into his protagonist's actions, even if the protagonist made a decision at the end that showed some transformation and change. As a result, he changed the ending of his story to allow his protagonist to show his viewpoint—that violence doesn't solve problems—a viewpoint that he began to feel was well worth showing. He didn't put his view into a long speech, but rather showed his character walking away from a violent life to follow another path.

The Audience Point-of-View Character

Sometimes a screenplay deals with incredible material, such as the supernatural, UFOs, psychics, or reincarnation. In many cases, at least some of the audience will be skeptical of this material. To make such subject matter work, it's important to choose a character to represent the audience's point of view. Perhaps it's a skeptic who says just what the audience probably is thinking at the beginning of the story. As this character changes, slowly finding the material plausible during the course of the story, the audience skeptics will be carried along by this character and change their attitudes too. This does not necessarily mean that the story has made true believers of the audience. But it has suspended their disbelief for the course of the film, so that they can identify with the skeptical character and be involved with the story as it unfolds.

In 1987, Shirley MacLaine's book *Out on a Limb* was made into a miniseries. The movie was about her spiritual awakening and belief in reincarnation. Since many people in the audience might not have believed in reincarnation, there were a variety of characters in the film that represented different points of view. Whatever audience members believed, there was at least one character with that point of view. Audience members could identify with characters who held a strong belief in reincarnation, or they could identify with characters who thought it was a lot of hooey. Or they had the choice to transform their attitude toward reincarnation by identifying with Shirley MacLaine.

Whenever dealing with subject matter that demands an audience suspend disbelief for the duration of the film, try to create characters who represent most of the anticipated audience points of view so that, wherever the audience stands, its members feel respected and can identify with someone who shares their views.

MINOR CHARACTERS

Mass-and-Weight Characters

Mass-and-weight characters inhabit small supporting roles that demonstrate the prestige, power, or stature of the protagonist and/or the antagonist. These characters might be bodyguards, secretaries, assistants, right-hand men, or gals Friday, who, by their very presence help us understand who's important—who's Mr. or Ms. Big. How many mass-and-weight characters your script may need will depend on your main character's power and status.

Most powerful people, particularly villains, surround themselves with one or two bodyguards, perhaps a chauffeur, and maybe an assistant. But be careful: If you add too many people, you'll have clutter, not apparent mass. If you need a lot of mass but fear adding too many characters, you can create a multifunction character. For instance, you might make the bodyguard also a confidant. Or the gal Friday might be a catalyst who propels the story toward its conclusion.

Sometimes it's necessary to focus on particular minor characters within a mass-and-weight group. This can be accomplished by creating immediately recognizable characteristics for one or two characters while leaving the others in the background as nameless, faceless, somewhat shadowy folk. These one or two recognizable characters might stand out because they are of a strange size or a different ethnic background from the rest, or possess some unique characteristic. If a villain needs a lot of heft behind him so no one questions his power, he may have five or ten beefy guys in his entourage, but only one or two ever come to the forefront.

No matter how many functions a character has in a script, it's essential that he or she have a place in the story and a contribution to make to it. Clarifying a character function can bring a story into focus. It can save characters who might seem unnecessary. It can help determine who to cut. It has saved many scripts that seemed muddy and confused and were refocused through an examination of its characters' functions.

THE CHARACTER FUNCTIONS IN
LITTLE MISS SUNSHINE

In ensemble films, it is often difficult to know how many characters and what character functions are needed. Look at the core characters of *Little Miss Sunshine* to see if everyone has a reason to be there, and if everyone is adding something important to the film,

Olive is the *protagonist*, since it's her story. Although we get glimpses into the stories of the others, the story is essentially about Olive getting to the pageant. But the story is also about dreams and desires and family and love. And everyone has something to tell us, positively or negatively, about these ideas.

Olive is the character with the pageant dream that focuses the script. At the end, she learns about things that are more important: family, second chances, unconditional love, and her own identity.

Richard, her father, is a *catalyst* character. When the story needs a new decision or a push or a new injection of energy, Richard provides it. He decides that they'll all go to the pageant, that they'll steal Grandpa's body, that they won't give up when all seems lost, and that they'll dance onstage with Olive. Richard also has a dream of his own—to get his book published and to launch his motivational speaking career. It is elusive, however, and things don't seem to be coming together for his personal dream, in spite of his determination.

Grandpa is a *voice of* encouragement and support. Although his wisdom is not by-the-book, he's the one who coaches Olive. He helps her come up with her unique act, and he encourages Richard when his book deal falls apart: "Richard, whatever happens, you tried to do something on your own, which is more than most people ever do... You took a big chance, it took guts, and I'm proud of you." Grandpa pursues Olive's pageant dream. But he also lives in his own dream world—he's a heroin addict. Eventually he dies from an overdose.

Dwayne is a *contrasting character*. Whereas Olive is engaged in life, in making things happen, and in going after her dream, Dwayne is withdrawn, waiting for life to happen to him. He has a dream—to become a test pilot—but rather than going after his dream, he's simply silent. He won't engage in anything, even important things, hoping his dream will magically come true. He's the opposite of Olive, who works hard for her dream.

Frank is a *contrasting character* too. He's so unengaged with life that he's ready to check out. He thinks his life depends on his former gay lover, but he transforms to realize that his life depends on family and love. His behavior contrasts with Dwayne's and with the determined behaviors of Olive, Richard, and Sheryl.

All of the family characters except for Sheryl, Olive's mother, are pursuing dreams. Sheryl is a *thematic character* who represents unconditional love. She doesn't give up on anyone—not Olive (she can always try again next year) or silent Dwayne, or the dreams of her husband or her brother or even Grandpa ("Honey, Grandpa's soul is in Heaven now. He's with God. Okay?"). Nobody loses out on love. Although Sheryl is not depicted as a typically nurturing or sentimental or perfect mother (she hasn't been able to give up smoking, nor is she much of a cook since they seem to have takeout most of the time), she shows the breadth of accepting, unconditional, family love. If we weren't sure what the story is really about, Sheryl's character points the way to the theme that dreams are important, but winning is not the most important thing—love is.

PROBLEMS WITH CHARACTER FUNCTIONS

Some films get criticized for having too many characters. An audience might be overwhelmed, unable to keep them straight. In any large film this is a problem. Although a large film needs many characters, the audience needs to know who's important and what these key characters offer to the story. So the writer must help the audience stay focused while creating a background of characters who give texture to the film.

Think about how much you need to learn in the first twenty minutes of a film. Characters need to be introduced. You usually need to learn their names, be able to quickly identify them by sight, and have a sense of what each contributes to the story.

During the writing and rewriting process, establishing story focus and clarifying character functions are mainly a matter of cutting and combining and honing characters. Once a film goes into production, this becomes a casting problem.

Films like *Platoon*, *Gandhi*, *Crash* (2004), *Traffic*, and *Slumdog Millionaire* need a lot of characters. Main characters need to be set against background characters who establish the film's environment. Usually the problems are solved in casting, through careful differentiation of characters.

When it's necessary to have a great many characters, it can help to find ways to quickly differentiate the characters so we instantly recognize each person. The fastest way to remember a character is through gender and/or ethnic type. And the use of characters representing many ethnic backgrounds expands a film's context. The world is not all Caucasian or all black or all Hispanic or all Asian, and writers can go a long way in helping expand audience awareness of real world demographics while also helping filmgoers instantly identify a story's characters. Sometimes writers ask, "Isn't that up to the casting director?" No. The casting director calls in actors who fit a role's description. If you write "Asian potheads" (*Harold and Kumar Go to White Castle*) or "African-American lawyer" (*Philadelphia*) or "Native

American mechanic" (*Fargo*), the casting director will call in actors who fit that description.

Characters can also be differentiated through weight (*What's Eating Gilbert Grape* or *I Now Pronounce You Chuck and Larry*) or height or physical characters such as tattoos or the way someone moves (Verbal's limp in *The Usual Suspects*).

In summary, a writer must pay attention to what each character contributes to a story. To keep us involved with a story, a writer must orient us fairly quickly to what it's about, who's important in it, and why they're important.

APPLICATION

It's always difficult to cut or change characters whom you've come to love. Yet the job of rewriting requires being ruthless at times. When doing a rewrite to clarify character functions, a favorite character often will need to be cut or combined with another character.

Questions to Ask Yourself about Your Script

As I begin my rewrite, can I identify the major functions of all my characters? Does every character in my script have a function?

Who is my protagonist? Is my protagonist driving the action? Does my protagonist achieve his or her goal at the climax of the story?

If I have several protagonists, do I have an equal partnership story or does one protagonist enjoy a bit more focus than the other?

Who is my antagonist? Who opposes my protagonist? If it's several characters or situations, which is the major one? Is my antagonist moving throughout my script?

Do I have a confidant character? If so, are my confidant scenes overly talky, or have I found ways to reveal and show rather than tell?

Do I have several characters with the same function? If so, how can I cut or combine them?

Am I missing an important character function? Perhaps I need another catalyst figure, or perhaps the audience will have trouble understanding my theme without a thematic character.

Is my protagonist receiving help from supporting characters? Are they really supporting my main character or simply hanging around?

Do I have a character who carries my personal point of view? If so, have I kept the character active and dramatic rather than talky? Does my point of view give insight to my story, or is it simply a message I've been trying to get across and thought I'd sneak in here?

Am I dealing with material that's open to misinterpretation? If so, have I included at least one balance character to protect myself?

Is there humor in my film? Does at least one character offer comic relief? Do I use humor to release tension or lighten the material or create greater audience enjoyment?

How many of my characters does my story focus on? If the audience needs to identify and keep track of more than seven, where can I cut characters so that viewers can easily follow my story and its various character throughlines?

Are my protagonist and antagonist clear? If I have are several antagonists, is one more in focus than the others?

Who are my supporting characters? How do they contribute to the story? If I have thematic characters, have I given them other functions so that they aren't merely "message" characters?

Do I have catalyst characters who help move the action?

If I have several characters with the same function, can I combine some characters?

Am I missing any character functions that my story needs?

EXERCISES AND THINGS TO THINK ABOUT

(1) Many films have failed at the box office because they had too many characters without clear story functions. Great scripts are clean, clear, and easy to follow. Characters take focus to perform a function, and each character has a reason to be in the story. Look at a few films that have many characters. Can you keep all the characters straight? What has the writer done to help you differentiate one from another? What does each character's function give to the story? Was everyone needed? Could characters have been combined?

(2) Think about the characters in this film and figure out which ones have a story function, and which ones help you understand the theme.

(3) Watch a film you consider to be a great film. Identify the functions of all its characters.

CHAPTER FOURTEEN

A Case Study:
Writer Paul Haggis in His Own Words

Paul Haggis has been in the film business since the early 1970s, writing for both television and feature films. He is the only writer to write the Best Picture Oscar winner two years in a row—*Million Dollar Baby* in 2005 and *Crash* in 2006. He is the only writer to be nominated for an Academy Award three years in a row—for *Million Dollar Baby, Crash,* and *Letters from Iwo Jima.* He won two Emmy Awards—Outstanding Drama Series and Outstanding Writing in a Drama Series—in 1987 for the TV series *thirtysomething.* The genres of his scripts are varied, from sitcoms (*Who's the Boss* and *Diff'rent Strokes*) to drama series (*thirtysomething* and *EZ Streets*) to a boxing movie (*Million Dollar Baby*) to war pictures (*Flags of our Fathers, Letters from Iwo Jima,* and *In the Valley of Elah*) to action-adventure features that include two James Bond films, *Casino Royale* (2006) and *Quantum of Solace.* He has sustained a very successful career for more than three decades.

It took Haggis three years, two months, and ten days to sell his first script.

In the Beginning

I began writing as a child. Most children write something or other, and we all think our children are terribly gifted in what they do, so I'm sure my parents thought the same. But I wasn't. They were mistaken. I do remember when I was in about fifth grade, I turned in a composition and my teacher, who was a lovely woman—a nun—gave it back to me with an "A" and said, "You're good at that." That moment really impressed itself on me. I thought, "Wow. Something I'm good at. I should do more of that," so I did a lot of writing from that point on. And when I was a teenager, I started writing plays—very, very bad ones—and producing them, which proved that they were very, very bad. And then, from there, it came down to Hollywood and bad sitcoms.

My dad always loved the theater, He found an old, burnt-out Baptist church, a tiny church, and bought it. We renovated it, he and I, and made it into this 99-seat theater. He lost a fortune doing so, but we had a great time.

I always loved movies, so I began to show films in our little theater. I put up a little screen and had a 16mm projector and showed all the films that I had wanted to see. Sunday at midnight, Saturday at two and seven... I showed *Persona* and *Breathless* and all these fabulous European films that we didn't get a chance to see in our town. I was interested in Antonioni and Costa-Gavras and even some of the Hitchcock classics that I hadn't had a chance to see. So I really got my education by booking films and watching them.

I then studied photography and went to a community college for a year and took cinematography courses. I really wanted to make movies. I just didn't know how to go about it until my dad suggested I move to Hollywood because there weren't very many opportunities in Canada, where I lived, to make movies unless you were very well connected in Ontario or Vancouver or Montreal. I wasn't in one of those cities. I was from the small town of London.

At the age of twenty-two, I moved to Hollywood.

The Preparation

I tried, unsuccessfully, to write film and television scripts in Canada before I moved. I had written a couple of sample scripts for television and was starting on a movie. But I wasn't getting anywhere. So I moved to Hollywood, and my Dad and Mom supported me for the first year with one hundred a week, which was a huge help. Then I worked as a furniture mover and my wife was a hostess at a restaurant. We had a child immediately, so it was a little difficult. Somehow we made it.

It took a while for me to become successful—a long while. My father said it took me three years, two months, and ten days before I sold my first script. I guess that's about right. I wrote spec scripts during this time. I think I wrote two movies and about six sample scripts for television.

I took a lot of writing classes—whatever I could find. There was a place here in town called Sherwood Oaks Experimental Film School. I went there and I took a couple of courses—a couple of comedy writing classes— and studied with Danny Simon. Whenever I would do this, I'd meet people, other students. And that was a big help. Through them, I got leads and sometimes I got part-nerships, and that would turn out to be a great success.

All this time, I would keep meeting people and writing letters and sending my work out. Although I didn't sell any of my movies or sample scripts, I did get work based on them.

I think the first thing I sold was to a Canadian sitcom. If you're a Canadian living in America, that means you made it and it doesn't really matter if you've never written anything or sold anything. So I was a Hollywood writer just because I was living in Glendale, which was close to Hollywood. And so I went and wrote for some episodes of a TV show in Toronto. And then my next real job was writing cartoons.

I had met with Michael Maurer, who was doing free-lancing, writing cartoons. We teamed up. We wrote a couple of samples, and then we had a job writing all the episodes of a series that only lasted a year. And then we wrote *Scooby-Doo* and *Richie Rich* and all sorts of different things for another year.

During this time, I just sort of schlepped along and pitched and pitched and pitched. I finally met a manager who took me on. He didn't get me very far, but he got me out to pitch. We'd get an appointment to pitch for a show and I'd go home and come up with twenty ideas or something over the course of a week, and we'd work about six into full stories, and all the others would be sketches. Usually by the time we'd get to pitch, they would have already sold it. I did that dozens and dozens of times before I actually got an assignment.

The Writing Process

I tended to write at night because I was working, moving furniture, in the morning. I didn't have a job full-time, I got work whenever I could, whenever they needed an extra hand. Usually that was during the days. I kind of wrote every second I could get. Of course, I had a young child, too, so that wasn't easy. So I had to write around her schedule.

I made sure I wrote every day. It didn't really matter what time. I just had to do it every single day—usually six days a week, but at the beginning, probably seven. And I would write around my work schedule. Even if I got home from work at ten o'clock at night and I had to get up in the morning the next day, I would still write, even if just for half an hour. I knew that if I wasn't writing, I was not going to get anywhere, and I was not going to get any better. So I just did it every day. And now, I still carry that with me—every day I'm not writing, I feel guilty.

When writing a movie, I jot down a lot of beats till I'm really, really happy. Usually I do it on my computer and then I write it literally on index cards. My daughter sometimes helps me if we're writing together. She'll write the index cards and I'll take tape and move those around until I'm happy with them. And, finally, I'll make an outline based on that.

Getting Ideas

I spend a lot of my time looking for ideas. That's frustrating, because they never come easily. Once I find something I want to do, and have broken it out, I tend to work at least five or six hours a day, writing, just breaking down the story. And then I try to hide myself away someplace. I go to New York, or I go to Rome sometimes, or I just hide out in the coffee shop here, wherever I can. Usually, I start around ten o'clock in the morning and I'll write until about five o'clock in the afternoon.

I just keep reading. I read and I read and I talk to people and I sit and think about what troubles me. I wish I had a big file of things that interested me because I could dig into them right now.

Of course, I also get assignments, and I love doing that. But I'm always looking for the next passion project—the thing that really stirs me.

Television versus Film

I did television for many, many years—twenty years or more—and the entire time, people would tell me, "You know, you should write movies." That wasn't a compliment, I don't think. Part of it was they were just trying to get rid of me because I was annoying, but I don't know if I ever learned how to write television, even though I made a really good living at it for a long time. It's a particular craft. I love writing television. I really do, and I love the medium. I'm just not sure if I ever got any good at it because I tend to be a really wordy writer, and you have to be pithy to write for television.

I learned a lot from television—I learned how to structure, I learned how to turn a scene without going on and on. I loved the fact that you had a page, or two pages, to get your character from A to B. You didn't have six pages, and there's great discipline in that. You either turn into a good writer, or you turn into a hack by doing so. I loved the challenge of it. I'm not sure I succeeded, but I loved the challenge.

Writing Challenges

Some stories come quite easily. I wrote *Crash* very easily and very quickly. I came up with the plot in one evening, starting at two o'clock in the morning and ending at ten in the morning. I had all the characters, at least how they connect. And then I researched for a year. I just read everything I could get my hands on. I interviewed when I could.

And then I wrote *Million Dollar Baby*. I had my friend Bobby Moresco come in to edit it and give me some notes. I didn't feel like sitting alone and writing again for a year, so I asked Bobby if he wanted to do a project with me and I gave him my twenty-five page outline, which was what I had, for *Crash*. He said, "Well, it's not a movie, is it?," and I said, "I don't know—I think it might be." And so we wrote a screenplay in two weeks based on that. And we did a reading, got some more thoughts from the actors, did a second draft in another two weeks and that was it. It was done. I had never written anything so quickly. But I think because I really lived inside those characters—I knew those characters, and personal experience was part of the research.

In the Valley of Elah and *Million Dollar Baby* both took about a year to write. One was based on actual incidents; the other was based on short stories. You would think those things would write more easily, but they don't. Both were really tough.

Casino Royale wrote very easily. I wrote that all backwards, actually. I remember they came to see me, the producers and the director, and I was in Italy at the time. I had read the script they had and I thought it was really troubled. I remember the third act was really problematic. It followed the book really carefully as I recall. In Act Three, Bond and Vesper sailed to Venice, and Bond went out shopping and came back to the hotel and found that Vesper had slit her wrists and was dead. She left a note that said, "Watch the TV." And Bond sat and watched TV for several pages. Vesper confesses to everything that had happened, and then sets them chasing after a villain we'd never seen before, who was at a bank. Bond went chasing after the villain in the bank, chased him down into a house that was weakly supported and once he got in there, it started to sink. And then he finally caught the bad guy and killed him.

So I said, "Your script has several sins, but only one is unforgivable. It doesn't have an Act Three. Would you like one?" And they said yes. I said, "Okay. Here's what I think I'm going to do... I don't know how I'm going to do it... but Vesper is going to be in that sinking house and Bond is going to want to kill her, and then want to save her, then she's going to kill herself and he's going to be unable to save her." And they said, "How are you going to do that?" I said, "I don't know. Go away."

So I wrote Act Three—thirty pages or whatever it was—and sent it to them. They liked that. So I went back and wrote Act Two. The early draft had a lot of good action pieces already, good poker playing stuff, so I was able to use that. Then, as I was about to go direct a pilot, they said, "What about Act One?" I said, "I've got to go direct my pilot!" So I pushed production of the pilot by a week, because we weren't quite ready, and I wrote Act One. And once I was finished directing the pilot, I did a quick pass all the way through and that was it. It was very backwards, writing Act Three first, but I found it was really a terrific idea because you do know where you're going.

It was a fun project because I was a huge Bond fan, but I hadn't watched any of the Bond films in years. I loved the early Bond films. And I just loved putting a twist on archetypal characters, bringing them into reality and watching that battle between an archetype and modern reality.

In this case, with Bond, I decided to start by asking some very simple questions of Bond, like, "What would it be like to be an assassin?" I don't believe you would shoot a laser, hit somebody across the room, and then say some smarmy line. I don't believe that's how assassins work. One would like to really get blood on your hands, to kill someone with a knife up close. We know that Bond has a lot of armor, there's a lot of reverse engineering with that character. We know where that character got to because we'd seen the movies. How does he get there? He built up all that scar tissue in his soul.

Then I said, "Well, how can this woman get underneath all that?" If you remember in that first train scene, she had to come in and deliver some money. Well, okay. In this first scene, we have to show that they fall in love. There's something in that one scene to make them fall in love. And I thought, "Well, what do people want in a relationship?"

I think you want to be seen through. We wear this armor and we want someone to pierce it. We want someone to look past our mask and see who we are and accept it.

Okay. So, I thought, "I'll start off with a game." Bond's really good at games. He's a spy; he has to be good at reading people. So I had Bond read her and tell her exactly who she is. Then I had her turn around and tell Bond exactly who he is. And in doing so, the last line she says is, "How is your lamb?" And he says, "Skewered. One sympathizes." And so he leaves there going, "Who the hell is this woman?" And she leaves thinking the same: "Who is this man?" And because you only have so much time in a movie like that, you need to continually move the plot along. You just can't stop and do big relationship scenes. They have to function and push the plot along themselves.

Advice for Writers

I love to write. Period. And I love to write characters, and I don't see a difference between comedy and drama, or suspense and mystery. I just like telling a good story, and I'll tell it any way I possibly can. I want to try and write something that has meaning, I want to try and hide that meaning, and one way to do that is to hide it in a genre.

I'd tell new writers, "Write your passion. Don't listen to your agents. Don't listen to your friends who tell you that the studio is looking for this thing, that actor's looking for this thing. Don't listen to them. You'll waste your time!" I wasted years and years chasing things like that. "Columbia is looking for a ghost story!"—so I spent months and months coming up with ghost stories. They didn't know what they were looking for. I wasted a lot of time, and I didn't succeed until very late in my career when I decided to write *Crash* and *Million Dollar Baby* because these stories deeply affected or troubled me. And they took four and a half years to sell. But they sold. And they got made. I think I've only succeeded when I've done things I was really passionate about.

I'm always thinking, "How do I find a good story to tell?" That's all that really haunts me—that I'll never find another good story to tell. Or I'll find a good story to tell, but won't know how to tell it. Success is something you can't really plan for. Your films will succeed or they'll fail and, often, it will have nothing to do with the quality of the script. You just have to keep writing the best story you possibly can. And if you're directing or producing, that's great. If you're not, you hand it over and pray to the gods that they'll treat it well.

Index

About the Author

Dr. Linda Seger began her script consulting business in 1981, based on a script analysis method she developed as part of her doctoral dissertation "What Makes a Script Work?" Since then, she has consulted with writers, producers, directors, and production companies on more than 2,000 scripts and 100 produced films and taught scriptwriting in thirty-one countries. Among her many clients have been Ray Bradbury, Peter Jackson, William Kelley, Tony Bill, ITC Entertainment, Charles Fries Entertainment, TriStar Pictures, and the Sundance Institute. She has given seminars for executives at ABC, CBS, NBC, Disney, Embassy Television, RAI television (Italy), and ZDF television (Germany), as well as for members of the American Film Institute, the Directors Guild of America, the Writers Guild of America, the Academy of Television Arts and Sciences, and the Academy of Motion Picture Arts and Sciences. She is the recipient of several awards, including the Living Legacy Award from the Moondance International Film Festival. She is the author of eight books on screenwriting. Her website is www.lindaseger.com.